Writing the Okanagan

NOVELS

A Short Sad Book (1977)

STORIES

The Rain Barrel (1994)

BOOK-LENGTH POEMS

At War with the U.S. (1974)

My Darling Nellie Grey (2010)

COLLECTIONS OF POEMS (INCLUDING GATHERED LONG POEMS)

Particular Accidents: Selected Poems (1981)

Sticks & Stones (1989)

Urban Snow (1992)

Blonds on Bikes (1997)

Vermeer's Light: Poems 1996–2006 (2007)

CHAPBOOKS

Two Police Poems (1969)

MEMOIRS

Baseball Love (2006)

EDITIONS

Imago Twenty (1974)

Loki Is Buried at Smoky Creek: Selected Poems of Fred Wah (1981)

And Other Stories (2001)

ABOUT

A Record of Writing: An Annotated and Illustrated Bibliography of George Bowering by Roy Miki (1989)

George Bowering: Bright Circles of Colour by Eva-Marie Kröller (1992)

ALL PUBLISHED BY TALONBOOKS

WRITING THE
OKANAGAN

GEORGE
BOWERING

TALONBOOKS

Talonbooks
278 East First Avenue, Vancouver, British Columbia, Canada v5T 1A6
www.talonbooks.com

First printing: 2015

Typeset in Jenson
Printed and bound in Canada on 100% post-consumer recycled paper

Interior and cover design by Typesmith
On the cover:
E.J. Hughes
Lake Okanagan, 1959
Reproduced courtesy of Heffel Fine Art Auction House

Lyrics from the song "Blue Okanagan" reproduced courtesy the Estate of Buddy Reynolds

Talonbooks gratefully acknowledges the financial support of the Canada Council for the Arts, the Government of Canada through the Canada Book Fund, and the Province of British Columbia through the British Columbia Arts Council and the Book Publishing Tax Credit.

LIBRARY AND ARCHIVES CANADA CATALOGUING IN PUBLICATION

Bowering, George, 1935–
[Works. Selections]
        Writing the Okanagan : literary/collections / George Bowering.

ISBN 978-0-88922-941-9 (PAPERBACK)

        1. Okanagan Valley (B.C. : Region) – Literary collections.
I. Title.

PS8503.O875A6 2015   C818'.54   C2015-904156-2

This book would like to commemorate

all the Bowerings and Brinsons who lie in

Okanagan cemeteries

I am struck by the frequency with which we encounter photos of me engaged in reading. I think it was because I never got to read the Okanagan that I got busy writing it.

The Okanagan.

This is where God said, "Finally, I got it right."

—George Bowering

Contents

Baby Bowering, circa 1935.

Introduction

I was born in Penticton and raised in the Okanagan. Like just about everyone else there, when I was a school kid I did not know what either of those words meant. I knew that there were "Indians" all up and down the valley, but it was not until I was really old that I knew that they were the Syilx people, though I did know that they spoke a branch of Interior Salish we settlers called Colville–Okanagan.

I for one found it interesting that many of the places around there had names that started with *O* or *K*. Omak, Okanogon, Oroville, Osoyoos, Oliver, Olalla, Oyama, Okanagan Falls, and so on—Kaleden, Keremeos, Kelowna, Kelleston, Kalamalka, Kamloops eventually. The abbreviation we commonly used for Okanagan was *OK*. Apple-box labels and tire-repair ads promised OK this and OK that. We called little towns up north OK Landing and OK Centre and OK Mission.

I loved stuff like this when I was a barely okay kid. "Words will make a world," the poet Robert Creeley would later write in the introduction to my first book. Yet in the beginning of what I hoped was my writing life, I thought it was the other way around. As you read through this compilation, you may notice the shift I'm talking about.

As a young reader I was at home in other people's literary landscapes—William Faulkner's Yoknapatawpha County and Thomas Hardy's Wessex, let's say. I thought it might be my duty as a writer to invent a small Okanagan town named Lawrence (which, like my very own Oliver, can be used either as a given name or a surname) and tell enough stories about people who lived there to populate it. But then I got sidetracked, wanting to portray Vancouver in poetry and fiction, eventually working my way as best I could toward Creeley's position.

I read what Margaret Laurence did with her place, what Hugh Hood did with his, and what Alice Munro remembered into fiction. They were more focused than I, more devoted to making their semi-rural townscapes real in the imaginations of their readers. I turned out to be a flibbertigibbet, a realist for a year, an anti-realist for the next, trying this and that, living in twentieth-century Italy and writing about eighteenth-century "Indians" on North America's west coast.

But by an act of the Oliver town council I was made a permanent citizen of that little municipality in 2003. With my wife, Jean, and our big dog, Mickey, I go there three times a year. I still get there that often at my writing desk, too. Despite the many changes that seventy years have brought to the town, there is a surprising amount of my childhood's stuff remaining in my home town. There may be two green golf courses and forty professional vineyards there now, and nowhere near as many fruit trees, but I can still drive around behind the school and look up the old skid trail even if I wouldn't think of climbing it. I can look at the top of Blue Mountain and wonder whether any parents these days would let their kids climb up there with no sunscreen and no water.

I do feel like a ghost once in a while as I enjoy a bit of shade under some desert elm. Maybe I've become my valley's ghostwriter.

I started this book by gathering all my literary writing concerned with the Okanagan Valley. I didn't even consider adding all my journalism about the valley. The manuscript came to well over seven hundred pages. Well, you know how editors are: the manuscript got shorter and shorter. I have been through this before—I know about repetition and space restraints. Still, I regretted the disappearance of some Okanagan settings from the book, and I know in my heart that some of the stuff we cut out had come straight from heaven to my writer's hand. Tough luck. I do hope that you will agree that the writing gets better as the author gets older.

But I can tell you one thing. If the book is any good at all, that is because my old-time editor, Karl Siegler, knows what he is doing, and my terrific wife, Jean Baird, spent many hours with a pile of papers nearly as tall as she is sitting down.

In my Air Cadet uniform, my kid brother Roger behind me.

Delsing

Delsing was the first novel I ever wrote. While I was an undergrad, I wrote a page a night after my studying was done. I would leave the page in the typewriter, having stopped mid-sentence for the curiosity of Bill Trump, the friend after whom the character Bob Small is modelled. It is an unapologetically autobiographical novel that records the memories of a certain George Delsing's life from junior high school's grade seven till his discharge from the RCAF at age twenty-one. I was studying the work of Ezra Pound, who had insisted that you had to learn to adopt a persona—to speak in a voice other than your own. George Delsing's character was somewhat modelled on my own. My home town, Oliver, became Delsing's Lawrence. Delsing also fancies himself to be in love with an English character called Frances in this novel. She is sometimes called Wendy in my other Okanagan writings.

The typescript comes to 550 pages. Roughly the first half takes place in the Okanagan, of course, and for our purposes I have chosen a chapter that is set in an orchard above Naramata. There isn't anything in the way of narration or characterization in this sample, but I thought it might show us something about orchard life there in the early fifties. If you go to the site now you will find that the fruit trees have come down and been replaced by relentless rows of grapevines.

As soon as I finished this bucolic manuscript I started graduate school at the University of British Columbia in Vancouver, and while I was at it, wrote a much shorter urban novel with the title *Mirror on the Floor*.

from Delsing

The alarm clock jangled him awake. Six o'clock on another long work-day, and he rolled out of bed, put his bare feet on the cold linoleum floor and reached for a cigarette with his shivering hand. Sam, the big black German shepherd, scratched on the door of his cabin. George pulled on his denim trousers and opened the door to let the dog scramble in and wrestle a good morning.

"Hey, you're scratching me, you inconsiderate mutt," he said.

With the dog impatiently trotting around the dusty yard, George sat on the stoop of his cabin and put on his thick red-and-grey wool socks and rubber boots, then stood up and put on his shirt and jacket. It was cool and sunny and moist now, but in a few hours it would be too hot to wear anything but pants and socks and boots.

It was the third summer he had worked at Uncle Norris's fruit ranch, fifty acres of military-positioned fruit trees—apples, cherries, apricots, pears, peaches, prunes, and all the experimental little groves of peach-plums, miniature pears, Eastern apples—moistly jungle-like now with all the tall wet grass at six o'clock in the morning. In years earlier he had been a kid, working there with his father during summer vacations, paid as a kid, expected to work as a kid. Now he was on full-time, a full-time effort expected of him. At six o'clock in the morning he had to go out and reposition hundreds of feet of aluminum sprinkler lines, straining and slipping and cursing for an hour and a half in the slimy wet long grass between the rows of trees, his fingers squishing slugs, water spurting in his face, his feet and pant legs getting soaked. He always felt squidgy as he walked back up the hill toward his uncle's house to have breakfast at eight, walked along the dusty road, the dust caking on his wet boots, a cigarette jammed in the corner of his mouth—too wet and hungry to pay much attention to the dog cavorting along beside him.

Then a huge working man's breakfast, but first dry socks, big wool grey socks that would be all grimy and hard to pull off at the end of the day, but in the morning fresh and dry and warm. Breakfast: three cups of hot sweet coffee, porridge, eggs, bacon, toast, and another cigarette cherished before going back out for eight more hours in the long grass of the orchard.

Uncle Norris had his breakfast earlier and was already out directing the other men—thinners, pickers, sprayers, tractor drivers. The two little cousin Delsings were already out in the long grass in their high rubber boots, scurrying around under the trees and around the busy men, picking up funny German and Russian expressions. He, George, was alone with Aunt Dorothy, once English schoolgirl and English Navy girl, now completely resolved to handling the men and children and dogs of a big fruit ranch, a woman still beautiful but in a tired way beautiful, still fresh but in a more robust way fresh. She still had a little of her English accent, or rather she had still resisted some of the more unpleasant Canadian way of pronouncing sounds. She smoked the way only an English woman can smoke, sucking, caressing, loving her cigarette, the way a wolverine would smoke if man could spread the disease to the other animals.

Breakfast time was one of the best times of the day. It was when he could talk to his aunt, find out things about England, about the Navy, use his time in finding out things while he had to eat, time that wasn't wasted. He talked to her about Frances, and she seemed really interested. He didn't know that she was identifying with Frances, seeing herself, the English *cum* Canadian girl getting involved with the provincial Canadian boy all over again. They would pick up the conversation where it had left off at half past eight the morning before, and leave it off at half past eight again, to be picked up the next day.

After breakfast he would walk down through the orchard or along the road with its foot-deep clay dust to find his uncle and find out where to go to work this day. Or sometimes he would find out from

A bunch of pickers having a sit-down rest.

his aunt at breakfast that he was supposed to go ahead with whatever he had been doing the day before.

Right after school, in the end of June and most of July they had been picking cherries, filling hundreds of boxes with Bings and Lamberts and the yellow Royal Anns from the giant trees. It had been an unusually good cherry year. Sometimes they had been able to set a twenty-four-foot ladder in one spot and bring down a hundred and fifty pounds of red-black cherries before moving the ladder to the next spot. But one night, near the end of the cherry picking, a lashing, howling storm had hit the orchard, smashing rain against the trees there on the slopes that came to an abrupt edge overlooking the forty-mile-long lake hundreds of feet down the cliffs. They had to work as late as they could that night, picking by the dangerous gleam of spotlights after the huge rolling black clouds darkened the valley. They had to work fast before the storm could ruin the rest of the crop, before the rain could get in and split the fat cherries. They got soaked through their clothing, he and his uncle and the twenty men. It was dangerous on the slippery ladders and trees. They had to shout up close to one another to be heard, rain in their uplifted eyes, through the almost constant howling of the rain wind and the booming of the thunder and the protest of the trees as the rain came through them almost horizontal. But they worked silently as much as they could, too hurried to talk, later too tired and aching to talk. But they quit at nine o'clock, and let the rest of the cherries go. They would salvage the remains the next day. Uncle Norris had made them quit. At nine o'clock huge white lightning had smashed through and into the top of the forty-foot tree he had been in, and he had come down, walking back and forth on the muddy road, half-blinded, shouting at the men to come down and stop for the night. Afterward at the house, after he had seen the boxes of cherries safely in the sheds, Uncle Norris had been very quiet, not joining in the conversation or offering to play cards.

Then after the cherries came the thinning of the apples. George made a game or war or contest out of thinning apples. Each man would be given a row of apple trees to thin, his job to break up the clusters of little green apples so that the strongest apple remained alone on each spur. After a tree was thinned the ground underneath it would be blanketed with little green apples, some of them mashed by boots and the ladders. George went to war against each tree, seeing the apples on the ground as his defeated foes, the apples left on the tree his army occupying the newly won lands. It was good to be finished a row of trees and look back at the day's campaign, and to look on the next day's row, to calculate how many days of fighting would win the war. Then there was the picking war with the peaches and the pears.

But by peach and pear season, halfway through August, George wasn't picking anymore. He was driving tractor. He really liked driving tractor. He felt as if he were a new kind of warrior, the officer on horseback, who rode all around the battlegrounds, surveying the troops and working with them in different theatres of war. Some days he would be hauling trailer loads of props, the long, skinned jack-pine poles with slats nailed into the ends to form vees that would be nudged up under branches on the apple trees where the growing weight of the apples was bending the branches down. He would load up the trailer from the huge wigwams of poles and drive his load along the dust roads till he came to the trees he was working. Sometimes he would have to use almost a whole load of props on one tree. You had to learn by experience which branches would need propping, but even after you got to where you weren't using a single extraneous prop, sometimes you would finish with forty props under a big old apple tree. It was a good apple crop that year, too. Or sometimes he loaded his trailer with empty boxes and drove down between the rows of peach trees where the men were going to start picking the full round peaches off the loaded trees. He would stop in the middle of the long wet grass and throw boxes off under the four nearest trees, then drive on to the next spot. For this too you got the system after a while, and it was a muscular joy to be smooth, wasting no motions, as if you could stand off to one side and watch yourself working like a smooth-working timberman or boxer. It was not so easy on the trip back. On the trip back he loaded the trailer with the full boxes from under the trees that had already been picked over. These he had to haul along the dusty road up past the house and to the highway, there to unload them onto the big platform, seven high, to be picked up by the trucks from the packing house down in the city by the lake. The full boxes weighed about sixty pounds each. The seventh one on the top of the pile seemed to weight twice that. He was always glad when it was time to load up with empties and drive back along the dusty road. After the trailer was loaded up with empties he would drive leisurely down the road, churning up a tall cloud of dust that moved along with him, white clay dust that covered his bare back and legs with a fine powder, that stuck to him because he was covered with sweat. It would clog in his mouth and sift into his eyebrows and his hair whenever he had his baseball cap off. Every time he drove down the road with a load of empties he had a cigarette. He would drive along with the long new cigarette in the left corner of his mouth, and every time he came to one sharp bend he would turn his head to look back at the load, and he would always burn his bare shoulder with the cigarette. He had cigarette scars all over his shoulder.

It was good to be working and saving your money to go to college. He liked to think of how he was putting out work and bringing in money, and when you worked it helped you, too. Already, after working two months in the hot sun he had a good dark tan and tough muscles on his arms, shoulders, and back.

And the nights were yours, all yours. No homework to do, or rather no homework you should have been doing. But they went too fast, the nights. He would finish work at six or seven, and then drive the tractor up to the sheds beside the big brown house (ranch house, he always called it), and then he would tromp in and have a shower, usually with cold water that never did get the clay dust out of the cracks, and then they would all have supper. Some nights there was a baseball practice down in Layton, or rather in the little suburb Tarawa, just a few stores and a packing house and a few old houses and a few new ones, and some nights there was swimming down there. Either Uncle Norris would drive them down, or maybe one of the other guys would get his old man's car or old orchard car. Every Monday and Wednesday night he would write a letter full of jokes and nudging endearments to Frances, and every Tuesday and Thursday he would get a letter from her. Usually he would take off right after work on Friday nights and climb up to the highway and stick out his thumb and be in Lawrence about nine o'clock. Sometimes he would get off work about three in the afternoon on Fridays, and get into Lawrence in time to have supper at Frances's place. But sometimes, when the Tarawa Terriers were playing ball up north in the valley instead of down around Layton or Lawrence, he would have to go through a weekend without seeing her. It was tough, but baseball was a good thing, and it was worth missing a weekend with Frances to go to some ball diamond up north and suit up and come out on the field in your spikes and your clean ball uniform and see how the girls that came out to the junior ball games in that town were. He was playing right field that year. He would have liked second base, but he was late trying out for the team, and he had to be satisfied with right field. They had him on the team because he was big, six feet, and he could hit well, and he was a good psychological weapon. A little pitcher from the other side

This is a picture of me adopting the persona of Lou Gehrig. There's my dad's 1936 Chevrolet. Blue Mountain is in the background.

would see him standing up straight and tall over the plate, and maybe get a little nervous. He was hitting in his favourite number two slot, and was about .330 that summer, which was better than he had done in Lawrence the year before, where there were so many guys going out for baseball that you couldn't get a regular place on the team unless you were there the year before or really good, or in the gang solid. And it wasn't too bad out there in the outfield where you could stand with your legs slightly apart, cool and graceful like Ted Williams, who was the greatest ballplayer of all time and not much taller than six feet.

The nights at the house went too fast, and there were too many things to do in the few hours between supper and bedtime. Some nights the three of them played canasta or hearts or gin rummy, and that was good, too, pitting your skill against high odds, losing most of the time against these older more experienced players, but knowing you were getting better and better all the time, and winning more and more often as the summer wore on. And there was the paper to read, the sports pages to go through. The Dodgers and the Yankees were sailing along that year again, just as in 1952, when they had met and the Yankees had won again. There were the sports magazines and the baseball magazines. And there were the science fiction books that had taken the place of the westerns a year ago. Max Brand and Luke Short and Ernest Haycox had given way to Ray Bradbury and Murray Leinster and Robert Heinlein. It made George mad the way everyone sort of looked at him reading science fiction and said stupid things about reading that Buck Rogers stuff about impossible things like space platforms. They thought science fiction was stuff about spaceships and bug-eyed monsters and zap ray guns and evil scientists with white Van Dyck beards and semi-naked daughters.

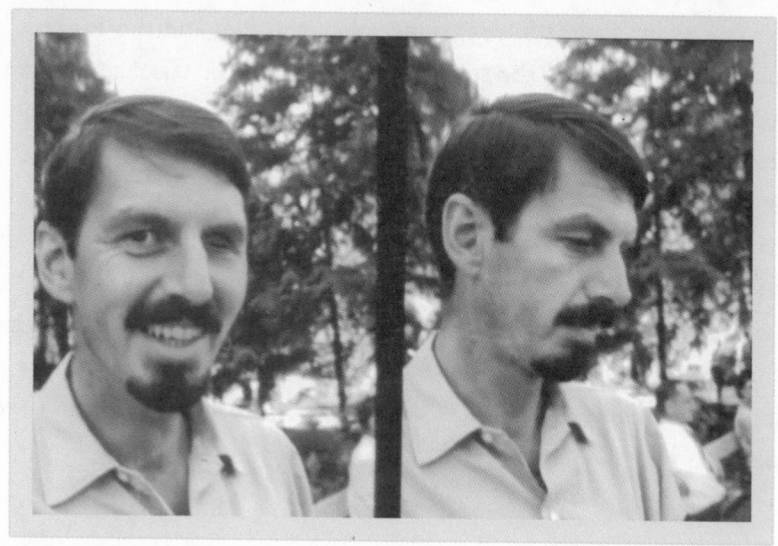

Robert Creeley

Illustration from Sticks & Stones by Gordon Payne,
a North Okanagan boy.

Sticks & Stones

We will remember that Robert Creeley wrote, "The words will become a world," in the introduction to this first collection of my poems. Yet in his editor's end note, Roy Miki remembers his interview with the author: "the main notion was that you built poems out of actual things," according to the poetic of William Carlos Williams, the poet I chose in my youth to be my poetry dad. Well, over time we came to know that these two assertions are complementary rather than contradictory. "Art is life's only twin," after all. Charles Olson, Creeley's friend and our hero said that.

So these poems, written while I was a student at UBC and an editor of a little poetry newsletter called *Tish*, are heavy with concrete nouns and simple verbs. "Locus Primus," for example (republished the following year in *The Valley*), shows two kids carefully swimming and rowboating across a small Okanagan lake. It is a poem that is carefully local and without metaphor (although "metaphor" does mean "to carry across").

Those who wanted to make something more of the title, which might be read as part of "sticks & stones may break my bones but names will never hurt me" were free to do so. My focus was on concrete nouns, out of which I hoped to make poetry.

Sticks & Stones was more a gathering of pages that were intended to become a printed Tishbook. In 1989 a true first edition was published by Talonbooks.

Radio Jazz

Sucked into the horn of jazz
on lonely midnight Salt Lake City radio
over to me alone in a big house
hundreds of miles in the mountains
fantastic piano then
key to me right hand left hand on silent radio sound
on a million radio America waves in the dark

Folks all gone folks
gone to the Coast leaving me and
the shelf radio in a hot night kitchen
old friends gone home three empty cups on the
table here
Gerry Mulligan meets Stan Getz
in the next one in the last one
on the radio award bandstand
down away on the truck coming road
sound radio bound Salt Lake City comes on

The Valley

For five decades I forgot about this item. My wife, Jean, found a messy typescript of something called "The Valley and the City. Part One—The Valley," thirteen pages of descriptive prose with poems interspersed. The handwriting on the cover sheet tells us that this was finished in February 1963. In 1953 I had graduated from high school and left town. Almost ten years later I was writing a nostalgic piece instead of studying for the ordeal that a student is supposed to go through in the last half year before earning his M. A.

According to Roy Miki's bibliography of my stuff, "The Valley" was published in a beautiful but doomed Montreal arts magazine called *Parallel*. That mag started in 1966 and ended in 1967, during one of the liveliest times for Canadian small presses and reading venues. If I ever wrote or even started "The City," I don't have any memory of it—1963 was a pretty busy year for me.

The person who wrote the prose in "The Valley" seems a little self-satisfied, but I have to say that the prose is better than the poems. There are ten short poems, five of which eventually made their way into books. One even became the middle of a print ad for the Hudson's Bay Company, showing up in lots of papers and magazines all over the country.

Actually, now that I think about it, I kind of wish I had written "The City." I'd be curious to see what Vancouver was like in the early sixties.

Looking north from the hills I used to hike in, west of Oliver, near the umbrella tree. Farther south is the ghost town of Fairview.

Another view looking north past the airport, circa 1940.

Part One—The Valley

The Okanagan Valley is a giant groove cut through the centre of British Columbia by a huge glacier of the last ice age. Two hundred and fifty miles east of Vancouver, the valley appears abruptly as a wide swathe of blue. Deep blue lakes are bordered by blue mountains and the wide blue Mediterranean sky the residents of the valley seem to think they themselves have painted.

In the spring the predominant blue is invaded by a huge garden of fruit-tree blossoms, as whole acres of pink and white, orange and yellow appear overnight. At this time the air is filled with the scent of blossoms, drifted north or south by the warm spring winds. But the blossoms fall away, and in the summer, the colours are wilder, more confused, as thousands upon thousands of tourists, including wandering Americans and restless Canadians, descend from the hills and cover the beaches and the lakes with their tents and sails, their Mediterranean costumes and their Okanagan sunburns.

Oliver is one of the hottest places in the valley. At the end of July the grass on the hills burns brown and the village dogs walk around with their tongues hanging out. For two months the temperature has been climbing higher and higher and there has been no hint of rain, no gathering of clouds, nothing but the wide blue sky and the huge white hot sun. White sheets hanging on lines in backyards are stiff and dry in ten minutes. The kids out playing sandlot baseball come in for ice water every fifteen minutes.

The heat builds up for week after week, and people begin to look toward the western hills before doing anything else every day, knowing that sooner or later the Pacific coast will send them a storm, and hoping it will be sooner. And finally one day, or one night, the storm comes,

OKANAGAN STORM
by George Bowering

forks of standing lightning
on the mountain crests
    as the dark rolling storm
      thunders on the edges of the valley
      overlooking mountains
light the night
and fill the forest with morning
in a second
    Valley is refuge
a trench in the storm
a dark
   blue
      balls of orange rain cloud
      drifting west
      up the hills
Letting up the pressure
for the first rain
creeping fast across the lake
     and the lightning
     goes out

HBC ad that appeared in many magazines and journals, with an illustration by Les Simoens.

and it comes so suddenly as to catch everyone by surprise. A great wall of wind-driven rain can overtake a motorist driving south along Highway 97, and threaten to wash his car from the road. Great jags of lightning spatter the mountain ridges, and huge detonations of thunder roll between the two edges of the valley.

And the storm is over—as suddenly as it had begun. The thunder can be heard rolling away into distant valleys until it fades from hearing. If it is still daytime the sun comes out again, sending back a million reflections from the quiet puddles beside the roads. Every still thing is glazed for an hour, and the air feels cool and clean. At this time the people come from their houses and do the shopping; the kids bring out the baseball things and pick their way between pools of water.

The old retired Russian across the street comes out of his house and resumes work on his wine bottle fence. Everyone says he is mad, a kind of local nut who wants to build a whole city of bottles. But sitting and watching him from the window in our dining room, I am convinced that what he is doing takes on some kind of constructive significance as slowly and steadily he puts one bottle on top of another. Every morning I see him coming up the street from downtown, with a cardboard carton full of bottles in his arms, and every afternoon I see him out in the sun, trowelling mortar and placing the bottles, slowly and steadily.

Returning to the valley after I have grown up is a strange experience. But it is not only the boy or the man who changes while the village remains the same. As the world moves, so does the old home town; but it moves a little slower, and it moves in its own direction, sometimes following the rest of the world, sometimes at right angles to it. When you go back there and notice the changes, you find it harder to remember how it all was when you were growing up there; and you think about it more consciously.

But it isn't the town itself that stays in the mind when you think back to the time when you were a kid and you could start your day without a series of commitments and complications, when you had a whole new day to do whatever you wanted. For me and my best friend, a straw-haired and round-nosed boy by the name of Bill, a long free day usually meant a hike in the hills. The hills around that part of the valley are a sort of medium colour, of a sort of medium height, with a sort of medium difficult rise, the sort of hills we always saw in western movies.

But they were full of snakes and cactus, creeks and caves, horses and coyotes. Sometimes you would find a creek bed sheltered from the sun, and in the warm spring there would be a pocket of wet crystalline snow, a chance for the last snowball fight of the year, or a place to leave tracks for the unknown pathfinders behind us. And there was Blue Mountain, a five-thousand-foot hump of rock and fir trees we had named ourselves. For years we talked of climbing Blue Mountain, and then one year we did.

Locus Solus

Attaching toes to Vancouver downtown sidewalks over-
sluiced with rain water
                    Under billowed concave black
umbrella dripping around me

                    eyes down on neon reflections
wiggled in the gutter
                    cursing & moving alone

next to shoulders of down looking strangers
soggy in the rain

I remember dried out lips & tongue
                    long trip without water-
bottle down the side of old Blue Mountain

It was a hundred & twenty
in the shade
but there was no shade

& coming down was harder than going up
down in the empty water-
drainage slashes

in dust now
& over boulder slides

Finally down
To lichen green rocks

& face first into the stream muddied
by the dog a few yards up

head pushed into the water
teeth aching & belly pulled tight by the cold sucking
down the throat

and the final walking home

respecting the sun & taking it easy
planting feet in the long easy strides

But Blue Mountain wasn't the only goal Bill and I had set ourselves. Another was Tuc-el-Nuit Lake, where his family lived. For years we talked about swimming across it, this little lake a half mile wide and warm as a blanket. Then one summer we decided to accept the challenge. For weeks we practised our swimming, Australian crawling back and forth in front of the little wharf at Bill's house, seeing how long we could stay in the water.

Bill's place on Tuc-el-Nuit Lake. We swam across it once.

We had seen quite a few people swim across the lake. In fact it was done every day, by the school kids older than us, and even by some our age. But we wanted to be sure. There had been too many people drowned in that lake. Our plan was for Bill to swim across while I rowed beside him in his battered and leaky old rowboat. Then on the way back he would row while I swam. Now the typewriter takes me back.

Locus Primus

The typewriter takes me across
& back
  there across Tuc-el-Nuit Lake
beside Bill in the boat
resting on the oars
    while I was treading water

  When we were ten we looked across the lake
  when we were eleven we looked across
  when we were twelve we walked in
  up to our necks
  & swam

I rowed while he swam across
We turned back
& I put my arms ahead of me in the water
while he bent in the boat
the water drying off his back

  The typewriter moves across the page
  laying letter by letter
  resting now & then
  begun: & unwilling to stop

I supposed when you are kids in the valley, everything you do on your free days is a kind of expedition, a journey on which you rest yourselves against the natural terrain and the elements. When you go hiking together in the mountains you are striking out like Lewis and Clark, discovering new rivers and mountains, exploring the virgin country the settlers and loggers and miners will follow you into. When you ride your bikes down to the American border and back, you are carrying the important gold dust messages through dangerous Apache country.

All down the southern end of the valley runs the irrigation ditch, a concrete channel eight feet deep and twelve feet wide. In the summer it is filled to brimming with deep green water that supplies the hundreds of orchards whose miles of sprinklers must be kept spraying water to the trees twenty-four hours a day. But in the winter the water is shut off as the orchards stand bare, and the irrigation ditch is empty. On the first empty day the kids put on their rubber boots and walk along the ditch, looking for anything that might have been thrown or dropped into the water during the summer. One time I found a .22 calibre pistol; another time I found a necklace of Dutch coins.

But mainly the winter irrigation ditch was the best way of getting to the old empty cement works, a dilapidated building surrounded by old concrete pipes and unexplainable machines. This is where the ditch was made, slab by slab. Why we went out there we never really knew. One time our dogs trapped a porcupine under the floor of the old building, and we spent the afternoon pulling the quills out of their noses and tongues. Usually we would just go out to the cement works and crawl around the place for a while, looking for mysteries in the attic and under the floor. But what sticks in the mind is the walk out there and back. Sometimes we took Bill's kid brother Sandy with us.

Patrol

Walking along the empty winter
irrigation ditch

below the blow of snow
drifting across above us

five miles and back south
of Oliver

the three of us
two from the city
and wearing city sweaters

suffering the cold wind the dry
air and enjoying it
the Boy Commandos

We paced off
the joining segments
of weedy cement

looking for treasures
and money dropped
in the water
last summer

doing ten miles that day
walking ten miles away that day

A few years ago I climbed Blue Mountain again, and whenever I go
back to the valley I manage to find the time to tramp around the hills
that seem much smaller now. But I have never gone out the irrigation
ditch to the cement works since the time ten years ago when I left the
valley for the outside world. For the man who comes back, the irrigation ditch has been replaced by Highway 97 that runs thru the valley
on the way north to the Cariboo and Peace countries. A man has a car
now, and his friends are scattered out in various cities a few hours' drive
from the old home town.

Winter was for maintenance. Here we see people pruning fruit trees before the sap starts rising.

One thing the drive up the valley brings back is the sense of size. The highway runs alongside the big blue lakes on one side and the striated cliffs or clay bluffs on the other. Driving up the road, you bring back the sense of what the valley means, how it got there, and why you keep coming back. You look for sources and beginnings.

There is a size in time as well as a size in space, and the ice that carved out the valley disappeared from the memory of man. So that now the valley is generally thought of in terms of its summer; it is vacationland for most people, a place seen in July and August, and left to the inhabitants in the winter. And for those inhabitants the winter usually means a time not of cold and snow so much as a time when the apple trees are bare and the orchard machinery is in the sheds. The winters are mild, or usually mild, and the idea of a Canadian winter under tons of snow is something you see realized in the photographs of Saturday magazines.

But every once in a while a winter brings snow, and the valley people get a sense of what the magazine pictures mean. A kid in the valley will probably see one winter of snow, and if he is lucky, two. And for the rest of his life he will remember it and talk about it.

I haven't seen the valley in the spring or fall in ten years, and I probably never will again. Every time I ride the bus into the village I see the same people on the street, the poorly spelled signs there year after year, the same baseball team in the same ballpark with the same spectators. One searches for signs of change and has to be satisfied with little things: the school has been painted, a sidewalk has been laid, someone has got married.

The only change has been in yourself, you think, that added height year after year, the growing out to new interests. That is why I climb the hill to the old umbrella tree every time I go back there. The umbrella tree stands on top of the hill that marks the west boundary of the valley, and for years it was my boundary. A climb to the umbrella tree was a reaching out to the edge of things. My friend Bill and I had always thought of it as our tree. Now when I think back on the time I lived in the valley, it is the umbrella tree that comes first to mind.

Points on the Grid

When I was a serious and hopeful young writer I said that I wanted my first poetry book to be published by Contact Press and my first fiction book to be published by McClelland & Stewart. I got my wish on both, and then I quit wishing because I knew my lucky streak could not continue.

I was living in Calgary when I got the telephone call from Raymond Souster to tell me that Contact was going to publish my book of poetry. For some reason I felt and looked completely calm, as if things were going the way they were meant to.

But I was very happy. I had a little collection of Contact Press books, probably the only such collection in Calgary—and I remember that it was pleasing to look at the Contact back covers and see that I was going to be listed in their catalogue with Louis Dudek, Raymond Souster, Alden Nowlan, and D. G. Jones. There was, I was convinced, a tradition in which the most interesting young poets would get their first big-deal Toronto publication by this press. I would soon be followed by Margaret Atwood and John Newlove, for instance. I breathed a poetic sigh of relief.

Points on the Grid had been the title of my M. A. thesis at UBC. So though the book is not what the thesis was, it is no wonder that there are poems based on my tyro's theory in it. That theory had something to do with what us young Charles Olsonites called *locus*. What we meant by that was the kind of writing, like his, that was grounded in the particulars of the place(s) in which its action(s) takes place. So the poems in this book are about the South Okanagan and the city of Vancouver. When it was published I was in Calgary, trying to write a book about Alberta.

Meta Morphosis

(a)

Squared off by taut
string tied to pegs
at the four corners
my quarter of the garden

brought forth every year
radishes. So that bending
over the furrows I
would know the seeds

would send back
leaves and later radishes
bulging out of the
ground. Every year.

(b)

This year my foursquare
garden squashes under
my crouched weight. I
dribble these seeds

into thumb-punched holes.
And I will water till
and weed them till they
are radishes for the plucking.

So each red wet vege-
table on this plate on this
table will have come
from this hole from this row.

                (c)

So shall the spring pass
So shall this come
this spring
this fair sister to them all
So shall this only
child spring
be sprung
So shall it come never again
So shall it come again another spring.

The Man in Yellow Boots

When I was in the RCAF during the fifties, I spent most of my time at a base called Macdonald, which was just south of the bottom tip of Lake Manitoba. In the winter there was a lot of snow, and in the spring there was a lot of mud, so we airmen wore big galumphing rubber boots with fur and laces over our regular footwear. Of course, when we went into the mess hall we had to leave them in the huge mud room. I got tired of trying to find my boots after meals, so I painted their toes yellow. This was one of the ways in which my items of service clothing became irregular.

This book is otherwise the sixteenth number of the fine poetry magazine *El Corno Emplumado*, edited by Sergio Mondragón and Margaret Randall in Mexico City. Every fourth issue of the magazine was a book, and as befits a bilingual magazine, this would mean that every eighth issue would be a book by a poet who wrote in English. Number eight was *Her Body Against Time / Su cuerpo contra el tiempo* by Robert Kelly. Number four was a long poem, *Màrsias i Adila*, by the self-exiled Catalan poet Agustí Bartra. Number twelve was *Ajy Tojen* by Raquel Jodorowsky, one of the leaders of Peru's Nadaistas.

El Corno Emplumada always featured visual artists as well as poets. On my wall now I have three ink drawings by the great José Luis Cuevas that were reproduced in an issue of the magazine. I would tell you which one, but I foolishly gave my run of the magazine to the University of Northern British Columbia library. You'll just have to look it up. It was not until January 2013 that I was able to visit the Cuevas museum just off the Zócalo in Mexico City.

In any case, I was very pleased that the great artist Roy Kiyooka let me include twelve of his photo-collages in *El hombre de las botas amarillas*. They were ovals, the shape that Roy was trying out in painting and sculpture at the time. I also persuaded him to give me one of his poems for inclusion in my book.

Because *El Corno Emplumado* had subscribers from Alaska to Tierra del Fuego, and there were lots of poetry bookstores in those days, my second real book of poetry sold three thousand copies. Sergio and Margaret told me that they always ordered a limited edition of leather-and-buckram bound copies that the author would pay for. I set a record for modesty/frugality, and ordered five.

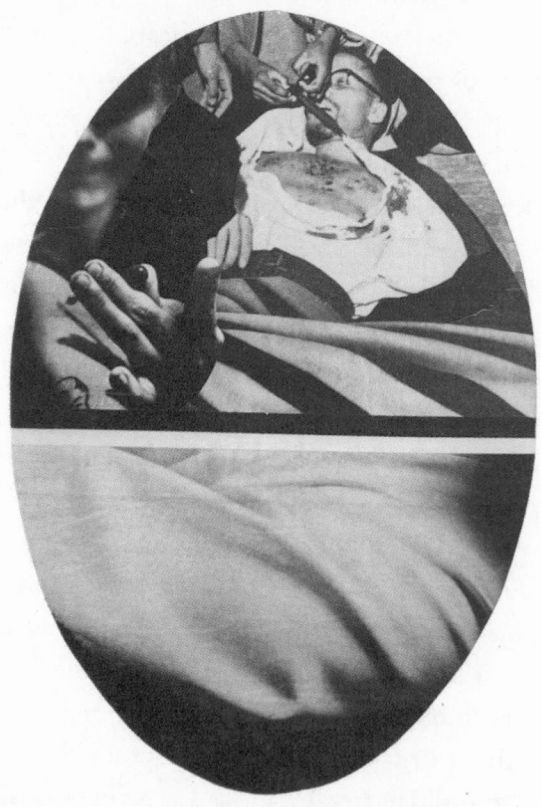

One of Roy Kiyooka's elliptical collages that appeared in
The Man in Yellow Boots.

Recharge

These peach trees
along the highway
emptied now, lean
away from the wind,

are not eclectic,
as I return to
origin, a matter of
choice, the orchard

country, or first
learnings in a later
wind. I sit in my
father's house and

read his dictionary,
picking it up, piece
by piece, forming
my own opinions again.

Painting by Gordon Payne, circa 1962. See those small letters of my name on the surface of the paint, above my head? There is also a unique manuscript of a poem under the paint. The painting appears on the back cover of The Silver Wire.

The Silver Wire

The Silver Wire, the title of which is derived from Blake's definition of poetry, is perhaps my least-known book of poems. It is a collection of lyric poems typical for the time. On the back cover I am referred to as "prolific and energetic," descriptions that would cover me for years to come, not always in praise. I was publishing here, there, and everywhere in those days, from the *Atlantic Monthly* to young David McFadden's *Mountain.* The acknowledgements page lists thirty-nine sources. My fellow *Tish* editors used to give me the gears about that.

Once again the book was graced by the art of Gordon Payne, whose portrait of me is reprinted on the back of the dust jacket. That the book was published in Kingston was due to the fact that fellow young poets Tom Marshall and Douglas Barbour were university students there.

The collection is eclectic, to put a nice word on it. There are the short poems of a recently married man, observations on the climate of Alberta, poems about other poets, translations, poems about Vancouver—and short poems about the Okanagan Valley. Looking at the project now, I see and hear the exercises that a composer writes before venturing into something I once called his symphonic age.

So the roadside in the Okanagan is subject to the same eye that looks at a clothesline in a backyard over False Creek. I guess the words were trying to make a world.

Reading these pieces now I find myself enjoying the brevity that obviously defined my poetic in my twenties. A few years out of the air force, I was still a photographer—a still photographer.

My dad did like sporty cars when he was young but by the time I was around he was driving four-door sedans.

Driving to Kelowna

you edge along the Okanagan
lake   valley   hills   and sky

blue
striated sense all pointing north

    to the source

        where ice loaded and spring south
        leaving a cut of clay
        and green knobs by the lake

You move your coloured car
on the highway that issues north

trace your beginnings

Baseball

This little book (I hadn't then thought of classifying my volumes as books and chapbooks) was the beginning of my happy relationship with Coach House Press during the radical years of its history. In those days, we thought of Coach House as the Toronto branch of Talonbooks. The manuscript was acquired and edited by bpNichol, who was not himself a baseball fan, but who would become the hippest Canadian poetry press's flagship author.

Though the book is a poem rather than a collection of poems, and though it tries to include the presence of the poet Jack Spicer, it does not really qualify totally as a serial poem in the open-ended Spicerian sense, especially in that it seems too conscious of its limited range to do that. I wrote it over the baseball season of 1965, starting in Calgary, continuing in Mexico City, and wrapping it up back home. Jack Spicer died halfway through the poem. He was a great San Francisco baseball fan. When he died the Giants were in first place in the ten-team National League, and their centre fielder, the best player in baseball, Willie Mays, was making a run at Babe Ruth's home run record.

I was a Dodgers fan, and as everyone knows the Dodgers and Giants drive each other's fans to murderous frames of mind, but after some friends from Oregon came down to Mexcity and told us that Jack had died, I almost wanted the Giants and Mays to do it. As it turned out the Dodgers beat the Giants by two games, and Willie got fifty-two homers (my unlucky number) and an OPS (on-base percentage plus slugging average) over a thousand.

The book became a little notorious because of its production, something that Coach House was then noted for. Its cover was green and textured to suggest artificial turf. When closed it was in the shape of

Jack Spicer

a pennant, and when open it looked like a squashed diamond. It was organized into nine sections to resemble a baseball game's innings. The words it uttered made form pay attention to structure. Because of its triangular shape, its pointy end often got misshapen in bookshelves, and people did not know whether the pointy end should go up or forward. The young poet Artie Gold solved the problem by nailing the book to the wall as if it were a pennant celebrating some green baseball team.

Remembering the poem now, I see that I was learning to work my contraries: the adolescent mind of a baseball fan and the flowering mind of a poet in the poetry world; the nurturing desert valley of my childhood and the exciting expanding city of my youngmanhood; Manuel Louie, the old Okanagan Indian chief shortstop, and Jack Spicer, heroic and demanding USAmerican bard dead in San Francisco at thirty-nine, his voice rumbling back from the afterlife. I was learning in this book that you don't cast aside your boyhood *locus*; it remains as part of the breath and sound trying to make what you are trying to make. Trying even now, forty-nine years on.

Here's Manuel Louie and family a few years before I knew him. Like all the "Indians" in the South Okanagan, he was a pretty good ballplayer.

3rd Inning

Manuel Louie, old Manuel Louie
is chief of the Indians around Oliver.
1965 now, he is 94 but he looks 55.
He's still got big black moustache, shoots pool
with his belly hanging over the rail.

Age 80, he was still playing Indian baseball games,
the chief, bowlegged running bases with turkey feather
in his hat.

The Wenatchee Chiefs, class A,
were spring training in Oliver then,
letting Manuel Louie work out at shortstop,
weird Sitting Bull Honus Wagner,
in exchange for his sweat lodge,
beside the creek, outside his back door.

That year the Wenatchee Chiefs finished fifth.

The Gangs of Kosmos

The title is Walt Whitman's characterization of the poets who would follow in his future. The book was edited for her House of Anansi by young Margaret Atwood. It, along with *Rocky Mountain Foot*, would get me the Governor General's Award that year. I figured things were going along as they should.

But I guess there is a lot more Vancouver and Mexico in the book than there is Okanagan, unless you count the land that formulated my imagination's character.

So, was I thinking at the time that I was growing away from the Okanagan's reach? Was that how you grew up in the poetry world?

I Don't

While my father emptied
I climbed around the town dump

looking, because so many objects
were nearly whole.

                                    I'm supposed
to say something here
about poetry & growing up?

Once I found a necklace
made of Dutch coins. I don't

know what became of them.

A fat kid with a dreamy look on his face. Me, in Peachland, with my mother, Pearl Bowering.

Autobiology

But no, the Okanagan would always reach out and urge me back, at least in thought. In *Autobiology*, which has been reprinted pretty often, we see why. I have often said that when I moved east to Ontario and then to Quebec I could no longer base my approach on the place around me because I could not see and understand the details that made a place. Instead of forest there were woodlots, for example. Instead of mountains there were lots of paved roads.

So I went inside, I guess you'd say. I did a long poem based on an eighteenth-century medico's diary of his voyage with Captain Vancouver. I did a poem based on the tarot deck. *Autobiology*, as its title suggest, is a number of Steinian improvisations on moments in my life when stuff that occurred to my body caused shifts in whatever you call the combination of memory and observation. The first piece was composed in the kitchen of a place in an Irish section of North London, England, but is about something that happened with raspberries in Peachland, British Columbia, long before. So I guess it makes sense that thirteen of its forty-eight sections were provoked by the Okanagan Valley.

The rest of the book was written back "home" in Montreal, and published in Vancouver at a press founded by the commune we moved into when we got there. Talk about home. That commune was just around the corner from the apartment we had lived in on Yew Street just before going to Calgary eight years earlier.

I have always thought of *Autobiology* as an important departure for me. It was to that date the most extremely language-centred (as opposed to place-centred) long poem I had written, and would prepare my way for the next few, *Curious* and *A Short Sad Book* and *Allophanes*, none of which have Okanagan stuff in them.

Like a lot of boys in the OK in those days,
I started smoking young.

The Raspberries

When I was thirty I had free raspberries in the back yard
and I loved them. In the back yard and I ate them. And I ate them
in the kitchen out of an aluminum pot. When I was thirty I loved
raspberries, I loved to eat them. I loved the way they were made
of many pieces in my mouth, and they came from the outside of
the bush and the inside. They came from the outside in the sunshine and from the inside in the darkness, and that is where they
went again. But inside in the darkness is where we are told the
subconscious is and that is why I could not eat raspberries. I could
not eat raspberries when I was three years old when we had free
raspberries in the front yard. In Peachland, where the free raspberries grow, and they grew outside in the sunshine where I could
reach them when I was three and a half. I could reach one and I
ate it, and I thought there was a bug on it. But I ate it too fast to
know for certain. Years later I saw a face at a girl's window and
I thought it was a man named Russell, but I went away too soon
and so I never knew. I never knew whether I ate a bug on a raspberry. I had never eaten a bug before so I didn't know what they
taste like. I could not eat raspberries for years after that day in our
front yard when I was over three years old, even though the raspberries always looked so good with all their round pieces in a
cone or bunch. But there is a hole inside the raspberry and it could
always have a bug in it.

The Bowering clan assembled, maybe for Christmas, outside the West Summerland post office, attached to my grandparents' house. Note that young George is front and centre.

Some Deaths

My cousin Russell died the night before and I stayed on the lawn and said I didn't want his saxophone. It was a death without sex because he was twenty and I was twelve and we lived twenty-seven miles apart. In Penticton he played the saxophone and in Oliver I dreamed of playing the drums and that dream was dead and the duet was dead as well and after that I played alone but not the drums. They offered me the saxophone but I stayed by myself on the lawn.

My aunt Dorothy died when I was a baby so I saw her but mainly in the photograph. She died of TB where she worked against death as a nurse. She worked against TB and she died and I never saw her photograph after I passed the age when she died and I had my chest photographed to see whether I had TB.

My grandmother Clara died at Easter and my grandfather Jabez walked on his crutches around the living room saying "Mother" as if she would not be resurrected. He said it as if she were his mother, and he an old man. He said it as if she would not be resurrected and he a former minister of God. It was Easter and the food she had cooked for the family lay where she left it and began to undergo the changes brought by death. Perhaps it was thrown away and perhaps the family ate it all.

Sally and Caesar and George. This picture is probably from grade one or grade two, but that is the dog I still had in grade three. What a cute dog, eh? He was so prickly.

Growing

In grade six I was interested in science but before I knew the
pleasure of its order then it was only a gleam. In grade nine I was
interested in science fiction for the pleasure of it was only a dream
not the order intended but all along I was practising a pleasure in
order but that was superstition and certainly not science fiction. In
grade twelve after the order of six and nine I was interested in fiction
and seeking an order that would be clean knowing superstitiously
that fiction was certainly not the novel it was certainly not news it
was moulding that is not science but something like movement where
you do not concern yourself with what you are riding but with the
present of where you are not going but you are right now, moving.
Science wants to know where you have been and where it will take
you. That is order and may even be orders though that sounds like
romance. Romance is not certainly fiction though it may be science
fiction. In grade three I was interested in my dog and his associations
with the animals in the orchard. I lived in a house surrounded by
trees in efficient lines so that the house was connected with Highway
3 and 97 by a straight gravel driveway and at the end of the driveway
was a garage behind which I grew wheat in hopes of feeding the
chickens.

This photo was colourized and used as the cover for Baseball Love,
another Talon book.

Working and Wearing

I discovered the working was a wearing away. In the orchard
at Naramata I removed my baseball cap every time and every time
it was a nest of hair and I was fifteen there. The working was a wearing away. On Sundays I wore the cap at baseball and lost no hair
and Sunday was the best day there. Who bets on Sunday lets his hair
grow. The machine that works is worn away and oiled every day.
When I was fifteen I oiled my hair and made a nest I was wearing
there.

In the forest near Merritt I carried two cloves in my jaw for
the holes of pain I carried there. There was no dentist working
where I carried my pain from forest to town. I used to drown the
cloves in beer in the parlours there. I wore the cloves in the widening holes & on Sundays at baseball I knew no pain save the times
I would err and never be forgiven. The working was the time of
wearing away.

The sun is dying to keep us alive. The fire in its place is
dying to keep us warm. What is working is being worn.

Gallagher Lake with Gallagher Bluff in the background. You can see the irrigation ditch crossing the foreground.

The Lake

In the water was a flat fish glimmering all its colours but
mainly yellow perch eating its brother on the end of the line. I
yanked him out and we cut him up and who was with me was I
think Fred whom I thought of today nearly forty but then I
thought of him hanging from the trestle by his fingers at that
same lake saying to his girlfriend Barbara she'd better call him
pet names or he would let go and drop to the rocks and she did.
Before that she was my girlfriend and he was an older kid from
Belgium. We cut up the yellow perch and used him for bait and
I never caught another fish but I killed a pregnant squirrel with
a stone thrown into the high fir tree and I killed a snake on the
golf course with my six iron and sent the six rattles to Amanda
or Angela the lady anyway on Vancouver Island, I sent them in
an envelope and she called me Saint George and soon Saint
George was removed from the list of saints. Fred and I made a
raft and sailed it on the lake reputed to have no bottom though
we never went in our lives to the north end where there was a
house lived in by six nuns. It was called Gallagher Lake and
was near Gallagher Bluff and I have never found out who Gallagher was but Barbara was Gregory, a saint still on the list.

The First Two Towns

What is a town, what is a town exactly that we have lived in
or a city, what is the city that we have lived in even less or a good
deal more depending on how we look at it. How do we look at it
and how did we look at it. Well in the first place it was mainly towns
and in the second place it was nearly all cities and you should say
time as well as place for town or city.

The first was Penticton. It was Penticton and I was born on
the hill but I did not look at Penticton from the hill and now when
I am in Penticton though now I am not in Penticton I look up at the
hill but I did not look down from the hill because I was just born
there where my father climbed to see me and now I am realizing
that he is old and if he hears this I love him.

The second was Peachland though it was really the first for
I because that was where I began to look at a town though really
I began to look at the lake or across the lake to the east side because I was fated to be in the west looking east in these imagin-
ings because I would always move eastward looking backward
to the west not really looking east but being there.

The Fourth Town

It is really a village. It is still a village. I was embarrassed that
Oliver or Lawrence was only a village and I waited for them to vote
and pay their taxes and become with pride a town or later with great
pride a city. I could hardly wait to live in a city. It is however really
a village. There were two populations, one thousand and five thousand, but four thousand lived outside the village in the orchards, but
I always said five thousand. Consciousness is how it is composed.
When they asked I said I was from Penticton, this was when I was
back East and Penticton got famous for the hockey champions.
There was no hockey in the village of Oliver and that is why it was
always a village. At first we lived in an absent soldier's house in an
orchard two miles from the village and he later became Conservative
member of parliament to my shame. Secondly we lived in an orchard
less than two miles from the village but off a back road not the highway now. Then we moved to the village and I had more pride but
the house was small and covered with tar paper and the owner lived
next door on the corner lot. We made the house larger and I became
friends with people who lived in the village and gave up my friends
who lived in the orchards. Later I went to work for people who
owned the orchards and they were strangers and my bosses.

The Pool

It was the empty pool and then it was the cool hospital. It
was ninety-nine in the shade and then in the hospital I was laid in
white sheets. There was no shade and I was not afraid I was too
stupid with the sun to be afraid. I was struck with the sun and in
love with my luck and I thought I was the sun of god. Simply, I
was in the hospital with sunstroke. My temperature was far above
ninety-nine but I was in the catholic hospital of sheets as white as
the sun and my grandfather's hair. That would have made him the
father of god but he was a retired preacher.

My job was to clean the algae from the empty pool made of
concrete in the hot sun. The blinding sun turned white and I awoke
to the sheets next to my eyes sore with sunstroke. Later I always
needed glasses but didn't have them. I squinted.

The sun god saw to it with his eye. Simply I was in the hospital half blind with algae in my eyes. Sun stroke brings on too
hard a headache for metaphor, simply makes you squint. My twin
eyes began to bend in different directions, son of man & struck by
sun, struck like a new coin, mint in the middle of the concrete.

The Joints

I could work in cold storage because of the heat. The heat
filled the peaches with juice and my hands afterward, especially on
Sunday when I did not put on my old winter air force clothes and
go into the refrigerated room out of the room into the railroad car
into the hot sun, the fingers curled around wooden handles of the
hand truck, curled till I could not open them like blossoms of the
peach trees. I feel it now in the back of my right hand, the tree of
arthritis, I could not sleep those nights without my mother's pills,
waking in the morning with my hands curled till I'd spilled the
coffee, yes it's working now, out in the sun and again at lunch. The
doctor, I forget his name save that he was not Dr. Bridgeman, told
me it was not crippling but it was arthritis and I was proud to have
it, age twenty-one.

When it rains, yes, when it rains, just like they say in some
pained humour they seem to need, when it rains, the tree grows
and shoots like arteries all through, like they say, arthritic smile,
it's the pain, totally private, it's mine, and I have it and am still,
I admit it, glad to have it, but later I will not and will try not to
have it, the numbing and wonderful private pain totally inside.

My serious teenage reading. With my brother Roger.

Flycatcher and Other Stories

I guess it makes sense that the events in my first collection of stories would take place in orchards and along main street in Oliver, or as I called it in my fictions, Lawrence.

In a small town like Oliver there were quite a few "characters" that we just assumed were part of having a town. The two best-known "characters" in Oliver when I was a kid were Squeaky and Flycatcher. We did not shy from telling funny stories about them, we did not think that they should be shut away in a "home" somewhere, either. You will note that the narrator, presumably young George Delsing, employs a common writer's trick, in which the boy who is most likely autobiographical, is more sensitive about such things than are his peers. You will see this in the first few sentences.

The first section of "Time and Again," on the other hand, was regrettable until I somewhat improved it for this volume. The story is, as one will be led to believe, nostalgic and pretentious, and that is likely why it has been anthologized quite often. But as a reader of writers such as James T. Farrell and J. D. Salinger, I figured that you had to tell stories about boys who were a lot like yourself—sensitive and curious.

"Apples," is an example of a short short story, a form that creative writing profs and other literati made a lot of back in the day. I am proud to say that quite a while ago it was translated and published in a Japanese school anthology. Imagine—Japanese kids getting a picture of Canada that featured an orchard rather than a Rocky Mountain or Niagara Falls.

Flycatcher

Maybe in their secret hearts all the kids felt sorry for Flycatcher, maybe, but I don't think so. I just know I did, though I sometimes used to put a lampshade on my head at a party and grab a bottle, slopping thru the room and hollering first, "Who am I?" and everybody hollering as if he were a member of the group rather than a man whose real name nobody knew, "FLYCATCHER!" and I would have a moment of success, recognition, be in the middle of the room taking the lampshade off my head, face slack in pretended modesty.

As if he was fair game, which everybody thought he was. He was a familiar figure in Lawrence in the old days I remember, and I can't remember when he went away, I guess it was probably when I was away at college or air force and only years later did I stop and think Flycatcher isn't around anymore.

Here comes Flycatcher along the street, tall bony man somewhere under that old torn flag of a blue suit, in his shuffling uncontrolled slap-footed walk like a comic takeoff on the dead march, his skinny arms hanging straight down, with the fingers dangling and curled slightly, palms facing behind him. The hands would have paddled at the air if the arms had moved, but they just jiggled up and down with each jolt of that slapfooted trudge that jarred his whole slat frame. His eyes were droopy and unblinking, looking straight ahead, without purpose, in his head that took its slight movement from the joggling of his body, the scrawny neck. His pointed chin hung down, leaving his mouth in a breathless gape, some brown and bubbly saliva pasted to the corners of his lips. Hence his name. We used to say he was paid by the town to walk around the streets engulfing fliers with that looming mouth. The awful part of it was: I thought I could see that given control he would be a thinly handsome man. But there was his voice, too. When he tried to talk the eyes would get excited, tendrilled from that unknown brain in there, and the throat would work, sending the saliva in sparkly bubbles, but the voice would come out as a hysterical mumble with great throat gulps and teeth clacks. And his hands would flutter from the hanging arms.

Flycatcher! Come and hear him talk! Got little snatch hairs under his nails!

Because there were the inevitable (as I see now) stories about old Flycatcher the unsatisfied lonely man, hanging in the gaunt shadows of the river elms, ready to grab little girls (or boys!) and feel in their pants. We never thought he would do anything more than that. There were stories that he lived nights with old Ruby the Hermaphrodite, and we conjured stories of old bat-filled kitchen with dusty wooden chairs and piss-covered bed mattress, but I don't think anyone ever found anything. I remember I tried to follow him home one time and sat for hours watching him stare at the river in the summer moonlight where the water twisted under the car bridge, but I finally went home. Before I left I threw a big heavy rock in the water and wondered why he didn't hear the splash. I thought he was communicating with something.

The story was that Flycatcher got that way from too much drinking out of the bottle, and playing with his dick. For a while I quit doing it, then I decided to take my chances, clenching my jaws tight when I remembered.

Old Flycatcher was always a hilarious sight at the ball games in the summer. He'd be sitting in the stands behind the chicken wire back of third base, trying to hang onto his awful brown cigarette and blubbering something he thought was a cheer when the Elks got a run, which wasn't often. There'd always be lots of room around him, not because anyone was afraid they'd get spit on them, but because it was a legend around town that he smelled like the top layer of his skin was dead.

It was at a ball game in July, hot old valley July, when school has been out long enough so it isn't a novelty anymore, and the temperature is in the nineties every day, and your mother is nagging at you about

Dianne Bancroft from the Coast was the lifeguard at the Oliver pool.
Bill and I had big crushes on her.

how you should be out picking cherries to make a little money instead of hanging around the new swimming pool every day, where we used to go gawk at the thin brown legs of the new lifeguard Diana from Vancouver, all of us guys dashing from the pool to the dressing room to comb our long sleek hair—it was at the ball game I first heard anyone decide to do something about Flycatcher, and this was Red Duncan, of course, the only kid in town with hand-tooled motorcycle boots, with a goddam bell on a chain hanging from them.

Red was talking to Chicken Malley, the Henhouse Man, as we used to call him, having circulated rumours about how he used to eat chickens without cooking them till he was old enough to start fooling around with them in different ways. Perfect pair of guys to do something about Flycatcher. I stood beside them, listening to the birth of their plan, a typical plan for Red Duncan. Anytime you saw Red talking with anyone you knew he was relating some sex lie about his last Saturday night, or planning to castrate a dog or some such harmless teenage stunt.

The notion was to dress somebody up in girls' clothes and thereby trap Flycatcher into a grim sexual adventure to take place in Flycatcher's house, where the ruse could be exposed at the last possible minute, and they could knock over poor slavering Flycatcher and grab the mysterious pile of loot he was supposed to have hidden somewhere in his shack. No pause over the choice of the set-up man: it was to be Eldon Bear. Eldon was the perfect choice, somewhat stupid, afraid of Red Duncan, and so indefinite and obscure in appearance that, while he didn't exactly look like he wasn't a boy, he didn't exactly look like he wasn't a girl either; at least it would probably fool the dim mind of Flycatcher. To me it sounded as if the plan was ignoring something, maybe something I'd seen about Flycatcher that night by the river. Anyway I horned in quietly, standing with head bowed interestedly, and I was unannouncedly within the circle of conspirators, the fact that I was an uncommitted observer known only to myself. I didn't have to give any outward signs of encouragement or complicity, though; Red Duncan didn't think much of my initiative. "You got no ambition, Delsing. That's why you're going to be a failure, just like you always been," he said.

As I tagged along behind the dingling motorcycle boots of Red Duncan in search of Eldon Bear, I couldn't help thinking it wasn't a Flycatcher sort of day. Back in the ballpark they were losing by seven or eight runs now, so I didn't feel too bad about leaving. I'd brought my ball glove to go after the ten-cent foul balls, but I'd decided to watch the game instead, and threw the glove in my old man's car, because I knew all the little kids were in a fighting mood that day, and I didn't want to lose a scrabble for a foul ball under the irrigation siphon to some kid three years younger than me. In fact it was a good day. Passing the tennis courts out past the left-field fence I noticed Katy Jeonard was playing tennis without a brassiere again, and I lagged behind the others, watching Katy go after a couple of hard returns. That was one of the nice things about a good July day.

It took about three and a half hours to find Eldon Bear, what with Red stopping all over town to talk to his circle of friends and associates, a fine group for me to be seen among, all the cigarette-wielding kids that would grow up to be the familiar faces in the old pub on main street years later when I'd drop in for fugitive beers of a noon hour. But we finally found him, and Red strode down on him as if he were going to award him the merit of the bunched fist, because Red hated to be kept waiting. Nevertheless, Eldon didn't run, and in a short time Red and Chicken Malley had Eldon filled in on the scheme, and we were waiting outside Eldon's house for Eldon to come out with his sister's clothes.

"We'll have to split the money even, eh, Red?" said Chicken Malley, indicating me with a nonchalant toss of his head.

"Yeah, we'll maybe give him enough to go buy a French safe to make a balloon out of," said Red.

I don't want nothing. I'm just an observer, and you guys are obser-vees, I thought to myself, but I didn't say anything, because I was actually afraid of Red Duncan. I preferred to ride the thin line between getting Red riled and seeming to quake. Red had never seen fit to push me, of which I was glad. So I just leaned on the wall of the sawdust shed and watched Red and Chicken like young weirdly masculine clothes stylists, arranging Eldon Bear in his sister's clothes. Eldon wasn't very bright; he'd grabbed a pile of his sister's winter clothes, including three pairs of thick brown stockings. When they were finished, I wanted to say at last Eldon Bear looked like a man.

"You forgot the makeup," said Red.

"She ain't got any," said Eldon.

"Then go get your mother's. You got to have makeup, you don't look sexy enough yet."

"I can't go in there dressed like this," said Eldon, in a voice high-pitched enough to be a real girl's.

"You're goddam well going to," replied Red, balling his fist with palm upward, holding it at his hip.

So Eldon, hoisting his loose skirt for the steps, went into the house. A minute later he came running back out, scrabbling at his loose skirt with one hand, closely followed by his skinny mother, a cluster of pin-curls all over her head. She was hollering at him, but as soon as she saw Red she started hollering at him instead. Red was famous among mothers in Lawrence.

"Aw, shut up, you old horse's ass!" shouted Red, and turned away with a lazy dip of his shoulders. Eldon's mother stood still on the front step, forlorn in her husband's old brown army jacket.

"You shouldn't talk to a guy's mother like that," I said.

"Up yours," said Red.

Eldon was twisting the lipstick tube—Red grabbed it out of his hands. I never saw a guy happier than Red Duncan smearing makeup on Eldon Bear's face.

Red and Chicken had a hard time with Eldon once we got to the weeping willow back of Flycatcher's shack. I didn't blame Eldon much: not only did he look awful in the clothes and makeup, but he was also pretty nervous about old Flycatcher.

"When he starts groping you, just holler Help at the top of your lungs," said Red. "Then we'll bash his bloody door down, and we'll have him."

"We'll be rich," said Chicken.

"Beyond your fondest dreams," I added, for the rhythm.

Lawrence gets one of the earliest sunsets anywhere: when the hills in the east are enjoying some good afternoon sun, the valley is in the shadow of the big hump of rock and sand back of the high school on the west side. The sun had just gone back of the hill when Eldon got to Flycatcher's front door. We lurked in the shadows, admiring the sudden talent of Eldon Bear, who stood before the open door, his hip stuck out, and a skinny hand plunked on it. Beyond him, Flycatcher, no expression on his face but the drooped eyes and hanging jaw. Giving him no time to grunt a question, Eldon sailed in, and Flycatcher looked outside for a while, expecting. At once I thought he was sniffing the air. Brown raggy hair hung in shards in front of his ears. He closed the door.

Whereupon a long silence ensued, and I sat back against the topply woodpile, hands behind head, looking at the faint light that rimmed the west hills, listening to the river frogs start their miles-long ruckus. It was harder on Red and Chicken: "God damn son of a bitch, yell!" said Red. "Maybe he's got him tied down," said Chicken.

"You mean Her," I said.

"Shut up!"

"Bastard."

"I love you, too," I said. I was feeling cockier, the strange valley summer gloom dropping in heavier all the time. An hour went by.

"What you going to do with your share of the loot?" I asked, copying a gangland movie I'd seen on Saturday.

"I'm going to buy a funnel and shove it up yer keister and pour in some hot jam and sit you on an anthill," said Red. So I looked up at the purple in the sky.

In that way we waited for Eldon to yell Help—once Chicken went up to the window, but the yellow blind was pulled right down. It was strange to think of Flycatcher living in a house, the anonymity of it, not to be noticed, because on the street he had to do what no man wants to do: stand out in a crowd all the time, that droop, that slapdap walk of his, nothing to hide behind. I imagined Flycatcher slapdapping into his shack, closing the door, pulling down the blind—Suddenly: his mouth snaps shut, his eyes brighten, his back straightens; he's a normal man, football athlete, Pepsodent toothbrusher, novelist pounding out type-writer story of the hawks and lobos that drop their defences around his droopy frame—a massive trick, man dedicates his life to finding out the helpless truth about people's weakness and pride. A Christ writer spying in the marketplace and secret provinces of Pharisee…

In the name of Flycatcher, our Lord, Amen—

My back was to the shack. The skin along the bottom of my thigh crept in cold networks.

So I worked it off my usual way. "Hi, you desperate-looking disciples of the Saviour," I said, to the apparition of Red and Chicken sharing a tailor-made cigarette between their squatting figures.

Out the door comes Eldon Bear. I'd actually forgotten he was wearing girls' clothes. They were messed up now, and Eldon's hairy bony knob knee leg was no girl's leg. Eldon was turned at the door, no Flycatcher in sight, but Eldon saying, "Good night, Stuart," and the door closed.

Immediately, Red Duncan pounced on him.

"Why the hell didn't you yell Help?"

"I didn't need any," said Eldon, absently or nervously adjusting his skirt.

"You're a worse nut and pervert than Flycatcher," said Red.

"His name's Stuart, and he ain't a pervert," said Eldon.

"I can see it all in my head," Red went on, balanced dangerously, with fists balled up by his hips, seen even in the dark. "You and Flycatcher, him groping you and you groping him. You're disgusting! that's what you are, Eldon Bear, Ugfh! Hairy old lousy greasy dirty Flycatcher, and Eldon Bear all done up like a little girl. How long did it take for him to find out you weren't a girl, Girly?"

"As soon as I got in. He gave me a cup of tea and asked me why I'm all dressed up when it ain't Halloween," said Eldon.

"And of course you told him," said Red.

"Sort of. I wasn't going to, but he was kind of nice, you know? He told me I looked funny in girls' clothes, and he said he knew I wouldn't have dressed up in girls' clothes by myself. But I didn't tell him it was you made me do it, Red."

"That figgers, Eldon, cause I never. It was all your idea. You're some kind of queer, I got a notion to warn the cops about you."

Across them, suddenly in light, the face of Chicken Malley, concentrated, expecting.

Too fast to see: Red's fist came up from his hip and thudded into Eldon's belly—Eldon whoofed loudly, his face came down to his waist, Red's knee up into it. Eldon lay on the dark ground—Red's motorcycle boot kicked dirt and gravel into Eldon's face.

"Little fruit," said Red, and he sauntered off, Chicken Malley like a squire behind him, following the jingle bells on his boots.

I helped Eldon up, taking an edge of the skirt and wiping off as much dirt and blood as I could from his face, taking the lipstick and eyebrow stuff with it, in one grimy substance. He didn't say anything, but I had to work between gulps of air he was taking.

Walking him home, I didn't say anything either. But I felt a kind of jealousy: he knew Flycatcher better than I did. Through a kind of night-time violence I couldn't enter into, he'd found out the things I'd never know, the things I wanted to know. A poor creepy guy in a girl's skirt: I'm walking him home, not saying anything, silent friend, envying him, envying Flycatcher, the things that can be known, you never find out if you don't become victimized, if you watch from a safe distance, your face not hit like that.

Time and Again

Back in Lawrence, he could feel the isolation again. He'd been a boy there, he'd gone to school there, he'd started to read novels there, and it was there that he'd first thought about writing—sports stories; his plan was to be a baseball writer for the St. Louis *Post-Dispatch*, he'd even sent a letter to Bob Roeg, the sports editor, and asked what he should do, and Bob had said to take journalism at the University of Missouri and look him up when he was through St. Louis, home of the enemy Cardinals—he would have been afraid to approach the thing directly, that is write to a paper in Brooklyn.

The paper in Lawrence was a weekly sheet he'd written basketball stories for when he was in grades eleven and twelve—Wildcats Demolish Red Devils, Selkirk Leads Winners with 25 Points—and when he'd been away at college he'd sent the odd story "of special interest to Lawrence residents," by George Delsing, formerly of Lawrence.

Now back in Lawrence, noted in the social page of the weekly. Delsing was back in town, nobody noticing, the victor returning; not noticed by you boobs, who's to care? But somebody could have. Frances for instance, off somewhere, not even known where this summer, married or separated, with one child two years old now; how could it be that he was once the theoretical father of that planned-for child, and now somewhere in a space, not knowing the other juncture?

He looked up and down the street, greengrocers with aprons carrying paper cups of coffee into stores with crude handwritten sale signs Scotch-taped to the window, cool Indians, in from the reserve, playing pool and drinking beer in the middle of peach season, riding ponies by night up on Coyote Ridge.

He turned and headed up the hill, home. The truth was, it suited him fine nobody knew about him, or cared, here, except his folks suddenly more friendly and man-to-manly now that he was a man of the outer world. Why be appreciated in Lawrence? Take umbrage if someone claims you as a Lawrence boy. That's fine. Up the hill.

His brother Reggie was sitting at the kitchen table, tall lean kid; what? Thirteen years old, reading a hot-rod magazine, gloating over chromium tailpipes on a red thought of a car, as George, Delsing did years before with sports magazines, knowing the batting average of Eddie Stanky, unable to remember that his mother had sent him downtown with a shopping list; unwilling to get work, but working like hell if it caught up to him.

"When I was your age I was working nine hours a day in an orchard, my son," he said to Reggie, who flipped the page to a reconditioned Essex Super Six.

"Ha, ha, ha," interjected his mother, standing at the sink, cutting the dripping stones out of a sink full of peaches.

He snuck over beside her and grabbed a sticky handful of sliced peaches and crammed them in his mouth.

"You've got a handy memory," said his mother. "You can remember any amazing legend if it recounts the hard life and times of George Delsing."

His mother had grown more adept at jabbing that way, which was fun, but she would never understand the things he had stayed up to tell her the night before, elbows on the late-night kitchen table, everyone else in bed, telling how he would steal money to keep from toiling while he wrote a great long novel on the blatant secret lives of three thousand people in Lawrence and other places, yours included. His mother had sat there, smoking cigarettes, listening to his brashness, reserving motherly knowledge about first son George later to marry and take a job and settle down, maybe in middle age bringing out poems for relatives to see, collecting fine music and books as recompense, staying close to the artist life, which after all does not inhere in people from Lawrence, but is the drawing-room air of people in mythical European cities located somewhere far off, at the

Atlantic Ocean's door, probably. A hobby is okay, as long as it doesn't lure a mature man away from the business of making a way, keeping up with expectations for age brackets, paying debts, establishing a post from which to get weekly letters, like all the relatives, immediately Delsing, with trace of Lawrence, modified by the job and the new town.

"I'd abandon my children and deny my father if they got in the way of what I'm going to do."

What a nit he could be.

"The ironic thing," he added, "is that I'm writing immense novels and poems about all the people in this town, and they don't know it. For them I'm a goof-off, with brains, but a goof-off, who'll probably amount to something medium, and not deserve that much. There'll be great pages and chapters written about this little town, known to every hamlet in the nation except itself."

His mother peeled a peach, the skin pulling off in utter silence belonging to the world of sweet tree fruit.

"Put yourself in the position of a Lawrence orchardist. Would you care?" she said.

And was right, as always, this a hard fact to shake, no matter how intelligent and insightful he might become in the swirl outside the valley.

"I suppose not. That's why I feel no compunction about giving them life or killing them mercilessly. Except I never do it mercilessly," he added.

"In fact, I wonder if you've ever put yourself in the place of an orchardist, for example," she said. "I wonder if you can, seriously."

He'd been wondering lately, once in a while.

"I'll go out and see an orchardist," he said, grabbing a freshly washed peach on his way out.

The highway between the overhanging orchards, it was a groove deep in the sensual part of his mind, the motor of the car running smooth along it, leading him down the white line of earlier drunken auto races when the road narrowed and the trees crowded in close, pushing against the edges of the windshield. He knew where he was going, turned in at the weeping-willow tree that hung to the ground over half of the dirt road winding a weedy-edged trail up to the house, where he stopped the car and looked. The old house still needed painting, and the screen that darkened the long verandas was still loose at the edges. But the flowers still crowded the wooden steps, and the screen door was propped open with an old wicker armchair.

He got out of the car after the dust had settled because he had his new canvas shoes on, and walked around to the back. She was there as always, digging in the garden with little green tools, Mrs. Ackerman, skinny old grey woman with amazing pink face, hair knotted and stained yellow in spots at the back of her head, heavy man's boots on her feet, cigarette hanging from the side of her mouth.

Seventy-one when I left, she's seventy-six now, he thought.

She looked up when he walked across the lawn, squinting at him as he stood between her and the sun.

"Georgie Delsing!" she said, and got up from her crouch as quickly as she could, brushed the dry soil off her hand before she extended it to him. That was the way she was, not like a man—an eager force, strength.

"Hi, Mrs. Ackerman. I told you I'd be back to see you," he said, not embarrassed.

"Five years ago," she said. She was right on, not like the old folks he contemplated for his saga.

He didn't have to say he was sorry. "I heard about Mr. Ackerman. I'm feeling kind of strange not hearing him." Mr. Ackerman used to sit and whistle loudly, filling the air of the orchard he couldn't see.

She rubbed the back of her wrist across her forehead, a habit. She was too old to sweat.

"He just fell on his face straight out of his chair onto the grass. Dead as a doornail," she said in the manner that she knew unsettled George.

"How do you make out here by yourself? I mean, don't you have any help around the house?" It was six or seven years ago that he would join the small desperate crew trying to get her peaches off the trees before they got ripe.

"Oh, I certainly miss all the heavy work Walter used to do for me," she said, dumping the garden tools into the green box with the curled-up hose.

He remembered coming to the house and seeing her standing on a sawhorse to reach the end of the twisted clothesline, her straight spindly legs, and Mr. Ackerman in his chair, whistling an opera tune with all the short piccolo noises.

"Come on in the house and eat up all my peanut-butter cookies," she said clumping with her boots up the wooden steps to the kitchen.

She poured the tea, much too weak, the English way, and he dropped his cigarette into the wood stove.

"There's talk in town that you inherited a whole lot of insurance money," he said, putting it accusingly, the old way, with the precarious delight of being able to talk to an old woman without making allowances for her oldness.

"In that town," she said, as if it were a hundred miles away, past the weeping willow tree, and it was true—the occasion when she would be seen on the street was some kind of visit, or visitation, from the duchess —old Mrs. Ackerman, never forgotten out there four miles from town; but mysterious, a kind of local myth, like an abandoned silver mine. "In that town you could start a story that Bismarck was living as a recluse in the hospital basement, among the mops and furnaces." She enjoyed the idea. He filed it in his novelist mind, then forgot it.

"Come on, Mrs. Ackerman..."

"Well, to tell the truth, I'm not poor, Georgie, we never really were. You never thought of that, did you?"

He hadn't. And that showed what? That he hadn't really examined all the hours he'd spent talking to them—in fact he never thought of an encounter that way—it made a sense record in his head, and that was all. So the peril here—he'd thought of the Ackermans as types, reacting to the condition they lived in as he'd seen it. Expectations become fact too quick if you get comfortable.

"I'll take another cookie, that being the case." He wasn't looking at her now, rather down, at the tea leaves in the bottom of his cup. "That is, how—why didn't you ever...?" He didn't know what he was asking, but she did.

She laughed lightly, in the tone that was as clearly dry and ridged as her cheeks, and he lifted his head.

"Have another cup of tea, and I'll tell you." (He didn't like tea generally, at least never a second cup, but he had always waived that when it was worth it, paid some attention to the fancy cup and the fancy silver spoon.) "In fact—have you got anywhere to go this afternoon? Fine, then—in fact I'll go back to the beginning."

Which she had done on many occasions before, and he had settled back apprehensive at first, but later eagerly happy to sit and listen to her hard factual accounts of childhood farm days in some English shire of a greeny sound.

"I never told you how I met and married Walter, did I?" she asked, doing something evasive with a napkin, settling. Surprised he thought, no, by God, and then, quit interrupting, brain.

"I don't believe so," he said, settling.

"You've seen him sitting in his chair, whistling as loud as he can, filling the orchard with some sense he can trust—hear, because he never did like the sight of peaches on a tree, they were work growing and money coming in, that's all, because what he wanted was to use work to get away from it. That has a lot to do with it.

"When I first met him, I was new over from the Old Country, and it was a good job I did find him, because it was the middle of the summer in the Niagara Peninsula, which can be a lonely time for someone not bred to the place or passing through on a honeymoon. He was wearing thick glasses then, those old round ones with the spidery legs clinging to the ears—I always swore his ears stuck out from the side of his head because of those glasses. And of course I loved him, about which I felt at first nonplussed, and later guilty, because I knew I made him love me, not in the way girls in That Town do it now..."

She didn't blush, and she wasn't digressing into scorn, just telling hard facts.

"... but the reason I felt guilty was becoming clear to me. He'd been working all his thirty years to save up enough money to get to Europe—he came from an old family of Ontario Loyalists, and he told me all about Europe, what was waiting for him, for a fellow, over there, as if I had come from Ketchikan, Alaska. And of course when he married me he had had to start all over again, which he did, thinking of no way to do it but to buy a farm, an orchard, in the peninsula, and pay for that over the next fifteen years if the crops were good; which they were, from that time till the Great War, six years later, and he tried to get into the army, it would mean going to a sort of modern Europe, but they wouldn't take him; his eyes they said, but there was something about the farm, too—not as if he was an oldest son, going off to fight for the peach blossoms.

"Then the next ten years were his own fault—the times were so profitable, even for orchardists, that he kept working and working, not now with the idea of a trip to Europe, but thinking about going there to live, which meant of course putting it off for a few years, and working extra hard, with a bigger orchard—so when the chance came to pick up a big piece of land in the valley, he jumped at it, moving us out in 1922, in the old truck all the way across the country, the wrong direction, west, but he always said in those times, westward was the quickest route to Europe; and so when he got out here he realized it would be a few years before the new trees yielded fruit, so we lost most of the little we'd saved after buying the new place, and kept our heads above water by raising cucumbers and tomatoes, good ones, too—have another cookie."

He let the names of the years skid off his attention, all this before he was born, happening to two people, and hundreds of people whose faces he didn't know—he was born in 1935—and he waited for her to get quickly up to that year, taking another cookie, and holding his cup out for tea in the meantime.

"All the time he was buying travel books, postcards, magazines, even road maps, marking the route between Paris and Vienna in red ink which after a while grew faded and even obsolete as the postwar highways cut across Europe in new swift lines. All the time telling me what we were going to see; he was always talking about buildings, parks, cities, bridges, farms, never mentioned the paintings and music festivals everyone else was pretending they longed to add to their memories.

"Then it was the Depression and he was in his fifties, and even the farmers were in trouble, sometimes not having the money to pay their travelling peach pickers, and afraid the desperate-looking men would set fire to their houses. He would read the papers and say no Depression in Germany that's where we should have been long ago, in Germany. Then Germany started the war again and of course the orchard was mature and business was good again, and Walter said we would leave for Europe as soon as the war was over; but after the war business was even better, and the pictures of Europe were old piles of bricks with kids climbing on them looking for dirty heels of bread, so we said 1950 no later. By 1948 he was completely blind."

He was nervous. The tea was too strong now and it felt like acid in his stomach. He lit two cigarettes and handed her one.

"So you didn't go," he said.

"Oh yes, we went. We went in 1950, not later."

"But, I mean—"

"He packed all the travel books and maps together, and off we went, sitting on the deck of the ship all the way, and he would get me to tell him what colour of sea it was and everything that happened on the deck in front of us. We stopped in England for a while and visited some of my relatives. Then we went over to Europe and stayed in Paris, and took the road from Paris to Vienna. And of course we didn't go to the music festivals, and we didn't go to the paintings. We used to sit at the table on the sidewalk, and I would tell him what the street looked like, and the buildings and the little French people walking by, and what the cars looked like, how heavy the traffic was. We went to every big city in Europe, and some of the towns and villages. Most of the time we walked along the sidewalks or sat for a cup of tea at a sidewalk café. It was very nice."

Then George remembered his feeling coming back into Lawrence, the walk up and down the sidewalk. The mountains were very close in Lawrence.

"It was then he started the whistling," he said.

"It was there he started it," she said. "But it was just once in a while, till we were back in Paris, waiting for our boat train. When we were back here, he whistled all the time."

"It's a funny thing," said George. "All the time I saw him sitting there whistling like that, I never once wondered what he was thinking. I suppose you usually guess or apprehend what a person is thinking when you see the expression in his eyes."

Mrs. Ackerman had her own expression in her eyes. "I knew what he was thinking all the time. From about two months after he went totally blind till the day he died, he kept a diary."

"How?"

"On his little typewriter. He used to sit in his dark room with the typewriter on his lap and type out his diary every night. I could hear it right through the wall, very slow typing. I wanted to jump up and offer to help, it got on my nerves so much, but of course I couldn't do that, having caused him to go blind and get into the peach business and never see Europe and all that. So I used to read it the next day when he thought I was watering the front garden."

"Can I ...?"

"No."

She was right, of course, and it wasn't entirely because he was from and going to the town, and he knew why, was glad she had said that; that she knew surprised even him who had thought he'd known how wise she was.

So he opened the car up on the highway back, not as he had done many times before, in fury and impatience to get home under the dark tree in the front yard, back inside the gates of the town where Frances was a stranger though she'd lived three miles from town more than half her life. Now he was in a spirit like a casual hope, and the pedal underfoot was a direct connection to and from all gladland. So he sang, rocking his head back lustily as he hit the high distorted notes, propelling the car like a lateral rocket toward the little town of his youth.

Fruit trees were a lot taller in those days. The ladder looks like a twelve-footer.

Apples

In the orchards outside Lawrence the sprinklers are always going, moved twice a day from row to row, & the sun shines every day, so the grass never stops growing. The farmers have to send their mowers down between the trees, cutting the weeds & grass continually. But around each tree where the machine doesn't reach there's a circle of tall grass, sometimes the height of a man, & in this grass the pheasants hide during the day.

Frances Sinclair was walking in her father's small orchard at dusk after supper. With her was a boy from high school who was not George Delsing. George Delsing was the kid from town who was telling her lately that he loved her & she was beginning to believe him. But she had known this other boy for a longer time partly because they both sang in the choir at the Anglican church. Both their fathers had been in the British services during the war, though in different branches.

They were walking in grass that had been cut a few weeks earlier & it was dry because it was two rows away from the sprinkler line. In the approaching darkness they couldn't see the sprinklers but they could hear them clicking with that sound that resembles grasshoppers. It was the beginning of summer so the apples on the trees were small green things & the props hadn't yet been put under the branches though the trees had been thinned and there were many hard green apples on the ground, most of them hidden in the grass.

The boy stopped and held her to him and kissed her with open lips. She was always impatient with the tight way George Delsing kissed her but these lips were large and soft and she put her arms around his waist as he felt their tongues on one another. They walked farther away from the house with their arms around each other's waists. She could feel his warm hard flesh through his summer shirt. He played for the volleyball team and he wasn't as graceful as George Delsing but he was stronger. The next time they stopped he put his hand on the front of her shirt as he had done before and she opened her mouth wider.

As they approached the tall grass under a tress a pheasant crashed up past their faces. It always happened that way. It's a shock because it's so sudden and so loud. Her heart was thumping so that it picked up the sound of the bird's wings as it disappeared in the dim light. The boy took advantage of this and brought her down gently in the grass and held her while he kissed her and put his hand inside her shirt and inside her bra—it had been repaired twice and it broke again as he was trying to undo it with his arm around her and she lifted her leg to put it around his leg but each time she moved she had to stop and reach around behind her and throw away one of the little apples. Her skirt was half undone and then lifted and he had his hand wet on her, his finger in her and she had grass in her face and his breath, who is this she wondered, and he had always wanted to do this, she had seen his erection under the dark cloth in the choir loft, but she had to, sometime, there was no real trouble because the pain was very little but so was the pleasure and it didn't last long and immediately afterward his kisses stopped and he just held her and that was all. With their parents seeing each other all the time they would be seeing each other all the time, too, and they would probably do it again or she would with George Delsing and as in the book it would get better as you went along, in the orchard or in the bedroom under the pointed roof in the attic or in the hills when he or another managed to borrow his father's car. Or here, in her father's orchard, filled with life or pheasants, mice among the empty boxes, and even the skunks you saw from time to time strutting between the trees. The liquid on her skin was suddenly cold now. She reached down and pushed her skirt down a little. They hadn't said a word to each other since they left the house. It must have been unnecessary because they were going through the necessary step in the pattern. Here I lie, Frances Sinclair, no longer maiden. Now she could hear the sprinklers, shik-shik, shik-shik, shik-shik, shik-shik ...

It wasn't long before he grunted and began to gather the front of his pants together and she reached for the broken old thing and reached to close her shirt. As she did, she saw the eggs. They lay on the broken grass well hidden by the tall stems. Isn't it late for eggs? One was broken and solid inside. The rest were still all right.

But the pheasant won't come back to them now. You are taught not to touch the eggs or the young because the mother will abandon them. She could so something with the unbroken ones. She could take them and put them among the eggs under the brooding hen. But she couldn't do it right now, she'd have to come back later before it got too cold in the night.

She put her old broken bra over a twig as close as possible to the bottom of the tree.

What are you doing that for? He asked.

Kind of a marker, she said.

He smiled in the dark, tucking in his shirt. What are you, proud or sentimental?

I just want to remember, she said.

My father, Ewart Harry Bowering.

The Catch

"Desert Elm" has always been one of my favourites among the poems I have written. I have always looked for ways in which I can write a poem that extends over several pages, and I may have decided ahead of time that this one would go to ten sections. I may not have, too. There are two main subjects: the Okanagan Valley and my father, who, as I did, grew up there. In those days I was working in stanzas and a lot of rime. By "rime" I mean similar-sounding words.

There was also another challenge I set myself. I had noticed that my poems and my fiction very seldom told you what colour anything was. This was so because I had worked on a poetic that tried to exclude description. For this poem I decided to mention colour as often as I could do so without being a nuisance. The Okanagan Valley, in the southern part of it especially, offered me three main colours: blue, brown, and green. "Blue Okanagan" was the name of a 1947 song by Buddy Reynolds:

> Between the mighty Monashee and the Coast Range of B.C.
> Where the rivers flow like fountains, on their way out to the sea
> And the apple blossoms splendour in no other land is found
> For it's heaven, really heaven, when they're blooming all around.

> *Chorus*
> Blue water, blue sky, blue mountains so high
> Blue valleys and hills, blue rivers and rills
> Blue dreams in my heart, oh why did I part
> From the great Okanagan, so dear to my heart.

See the lonesome river, slowly winding its way
Just like the river, I'm leaving today
I'm headin' back now, gonna feather my nest
In the Okanagan Valley, pride of the West

"Blue Okanagan" was also a slogan much favoured by Okanagan chambers of commerce and real estate companies. If you got partway up a mountain near Oliver, for example, and looked south toward Osoyoos there seemed to be a light blue haze over everything. If you looked at the ground around your feet you saw bushes that were grey and brown, dry soil likewise. If you looked along the valley floor you saw a mile-wide band of green, the orchards that made for the area's biggest economy.

So the phrase recurs through the poem: "They found a desert and made it green."

"Reconsiderations" was an interesting project that I thought would go on for years, but which lasted for about ten poems. I would return to my earlier poems and do a radical editing and rewriting job. The new poem could not exist without the earlier version (see "Driving to Kelowna" in *The Silver Wire*), but together the two would try to be a kind of a short history of my attitude. Often, as in the one reprinted here, there would be a critique of an earlier naïveté, of both person and poem.

from *Desert Elm*

II

The earth he made me on, we dug into
side by side, has not long been there,
has been carried there by the glacier,
all rocks and all round rocks, all stones
rolled together.

We toiled among the stones, that rattling
sound is my earth, where I grew up looking like him. There was some light falling always into the valley, always blue,
the blue that hovers over heat, a blue
I saw cooling the Adriatic shore.

It is the blue fading in his eyes, they
are not startling blue, it is the family
colour I never got, they are not bright
blue but fading to a transparency you
will notice only if you are watching
closely, I mean within a few feet.

They found a desert and made it bloom, made
it green, but even the fairways seen from
across the valley are under a blue haze,
the smoke of space it seemed on high summer days, not a cloud in the sky, no mote
in that eye.

The earth is not brown but grey, grey of
stones, the flat stones round to the eye
looking straight down.

V

I thought of a rock, not quite round
sticking half out of the earth where I
would put the ladder's foot. In a hurry,
without patience to place it safely, to
be up that tree and working.

And working. Never half as fast as he could
do it, but in some ways inheriting his
quiet efficiency and turning it to grace.
He said he could never play second base
and I found it the easiest position, bending
over occasionally to pick stones off the
ground.

Even this summer, a month before his fall,
he picked twenty pounds while I picked
eleven, just more than half and I am more
than half at last, thirty-seven, moving
around to the other half of the tree,
but someone guessed, that is under the
ground, the root system.

A tree, growing downward as I dreamed I
would or desperately hoped I would, to
become this child again, never having the
nerve or wit, age four, to follow that to
its home, from one hundred back to the
seed, and then what. A new lease on life?
For him?

The earthly tree grows downward, we do it
after all, bypassing the womb, back where
we came from, down the rabbit hole on the
golf course, above the shade of the old
cherry tree.

VII

I woke and again I woke, to find her smiling
at me, and turned to return to soft sleep
in the green pillow. A tree, growing downward as I dreamed we all would or hoped
we would, against my god or what they
gave me as my god, their god, given them
against their will, we punish the generation that succeeds us.

Did I mean to say he did that. No, he
never tried to bend my life, never stood
between me and the sun, this tree grew where
the seed fell. A new lease on life? For
him? In the thick dark forest the trees
grow tall before they extend wings. Tall
green pillow.

They found a desert and made it bloom, made
it green, but even the trees feel blue
smoke curling among their branches, the
smoke that holds away the frost, the early
message that fills our hearts with ice,
lovely to taste fresh from the branch,
but it doesn't travel well. All stones
rolled together, long enough and they will
all be dust, hanging in the air over our
blue lakes.

Prophecy is finally simple, and simply a
pair of eyes through which the blue of the
sky travels, an observation through a lens.

Men who love wisdom should acquaint themselves with a great many particulars.
Cutting the crisp apple with a French knife
I saw that the worm had lived in the core
and chewed his way out, something I've seen
a thousand times and never understood and while
I'm looking he's on the other side of the
green tree picking. One two one two, the
wisdom of the tree filling his picking bag,
its weight strapped over his shoulders. He
showed me, you cross the straps like this
and keep it high. Get above the apples and look
down at them.

And I still do it wrong, reaching up, picking with sore arms, strain rather than wisdom filling me not the bag. He said the
safest step on the ladder is the top, he
was trying to get me up, and always right,
this one I have learned and Saturday I was
on the top step picking apples, wanting
someone to advise. That is how one becomes
acquainted, working to gather.

It could be a woman but is it a woman, is
it a woman you can work together with, is
it a woman you know doesn't feel the particulars as you do, they are apples, not the
picking of them, the filling. She has been
without a man for years, she offers ladders,
tools, bags for the apples. You want someone to advise to be him, but do it silently
knowing your expertise is somehow, known.

X

I did not see him lying on the grass. I
may as well have been under the ground,
perhaps entangled in the tree growing downward, an earth. His earth, our particular
earth, as it sifts back and forth, composing
like dust on a piano. The piano is black
but where it has been rubbed it is brown.
He never sat at a piano, only an old black
typewriter with round keys, making faint
words.

So faint they barely heard him. It was August and the grass dry, the thin words rose
like a tree into the air, lightly, as blue
as the thin smoke hanging over the green
fairway. It has nothing to do with justice.
He spent thousands of hours in those trees
picking pennies for me, this day he was
knocking them into a hole, I'm glad to hear
that.

In the ocean light of the ward window his
eyes are barely blue and deep in his head
like my daughter's. He woke again to see
me smiling at him, his head straight in
the pillow, a rock nearly round. In the
desert the rocks simply lie upon each other
on the ground, a tree is overturned out
of the ground, its shallow widespread roots
coiled around small rocks. By these fruits
we measure our weight and days.

Reconsiderations II

You edge along the Okanagan
dying in your car, dying

with the water, the green
lake where there had been
a blue lake, where

there had been a blue boy
climb out shivering, eyes
wide open.

        The eyes in that water now
        are closed shit eyes
        of peculiar worms

        and they wait

for you to return to your source.

They trace your beginnings for you,
from the decaying baseball park

to the West Summerland grave
where your headstone will be
a colour TV.

Protective Footwear

There's just one Okanagan story in my second book of short stories. Unlike the majority of my stories of a later time, it is almost a transcription of the events during my high-school class's twentieth year reunion. I even kept Ordie Jones's real name.

There is a certain amount of irony in it to go along with the realistic dialogue, and I believe that the title will make any reader wonder why the word has been cut in two, and then guide the curious reader to turn his attention to the word "union" as applied to a marriage.

One thing that still impresses me a little is the way the writer managed to get a first-person point of view into a third-person narrative.

Re Union

They would have to get together because it was a reunion, it was his anyway, and she was part of it now, she knew of the folklore of his valley upbringing, and resisted it, but was placed into it, at least beginning with his family. She was always relaxed, it seemed to him, there, maybe bored? And four and a half years younger. It was his reunion after all, these people would not be in her class.

"About as funny as usual," she said.

He'd been eager for this, always savaging his past, that mythology of his, for material, he said, but really, why. And afraid there wasn't going to be one after all. I mean twenty years! They are all alive as hell in my mind, walking around in V-neck sweaters. The morning before

Class reunion? Sure, I'll be there, circa 1970.

they were to drive up there, he woke up and looked in the mirror and there was a small boil on the end of his nose. He was a famous poet and that is exactly what he wanted to be when he, they, got there. He began to do what he had often, habitually, done twenty years ago, pray to God for personal help. Sylvia would be there and he hadn't seen her for twenty years. I can wait forever, he'd written on the note he stuck through the vent in her hall locker.

We realize that you have all been anxiously awaiting further news of our class reunion planned for the first of July weekend. We have now finalized plans and are anxious that you should know what a terrific time is in store for you!

"Got the old nose boil again, eh?"

"Yes, Jesus Christ!"

"Exactly, or nearly exactly," she said. "You should know by now that I do that, every time you're going to see one of your old girlfriends."

Maybe she does, but she doesn't understand after all, it's not any girl I worry about. I want them to see what they maybe only feared and suspected, that they scorned me but I wasn't just a fool in their midst, I had more potential than any of those monitors, those small dusty town not a real town somehow student council presidents, basketball heroes in green satin, rustlers of Yankee girls and whisky across the border in those towns I never visited at night. I haven't told her everything, couldn't really, though she says she's heard the stories dozens of times, every one. Well, here goes another.

"'The "beer garden" in the community hall in Okoneep provides an excellent informal atmosphere for those of you who are able to gather Saturday afternoon. Remember that children are also welcome here.'" He read it out loud.

She is again beside him, to his right, riding, and she, now, too, is learning, in her little car seat behind them, beside the bags of her stuff, toy animals with long necks in places around the car.

"It'll be ninety or a hundred up there today," he said.

"Well, I hope your parents have the air conditioning on." She was from the Island. That was another thing. In the desert she always wanted him to drive at night, sleep by day. Like the pursued in the western novels he'd read twenty-five years ago.

Driving into the hot sagebrush country, he thought over and over, at Princeton, at Keremeos, I hope they're all fatter than me, I hope they're balder than me, the men, anyway greyer than me. I hope they huff and puff and their shirts spill out over their belts. I wish there was going to be a ball game so I could show them how adept I am, how lithe. He never played on the ball team or the basketball team, this is later, the new incarnation. His flesh felt better in the little Japanese car than it ever had in the big swaying Chev.

Still, it was a distance from hers. The best thing about being an adult was to learn that you too could handle it, making love, late to come to it, but to come out of the self-doubt, listening to Red, for instance, talking on the pebbly soccer field, about it, as if some guys, like animals, could just do it, without self-doubt. He'd done it, and probably he could have driven himself harder than most, and made the basketball team, too. But now he was batting what, .375, and they weren't doing it often.

What thoughts am I putting into this man's head while he's driving, and where did they come from, buried so long? I love you, she suddenly says once in a while, hardly ever as a response to something, rather something that comes at the end of one of those long complicated arguments inside her head. Where I can't really go.

"I love you," she said.

"Me too you," he said, and he loved shifting gears then, up the last hill at whose crest they would be able to see the lake in the valley, and the isthmus, where in all likelihood "they" would be.

Walking home from the little strip of downtown where he's gone to get cigars though he had enough on the kitchen card-playing table at his parents' house, he saw that the garage across the lane from the United Church manse was gone, nothing there but another of Lawrence's vacant lots, dust on hard earth, with loose round stones and clumps of couch grass. It was a story he'd never told her, probably because it had happened one summer while he was on leave of absence, up the valley where his parents had gone to help his youngest uncle, hands in the trees of the orchard on the clifftop on the east side of the lake, another story, and prodding yet more, most of them told. His gang, the Coyote Kids, led by his second-in-command, eleven-year-old Bob Small, were holed up in the garage, busy as hell and then lying in wait for marauding Red Duncan's gang. Small's men (what tactical genius his unsung friend had!) had acquired a bundle of laths from the downtown lumberyard (oh more stories, oh graduating class, before the popular memories of lemon gin and drive-in movies) and from anywhere a bunch of empty soup tins. They nailed the soup tins to the laths and filled them with ashes, then they tied their catapults with binder twine. (Did I ever tell you about the time we contrived to have Red Duncan and his corsairs make us walk the plank at sword point, into the fire of packing cases set to the torch by a flaming broadsword, and this in his parents' basement?) When Red Duncan and his men broke their way past the deliberately flimsy barricade at the Rev. Richmond's garage door, Small and the few others cut the twines and in the smoky confusion laid on astonished Duncans with their wooden weapons, then retreated, outnumbered, up the alley past my place. This story was told to me by Bob Small when I got back into town, and that was a real reunion because I had not only belonged to the Coyote Kids, I was their chief. I loved and envied my lieutenant for his complex gambit in the long war over the imagination of Lawrence.

"No, you never told me that story," she said. "Probably because you were not the hero."

"You fail to understand me," he replied.

"No, I understand you, and I understand the meanings of your stories. I just don't understand why you are so fond of them," she said.

"As a man reaps, so shall he sow," he said, and completed the longest conversation of the Friday evening.

Still playing armed games, too. Friday night he sat at their kitchen table as always, playing cards, looking only briefly in Jack's one eye, thinking inexplicably of a classmate, Tibor, blond Hungarian fatty, who died in grade eight, the only one who fell away that deep, reputed to have said as he was going, "I love Jesus, I love you, Jesus," this reported by some girls in the class who had the nerve to visit him in the hospital just across the barbed wire and the irrigation ditch from the school, how could they. Dead twenty-four years now, in the rocky soil near Okoneep. The idea came that they, or some others in the class, are in and around town right now, seeing their parents in shadows of old German or Yugoslavian ways. Wonder who'll be the first I meet. (Sylvia? No.) At eleven-thirty his parents went as usual to their white bedroom and he shuffled, who thus cut loose could watch a late movie from someone else's past, or it's Friday night, horror on TV, small-town life in the pub. He walked down to the beer parlour, ostensibly to get cigarillos, again, and his heart was going when he entered the hallway with its chubby Indian women, but there was no one there but his long-haired brother, and that wasn't right either, too much of now, at the coast, and his brother's crowd, smoking dope out back and then looking at each other over the terry-cloth tabletop. He didn't even think of their sweet flesh, their small-town eagerness to be impressed, he was after his own shadowy superstars.

Walking home, he was aware that when you get away from the streetlamps the sky is filled, a half sphere of thousands of large bright separate fires. Just before he'd left Vancouver Tenny had told him, look up, in the Interior you'll always see sky activity.

Activity? What a funny way of saying it.

Satellites. Other lights. Comets. Meteors.

As soon as he looked up, ready, he scanned, fast. A shooting star. The cheese stood still.

I'm home. Don't kid yourself, twenty years, each one slimmer. I'm home, where tomorrow they'll say Jesus you did it after all. I wish you'd been a comedian, said Leonard Kovak ten years ago, you really had the talent.

Talent?

He had been predicting rain for the weekend ever since the month had been moved into, the house of excitement. It always rains there twice a summer, once around cherry season, to split the fat black Bings, and once again around Labour Day, on the double-header against the Kamloops Elks. Here Saturday morning it is windy, and there are grey clouds slopping down over the western hills to shove out the ninety-degree air of yesterday.

He walked down the hill to the pool hall to get the Saturday paper, past the old shingled police station where he'd daringly played at some age with a girl named Brenda, hard to credit, now recognizing old familiar Delsing of recent years, going a few blocks on old-fashioned legs. These feet have covered everything from horizon up there to horizon up there. The town is full of Saturday late morning, you recognize their family faces, familiar visored hats and how funny it now seems to see these old farmers with tailor-made cigarettes, or even cigarillos, there they are, the regular Central European apple growers, and now the recent turn of the Interior, pickup-truck hip kids, communes failing somewhere on back trails he must have walked along twenty-five years ago, making space time rather than the other way round.

Now he's afraid he *will* meet one of those Yugoslavian farmer's sons, the first classmate. It's the excitement building up, impatience not at *all*, he wants to avoid it at the last minute, looking now at the back of a fifty-five-year-old head, wondering if it's anyone from old grade twelve.

At bottom we are all one, the world, and the deeper we go into each, myself, the wider it becomes, the more total, I am not I, and I don't mean to say, I am you, brother, down there, it is that down there it becomes the world, a possibility each contains. Jesus, if I can't say it here how could I ever hope to say it to one of them in a pair of bell-bottom slacks? The world—and that's possibly what I'm reaching for, this trip, these little trips. While acting out the desperate, one.

It is not 1973 and yet it is not 1953. It isn't a year I'm looking to pick up and examine, it's not *that* I was looking forward to before 1953. Whoever was so busy and busybodied to lay that on us. Not a time at all, but maybe seventy-five hundred pounds of flesh.

"Did you?" she asked when he got back, know-it-all.

"Not a person," he said. "Not a one. Thank God."

"You dumbbell," she said.

But of course she was his reunion to begin with, out of particulars, to make a start, you neon in the city left behind, blink, you'll never know, glamour of my first leaving this place.

At the "Beer Garden" in the afternoon, a patch of grass fenced off next to the lake, water-skiers out there on the darkening water, he was standing with her to one side, his daughter skipping among the upright adult legs. Seeing the guys but not the girls from the class. They are, there's Ordie, crewcut, there's Rob, deep lines in his cheeks, healthy, they are, all at least ten years older than me! Grey, and as Amanda said, "stolid," and they all have short hair, as if—what do they all do for a living? They all do for a living. It is as he'd expected, and it is a disappointment, and he is proud of himself.

He thinks if they ask him, he'll say some writers are like skiers, hoping to move miraculously over the terrain, and not run into anything, and that's good. Some writers are like basketball players or boxers, hoping to hit a target right on, whether it's moving or still, and that's okay. Right now, fellows, I'm writing like a halfback, gliding off tacklers and hoping to make a few yards with each carry.

Actually, Ordie said, "You still writing? I saw your story in *Maclean's*, wasn't it, a couple of months ago."

"Sure (that's what I do for a living)."

"You got any books out?"

Later he thought I should have really said, yeah a few, but not well, around fifteen. He could feel Amanda at his side. And he didn't say how many contracts have you sold. Ordie's kids were standing around, tall as himself, and there were more kids than parents, and every family had an oldest son named Bobby. Sylvia didn't make it, but she sent greetings from herself and her four kids.

The next one who asks if I ever made it, I'll say to him I generally use my telephone receiver as a paperweight. He drank a few beers and talked a little with Ron, whose wife told him he was the only one she wanted to meet. That was the best he could hope for. When the large warm valley raindrops began to fall they got a hamburger and ran for the car. At home their feet tracked creosote on his mother's living-room rug.

Tracks, yes, but wasn't he looking for more than that, himself, really? Not quite, but something like that. I mean you might as well lag back unexpectedly to have a peek at the back of your head.

"Oh, I guess in four or five years I'll be going through what you're going through," she said.

"Hardly," he answered. "Impossible."

Oh what a boring story, nothing happens.

Well, this is my story. It is always most interesting when nothing happens. Of course it is. You want a naked man hacking away with a thin whippy sword, that's always the most boring thing of all, another plot. Who needs yet another plot. It is always most interesting when nobody is doing anything.

If this is still me talking I think the experience is already too much for you, she said.

And yet it is strange, he thought, I haven't heard yet anyway of any of my classmates who have died since, yes that is strange. It must be beating the odds. I have known many others, friends, who have died every year. The valley sun and valley wind make our skins tight and tough, the weathered women with marks on the corners of their faces are beautiful. No one dead, but just Tim W., who last year broke his back in a skydiving accident. He was a poor boy, a Russian who moved here from the prairies, and now he's been into the army, guaranteed supper, then glamour, now bed sores.

Saturday night it was again down south, thirteen miles on the familiar highway where he had sometimes courted death between the tame fruit trees, to the dance, yes, in a ballroom over the cinder-block storeroom of a beach motel, what else. It was a lot like the northern part of the state of Washington, only newer, in better condition. He eyed this one and that one, a roll of drink tickets in his pocket, talk with an old teacher who's busy looking around the room to see who else is there. The six-foot-six star of the basketball team. I haven't changed at all, he saw, standing alone with his drink beside the amateur bar, a little to the side, looking in. Well, destroy that schmaltzy icon—he began to talk animatedly with three classmates he's hardly known because they were in the C or D class, not the A's, and they probably didn't graduate—two of them were running their fathers' orchards. That would be honourable and exciting in France or Laos. Not here. The other had a machine shop. I'm getting there, he thought, I'm down to about twenty-four years old now. He got some more drinks and sat with his wife, his wife was talking with another, and another. He sat down and wrote a drunken note in his notebook. "What a drunken note!" he wrote, and would do so again, he thought months later, where is all this leading. The little band struck up a polka—1949!—and his big classmates were really turned on, they came stomping by, sweating faces in the desert, just like the old days. She nudged him and he looked—there was Mickey M. the basketball star with his old green singlet on, number thirteen. It was beautiful.

She knew, that is, the folklore of his valley upbringing, and sometimes resisted it, but was placed into it, and right there now, with the colours, green and gold, and in the sky traditionally blue, the Mediterranean, they always said, who had never been there. Now it might be raining outside, twenty years, really, later. Well, now it was nearly time to eat the smorgasbord, and the speeches were starting. He sat there and listened to the ribald jokes, teachers and students now all one in their weakness sitting in their mortality and standing to assert their commemorated youth. He who had spoken more solemn words in public than any of them, he listened. "Will the father stand up," one of them interjected, to cap a joke. He heard all the words, and the impromptu ones, too, that said I was there twenty years ago as well, don't forget me. Someone referred to him as "the original hippie." He imagined himself turning proudly to her gaze, and though he didn't he knew she imagined the same. And then they were close, sharing, a knowledge that removed them both above the gaucheries here, except this moment when they deigned to be among them.

Their response to me was, is, essentially is, mainly to my long hair or other ways of, in their words, "being different." I find that was the image they have carried twenty years, that's all, just that dumb thing. Well, I certainly was, and wanted to be, right back there. Except at the bar, where he yearned again for their ears, for respect. But that was why he was different, why he went away, to get something more than that, poor thing. Oh drink your drink in the clear plastic cup and forget this shit. But he felt it and admitted it, though not to her or anyone else, he felt a little envious that some of them still knew each other, were apparently acquainted on the coast where most of them, he was surprised to learn, lived now.

The floor filled as more and more took to, what else could they ever do, dancing. The trio was a surprise, at least to his drunken and snobbishly indulgent ears. His classmate Ray was on stand-up bass, with a piano and drums he didn't know, Ray's weekend band, playing new danceable jazz and 1953 favourites. In the middle of the rum and coke it was acceptable and beautiful, a beauty, it went with the dim pink lights. Outside himself it was happening more and more, and the inside was where he was, resting heavier. It came to him that there was no dope at the party, no dope all weekend, lots of liquor, and it was not at all sexual, a disappointment, what happened to that famous repressed back-seat sex of the fifties. He danced with Amanda, he had a hell of a good time, he stopped occasionally, sweating, they jived, expertly, as he had never done till he was out of school for two years, did they all notice this now, the man with his name on the radio. He danced once with Ron's wife, a shorty, who said again he was the only one she wanted to meet, his second wife, from somewhere else far off, Ron is in the navy, twenty years. Then he returned to Amanda and they really showed them. He was aware of his father, and his mother, they had gone home early, right after the eats, before the drinking really set in. The lake was out there, free of its algae now, young as it ever had been. The glacier long melted, the ice cubes, too, ran out around one o'clock.

In the Big Little Book Apple Mary was pretending she hadn't got her fortune back.

"What did you say? Not that I'm sure I want to know."

"Something I was reading while you were reading *The Wind in the Willows*."

"What were you really thinking, a minute ago. I was watching you," she said. She was smiling, with her eyes, indulgently, the way he loved.

"They've all got too many kids," he said. "Nobody should have that many kids. Each one of them has a tall son named Robert. Mainly teenage kids, too, I mean. They take up so much space."

"Oh you," she said. "I know you."

"What I see, is my classmates are now the parents. We used to be the kids, and the parents were the parents."

"As it should be?"

"And just about the same as *their* parents, except better off."

"You came all the way here to find that out? Why didn't you just ask me for a book?"

"Most of the ones that were the most intelligent, and most interesting, and the lovely troublemakers—"

Now you're getting to be a drunken maudlin class reunion.

"—well, they didn't come. At least I hope so." He felt what, redeemed.

He thought of the shouting at the supper, and some of it was not over, the loud in-jokes he explained to her from time to time. They danced, drooping into each other, finding the frames of that year, those years. He found it wasn't sentiment, it was relief, the bodies falling into their favourite easy chairs. They danced on the flimsy floor of the drab modern motel he had to accept because really he didn't live here now, let them have it.

He didn't enter the in-jokes. They had been a class that marched together, across the old playground to the newly built school in 1948. It was an E-shaped modern two-storey yellow stucco building, squatting upon a field of hard grey pebbles and round stones, the deserted bed of the glacier disappeared some eon in the past. It was a desert and they were used, expected to make it bloom. John Cairns the eternal prefect led the way, just behind the principal and teachers, that league, Moses, I suppose, Joshua and the staggering tribe.

Every time you were caught, they, the prefects and their friends the wardens, put you on the "rock pile," you picked up and raked up, pebbles and stones from the baked grey ground, and you hauled them in heavy cement-spattered wheelbarrows, I can remember their squat pneumatic tires bouncing, down to the ditch, where you dumped them and wiped the desert sweat off your temples, and cursed the ones who were making you do this.

So the in-jokes are about the "rock pile," said John Cairns the prefect, now of course a Vancouver doctor, grins, he doesn't look a day older and he never hauled a barrow of rocks, and the principal grins and he still isn't your pal, no matter how you spell it, he's a frail man with a disease called by a proper noun, the name of a person place or thing. They, the male voices, are shouting quips about the "rock pile." Is that still animosity, resentment, in the air. He is a doctor, and they are owners of their fathers' stony orchards.

At the table now, they were talking with some of his friends, drunken adults who used to get into trouble with adults. Here as on the family beer lawn yesterday, she was truly interested and happy to learn, to have it affirmed, that when he was having his school days move through him, he was a sneaky organizer of other people's activities and reactions. Happy that she didn't imagine that herself, that she didn't, as he suggested, cause him to start doing that. That she had not, after all, changed him, seeing what, if she had, she would be accused of changing him into. God, he was drunk.

It didn't matter, not now, much. There wasn't any *conversation* about those years or about the more recent past, no catching up at all, except with his one friend Joe Horvath. Only remarks, now, and present time running out. A cool first of July weekend where there weren't supposed to be any clouds, bodies circling by in the cheap pink light, he'd promised, but no talk either of the future, as if this was an indulgence. He'd half-promised himself there'd be renewed interest, they'd keep track from now on, after this interlude. But there was an unspoken agreement that they'd stay out of each other's, this would be the last time. He felt so old. Just for now some wry adult remarks, about producing kids, or fat ...

Racing to the end. Of this, too. So the next afternoon the hilarity was a strange gentility, the family picnic at the disappointingly but aptly cool beach was as pleasant as possible, with bending paper plates, Fred Mullins barbecuing paid-for salmon, eyes on children all along the sand. Someone was nice enough to photograph him with his daughter, knee-deep in the cool water. He had a valley hangover and his parents had let him sleep in as was his custom at home.

"I'm sorry it wasn't blazing hot for you this last day," Amanda said.

What can I do, I'm only the chronicler, he said, loving her, the first time either of them had been on this beach. During his childhood it had been unreclaimed marshes.

This afternoon he didn't try to connect with anyone. Back on the coast he was batting .375, but he gave up his plan to pass this information to the captains who'd seen him retreat chicken behind a collection of sports magazines.

There were no tables, so they gathered with Joe and his wife and daughter in the sand, sand in the potato salad, of course. He was never happy at picnics or parties, anyway, though he insisted on going. The two daughters threw sand at each other and dropped wet hotdogs among the discarded rubber sandals. The sun settled behind the clouds and was not to come out again all day. Noisy outboard engines roared in and out, and a faint odour of consumed gasoline filled the air. His wet feet had sand between the toes. The wind lifted the corners of their blanket on the sand.

Are you having any fun, she asked.

Yes, as a three-member family on an outing, he said.

You must have some friends here.

You, you're included now, the three of us, in my old isolation. Because of what?

It's—

That these people are familiar but out of our world, like the cousins you don't see anymore after the choice is your own and not your parents'.

You want to go home soon? she suggested.

Home?

Back into town.

I'd like to go and read a 1953 newspaper.

It's not 1953.

It's not 1953. It's not 1973, either.

West
Window

Back in the day, I used to publish book-length poems (say, forty-eight pages) with the really good small literary presses, such as Coach House Press or Talonbooks. Then a year or two later I would gather, say, three or four of these longish poems into a volume published by McClelland & Stewart. M&S had also published my first novel, so when I finished *Burning Water*, I sent it to them. Well, we had an argument about the ending of the book, so I went to General Publishing, and they published it, after I agreed to change the beginning.

So I figured that I was no longer an M&S author, too bad, and as I had a standard contract with General, meaning that they got first dibs on my next manuscript, I assembled four longish poems that had been published by Coach House and Talonbooks, added some shorter poems, and published *West Window* in General's Spectrum Poetry Series. I was pleased about this turn of events because that series had published other gathered books by Robert Kroetsch and D. G. Jones.

One of the shorter poems in my book was a little sequence titled "Four Jobs." Each of the titles was made up of a verb participle and its object. One of them, "Taking Pictures," is about my job in the RCAF and is set in Manitoba, but the other three are about working in and near Oliver. In fact, two of those have to do with the main activity around that place during my younger days—growing and packing tree fruit.

In the late seventies there was a small movement in Canadian poetry, extolled by some poets who resisted the experimentalism that

Oliver Co-op packing house where I worked in cold storage.

had crept onto the scene in the sixties. They called their product "work poetry," and promoted "content" over form, anecdote over uncertainty. Most of the champions of "work poetry" were creative-writing teachers at universities and colleges, though a few were ex-loggers on welfare, and so on.

It could be that my job poems were a gesture toward these folks. Here's one of them.

Trucking Peaches

The smell of peaches in new boxes,
seven boxes piles, I had to keep up
with the women on the sorting belt, pile
seven boxes and move them, my hand truck
leaning back over my head.

                    The women
were mothers in kerchiefs, same last names
as kids in my class, German names. They
said I was the hardest worker
in Mac & Fitz packing house and it was a shame
the way they made me run, and get rid of those
sneakers, wear boots in this place.

                              I was fifteen
but the union and Mac & Fitz agreed I was eighteen
because that was the rule. They had to give me
my 68 cents an hour.

                        I was scared shitless, Mac,
I would spill seven boxes of culled peaches
on the oiled floor and get behind hopeless and fired,
and I loved the neatness, seven boxes added to
seven boxes and back of that, how it all fits,
production.

                    They taught me the rules of poker, too
in the lunchroom, how to guard myself from too many
65 cent bets during that one
half hour.

Smoking Mirror

In 1980 I published a novel titled *Burning Water*, and two years later a book of poetry titled *Smoking Mirror*. I guess they are not synonyms, but they do resemble one another, in that where there is smoke there is or was fire, and it was not only Joseph Conrad who noticed the mirror of the sea. If we are lucky enough to experience calm.

The concept of burning water, its contradiction and mystery, comes from Mexico, the first country I ever visited where language and history were truly foreign. I was introduced to the concept by the Italian-French-Mexican archaeologist Laurette Séjourné, who lived in Mexico City and transformed archaeological attitudes there when she excavated Teotihuacan. Her book *Burning Water* is the great pioneering text on religion in Quetzalcóatl's time. I stole her title, and took the liberty of taking burning water as an image for the creative imagination.

Smoking Mirror also is Mexican. His Aztec name was Tezcatlipoca, and he was an important god in the Aztec religion, but he had been around for the Toltecs and the Maya and other civilizations in Mesoamerica. He is always associated with obsidian, the hard black lava used as a mirror, and with the night. If you slept through the night and woke with a little black footprint on your face, you had been visited by Tezcatlipoca. What was likely to happen to you I don't remember, probably by choice. I always thought of that little footprint as writing.

Smoking Mirror is one of my least-known books. It has three Okanagan poems in it, and I find them, or at least two of them, interesting for the following reason. They start as if they were the simply stated poems I had written in the late fifties and early sixties. Then something happens to lift them out of occasion and setting. I think that the ending of "Calm After" will give you a notion of what I mean. The Okanagan made this poem happen, but finally you are meant not to know the Okanagan so much as to know the poem, how it is not the route to a place but a place in itself.

A lot of my earlier poems were set in Mexico and seemed to have a mission to make spots in Mexico clear, to illuminate them as with daylight. The nocturnal mystery of *Smoking Mirror* probably did a lot to move one's attention from writing about toward writing itself.

Looking down toward Fairview from the stamp mill.

Calm After

After the storm
the apples hang on these branches
in front of my face ·
wet with rain,
sun round other side.

Ah, your face my
favourite poet
friend, our highways together,
our looking for work.

You, too, reader,
don't go on to the next poem.
Stay here for a minute,
stay.

The Smooth Loper

I was a kid
watching Coyote
run across the rise,
his tail straight behind him.

He was my favourite animal
but I didn't know
I imitated him
till recent years.

Moonlight becomes you
Coyote, and I, among other things
go to bed only
for the morning sun.

Also I have friends
who tell me I am wily
to my innocent
hairy Face.

At Fairview, Burnt to the Earth, 1902

for Frank Davey and Lionel Kearns

On the grassy site
where ghost Fairview once lay
I squat before a three-year-old rattlesnake
sleeping in the cool air
among burnt cans and a pair of pink high-button shoes.

I'd expected to see him or
see one. I was there alone
for an hour.

        It's not often you get home,
not often you are alone. Enough of that
for a while

        until I brought around
the camera I bought second hand
thirteen years ago on the prairie.

Home home home home home home.

He was still lying there with his head
resting on himself
when I walked back to the dirt road
going just about nowhere.

A Way with Words

A Way with Words was an early collection of essays about my favourite Canadian poets, including Margaret Avison, Roy Kiyooka, and Fred Wah. "The Memory of Red Lane" is more a memoir than it is a critical piece, because Red was a very close friend and a tyro poet before he died. Whenever I go to Vernon, I visit his grave overlooking the city where he and his two writer brothers grew up.

Fifty years after his death I still mourn him and the fact that we never got to read or hear his mature writing. Pat Lane, his kid brother, is an accomplished poet, always an earnest autobiographer and commentator. Red was a different bird; he did everything with wit and cool flair, if you can imagine that seeming contradiction.

I don't think that the people of the North Okanagan know these brothers well, but the valley itself does, I am sure.

The Memory of Red Lane

I can't write a critical essay about Red Lane's poetry. He died at the age during which a poet is learning to throw off his adolescent bad habits and ambitions. But I must count him among my contemporaries and brain cells. If on this subject I am a little mawkish, that is due to his influence upon me, and I am not sure that is a bad thing, for once in the life of West Coast poetry. If I repeat my words I am returning to the primal habit of the poet, perhaps: memory and mumbling. When Red Lane died he had done just his early words.

Red Lane, second from the right, in front of my parents' house.

I met Red for the first time over a poker game in the barracks at Royal Canadian Air Force Station Macdonald, Manitoba. I lost my whole two weeks' pay in one sitting. He likely lost his, but you would never know it. At four in the morning he got up with his nifty bare belly-button manner and hied off to work, whatever hauling and cutting he had to do in the airmen's mess. He was not a cook, he was a cook's helper. I forget what they were officially called.

We quickly became best friends, and there we were, both from the Okanagan. I had just turned twenty and he would soon. I knew more than he did because I had flunked out of a college course in Victoria. He knew more than I did because he had been around. We wanted each other's knowledge, and we freely handed it to each other, dramatizing ourselves to each other always, as fated-to-be companions always will. We broke more than bread together.

We were best friends from then on. Really, it had little to do with literature. It might have had something to do with the fact that we were both from the valley. He was a strange person, and not simply because he wanted to be; it had a lot to do with that, for me. Probably for him, too. I was writing then, in the barracks, and he was, too, in a different way.

We shared his little Underwood typewriter, and we often drank together, whatever there was, and played pool, and sat up literally all night, talking. I talked him into getting out of the air force, and a year later I got out, too. I went to Vancouver and the university. He went on the road.

When I have been on the road (my favourite part of America) for a while, behind the wheel or sitting in the ditch, I think a lot about Red Lane, whose poems ride with me, westward or eastward, toward the interior of British Columbia, where we grew up looking at the same water. After his childhood his normal habitat was the Trans-Canada Highway, where he lived either as a hitchhiker or driver of a malfunctioning 1947 Chevrolet, with his thigh tied to the gearshift to hold it in the only functioning gear. When I smash my car on the Okanagan highway I think of Manitoba, where our friend was killed in a car. In Manitoba I was writing stories and borrowing his unusual typewriter. He was away in the mess hall, stirring something and smoking a cigar. It was and is all very romantic when I come to think of it.

And I curse
this broken white line
I must follow
that leads
seems
morse-coding me
over the blackness of the highway
chaining me
to the passed

So ends a poem called "Margins VI" from *Collected Poems of Red Lane* (1968); and I suppose many poetry folks will say unsophisticated, and so on.

Some of his poems are not in that book. He also wrote a novel or two. Lionel Kearns was probably right when he said that Red's best writing is in his many long letters. I also wish you could see his drawings and cartoons.

But in an ordinary air force barracks he had a typewriter, of all things. I had a record player and a camera and drawers full of Signet novels in my room. I was already full of that small-town dream of becoming a major writer of the twentieth century. I was writing awful short stories about tested men, and sending them to the magazines, *Saga* and the *Antioch Review*, and acquiring rejections slips, which I may have taped to the inside of my closet door along with my picture of Mitzi Gaynor. My most intense reading was James T. Farrell's Danny O'Neill novels. I called myself George H. Bowering.

Pretty soon there was Red, or "Rick," as he encouraged people to call him (this was in the mid-fifties), over in his room, also writing stories; and I thought I had something to do with that. I was later tempted to think of him as my Dean Moriarty. But I also knew that his mother, who called him "Dick," was a writer of children's stories. Or at least I knew that Red had told me that. I rushed to believe everything he told me, even after I found that some of his marvellous cartoons had swiped their lines from *True*.

He got out of the air force, after months of urging by me, in the summer of 1956, and I went on leave, so we covered his turf, the North Okanagan, and my turf, the South Okanagan, together. He even sat in the back seat with my girlfriend's kid sister on, as they said, double dates.

You've made two mistakes in your life
and everything that is happening to you now
is a result of them.

The first is that
you didn't make love to the hometown girl.

The second is that
you argued with me that
intelligence came before knowledge
and went away
believing you were right.

(Yes, well, okay, maybe, Red.) He introduced me to his kid brother, Pat Lane, underage in a Vernon pool hall, and I introduced him to the suckers in the Lawrence pool hall. We blew the winnings in a floating poker game across the line in Oroville, and there we were again. So we were close, we were by my measure best friends. He wore his blue suede shoes and I my white bucks in innocuous low-life from Winnipeg to British Columbia.

I got out of the air force ten months later and worked in the Okanagan for the summer and went down to Vancouver to try college again in the fall of 1957, having read all the twentieth-century American novels. While I wore my old air-force duds around UBC and became the mysterious young writer Delsing, Red was running between Calgary and the Interior, working at jobs and rackets. And while he was always present in my stories, my red-haired pal, there were long stretches when I did not see him. In 1960 his letters to me started.

> Sweepings, George, I don't believe my time will ever come— my time, I mean of course my—well, I don't believe that I was meant to be a something for somebody but I think more probably a someone for somebody—you know what I mean or will—like, a man can't really say: "I used to work in a candy factory" but rather "I have worked in a candy factory."

Then we would see each other from time to time, usually when we were back in the Okanagan at the same time. He was more often roading back and forth across the west, taking meaningless jobs or other advantages here and there, but never staying long in one place. But he was, it turned out, always writing. His wonderful letters went to make his reputation, and Lionel Kearns was right. Red still had his typewriter, though, and all that time he was making poems and stories, and from time to time I would see them. I did not appraise them, and I still don't. I don't think they were expert poems and stories, but they were interesting and they are true.

In the early sixties some of us in Vancouver started the poetry newsletter *Tish*, and I sent copies to Red. After a while he sent me some more poems, and I showed them to the other editors of *Tish*, who were all in the university, and interested in very technical things about poetry. Red's poems were unlike our usual concerns, but there is some principle that results in the fact that very conscious concern about poetry and very naive making poetry out of life arrive at the same place of honest writing. The other *Tish* editors began publishing Red's poems without the untoward urging from me.

After *Tish* had begun in 1961, I had tried to get those two sides of my life together (and am still trying), Red the Real, and the sophistications of Projective Verse. It was after a struggle with my own doubtful poetic principles that I had managed to get Red's poems to the other editors and thence into the magazine. They were soon followed by Red himself, at last down here in Vancouver (where he was to die). So for a while I lost him again, to my friends with raunchier downtown pads, 1962, and more daring departures from the student life. We faced one another, when we got together, with the tacit understanding that sometime we would get away from all these people and tear down each others' lives, meld, and become a creature such as they had never seen before.

But for the meantime Red had more or less moved to Vancouver, and good exchanges had begun. Red learned more and more about poetry, and moved with ears into the West Coast scene, which at that time was remarkably active for the poets. The poets took quickly to Red, too, an unacademic presence that they needed, but not a scoff-art. The Vancouver poets—Jamie Reid, Sam Perry, Dan McLeod, Lionel Kearns, Frank Davey, Peter Auxier, and later Milton Acorn—will tell how important Red was to them, as a human being. I, too.

Vancouver in the summer of 1963 was the scene of a great New World poetry conference. There were hotshot young poets from all over the continent seeing and meeting and talking, all about their craft and profession and contentions with the rest of the world. Many of us thought ourselves to be insiders, and wanted to rub minds with Olson and others. I was happy to see that Allen Ginsberg was listening to Red, and I thought I could see why. Red showed him innocent poems that wanted above all else to convey the fact of his own life in the fire halls and forests of interior British Columbia. The *Tish* poets had often talked of such a thing as an ideal or a rationale for their poetics. Red just did it, woodenly to be sure, and those of us who had eyes to see knew that he in his way would satisfy the desire of Williams, who said once in Seattle that you get to reality in the *way* you say your piece. Red's way was not arrived at through doctrine—he was just open, the way Ginsberg asked us to be.

> and I pick up a few stones
> and on the strength of my companions
> throw the stones into darkness
>
> and I no longer hear the hooting
>
> on the road I'm walking.

We never got a chance to meld, not totally. The closest we came to living for each other was in our letters. Everyone who got them got great enjoyable letters from Red. I never forgot what Lionel Kearns said, and in 1976, Caledonia Writing Series published *Letters from Geeksville*, a selection of letters I received from Red in the last five years of his life. It is a shame that in that book you cannot see the real pages, the unreproducible, the drawings all over and through them, the words themselves drawn rather than written, the ten different sizes of the capitals and the various styles of handwriting as the news becomes theatre. The originals and others are stored in the University of Calgary Library. But for the book I chose to present the one aspect that is words, typeset. I tried to lay out a range of Red's appearances, as wordly fabulist of the Okanagan motels, as naive aspirant to the Canadian literary stage, as disguised petitioner for help and care toward the end. More than once I have heard people say that *Geeksville* is a terrific novel.

In 1955 I dug Kirk Douglas and Red dug Burt Lancaster. More than likely he was right.

In November 1964 when I was living in Calgary, I received in the mail a typescript so meticulous that it looked like the single copy of a book of poems. It had been fixed into decorated covers, and it was entitled *The 1962 Poems*, and it was of course by Red. In the early morning of the first of December, 1964, my twenty-ninth birthday, the telephone woke me up, and a working stranger told me that Red was dead in Vancouver. Since that time I have often dreamed that he was alive, walking back in through the door, smiling. Sometimes I used to try to believe that he had done what would have been a typical Red Lane trick, pretend he's dead and then appear suddenly one day, unchanged. By now he would have been a wonderful poet, I think; his poetry never got going in the higher gears, but I still read his advice to me and others, and sometimes it is wrong because he did not know enough yet, but much more often it is right. Ask Jamie, ask Lionel, ask Pat. Ask me.

In the year following his death, Red's poems began to appear in the magazines, as they seldom did during his lifetime. And in 1965, bpNichol published the manuscript Red had sent me just before his death. It was Red's first book. Three years later Pat Lane and Seymour Mayne published the second, *Collected Poems of Red Lane*.

That volume starts with a section of children's poems called "The Surprise Sandwich." It sounds trite, but Red was a kid. He was never taken in by the fifties watchword, "maturity." In the fifties parents, teachers and others were always after you to be "mature." Eisenhower was president, a nice old man but a severely tested one; and we had Louis St. Laurent. One was supposed to grow up (even your high school girlfriend would urge you to do that) and assume our sober responsibilities. Pat Boone, the white bucks man, was very big. But Red, thank God and James Dean, never fell for that. While I wore my white bucks, dirty as they were, he wore actual blue suede shoes, and yes I did step on them, out of jostling love. Being a kid might have made it hard for him to "adjust" (another fifties word) to the roles of husband and father, but he was in fact not interested in roles that he was not contriving for himself. Rick invented Red Lane. So when he addresses kids in his poems he does so without the condescension of even the well-intentioned grown-up trying to do the same thing.

So when he came to putting together a "book" of kids' poems, he did so with the same innocence of all the procedures that any kid is likely to bring to reading a book of poems.

Hi

My name is Red Lane
because I have red hair
and my father's last name is Lane

I am a poet

And I wrote all these poems
for you
and I don't even know you
and you don't even know me

What do you think about that?

If you are an ironist, what do you think about that?
    Jesus, I love him. Excuse me.
    Because, you see, it might seem that Red is pretending to speak from a kid's consciousness in these poems:

When I'm walking down the sidewalk
I do all kinds of things
like
making sure I don't step on any cracks
or
making sure I step on all the cracks
and
sometimes I walk Giant steps
or
sometimes I walk Baby steps

But I walked down numerous streets with Red, and I can tell you that he did just what he says. Are kids supposed to trust him because of that? I don't know whether they are supposed to, but they did, and do. I did. It is not usual to speak of trusting a poet. But here Red's skill is his truth of the matter. I trust him as I trust a veteran timber-topper.

The second part of the *Collected Poems* is his sequence called "Margins I–XXX," perhaps influenced by all the talk of margins in the earliest issues of *Tish*, or a sardonic comment on it. Red had a penchant for neatness—a neurosis, I might allow, because I have shared it. While walking down the street he would make an even number of steps between curbs. In his drawings there would be stark symmetry; in his poems a parallel structure of images and syntax. If he tells you what he saw he will use a similar sentence to tell you what he heard. The bare facts of his life might suggest a sense of chaos or at best of things left unfinished. It is in his personal ritual of beauty and order-making that he came most forthrightly from his everyday activities to his poems. You should have seen the beautiful fried eggs he made—yolk never broken, white part perfect circle, whether he was making forty-eight or two, and all the time he's doing a manic but perfectly symmetrical dance. So the "Margins": he wanted to push against them, but to make sure that they were clearly and evenly defined, too.

> I remember
> One winter
> I was walking her home
> and we came to an open
> untravelled
> field of snow
> and we walked out into the field
> and made love
> there in the middle of it all

> *

Heat heavy on my head
standing here on a rock by a lake
casting my line
out over the water
I watch
the small artificial fly
looping out
to the limits of the line
and falling
to lie on the surface of the lake
motionless

The "Margins" poems were written during 1962, in Vernon, Kamloops, and Vancouver, British Columbia. There I see Red standing on
a right-angle street corner, at ease with his idleness, knowing that he is
making discoveries for the future. The bad part is that Red knew that
he was just learning to write poems, that it would be ten years till he
was the best in the country. Or a necessary part of it.

Red was the raw stuff out of which John Newlove weaved himself.
Where Red just naturally saw

Black night
outside
my window

Newlove was practised enough to see that it is a "Black Night Window."
You do see the difference, but if you don't, pass on to the next thing I
say. That is, I loved Red Lane as my best friend, and John Newlove is
a very good poet who was born around the same time.

In 1965 the federal government, from its home in Ontario, desig-
nated the Okanagan Valley a depressed area. The people living there
would not allow the term. We have been sending poets to Vancouver
for years, and they are never heard of in the Okanagan, where there
are no bookstores.

Another section of *Collected Poems* is called "Marchlands I–VII."
These are dramatic small-town poems, with dialogue. They deal with
the tough times of theft and brutality, self-destruction and social
war. They give a hint of what Red's fiction is about. Though situated
in the world of the non-powerful, they do not preach. Rather they
end this way:

"Nice to see ya, Red."

"Nice to be seen
Man
Nice to be seen."

There are some more "sections" to that book, notably the one called
"Acknowledgements," Red's literary criticism in verse. It takes as its
subject or target the Canadian poetry scene of the sixties, especially in
Vancouver, "Land of Tish."

Finally, he is speaking of (a) job-seeking, and (b) grammar,
when he says

I give you no references
I give you poems.

That sense runs through the book, that Red Lane was (and later saw it
his gift to be) the voice of the home earth working a gravity on those
(poets, especially) who were beginning to float among clouds of their
own fashioning. We Vancouver writers owe him something, and we will
periodically read his books and let their attraction work on us in our
few and fugitive moments.

The 1962 Poems (Toronto: Ganglia Press, 1965).
Collected Poems of Red Lane (Vancouver: Very Stone Press, 1968).
War-Cry (Trumansburg, NY: The Crossing Press, 1970).
Letters from Geeksville (Prince George, BC: Caledonia Writing Series, 1976).

A Place to Die

My original title for this collection was *The World as a Place to Die*, but the publisher Michael Macklem, who had some strong and odd opinions about book design, liked this shortened version better. Being a genial person, I gave, as I did on changing *The Dead Sailors* to *Burning Water* a few years earlier.

By this time I had moved away from autobiographical realism to a kind of constructionism. Instead of asking myself "Was it like this?" I began to ask myself "Can I get away with this?" So in "A Short Story" I may have got "right" some details about an orchard home somewhere around Summerland, but my primary trope consisted in illustrating the main facets of the short story, as they were explained to me by high school and university teachers—plot, characters, theme, etc. I was, at the time, quite enamoured of John Hawkes's statement: "I began to write fiction on the assumption that the true enemies of the novel were plot, character, setting, and theme."

Ironically, this is my most-often anthologized and reprinted story, and it is the one that is most often taught in high schools and universities.

A Short Story

Setting

It was that slightly disappointing moment in the year when the cherry blossoms have been blown off the trees, or shrunken to brown lace out of which little hard green pebbles are beginning to appear. The orchardists were running tractors between rows of trees, disking the late spring weeds into the precious topsoil left there by the glacier that long ago receded from the desert valley.

Starlings were growing impatient with the season, tired of competing with the season, tired of competing for scraps behind the Safeway store in town, eager for those high blue days when the cherries would be plump and pink, when they could laugh at the sunburnt men in high gumboots, who would again try to deceive them with fake cannons and old shirts stretched between the branches.

High over Dog Lake a jet contrail was widening and drifting south. The orchards on the west bank were in shadow already, and sunlight sparkled off windows of the new housing development on the other shore. The lake was spotted with brown weeds dying underwater, where the newest poison had been dumped by the government two weeks before.

Evening swallows were already dipping and soaring around the Jacobsen house, nabbing insects in their first minutes of activity after a warm day's sleep. The house was like many of the remodelled orchard homes in the southern part of the valley, its shiplap sides now covered with pastel aluminum, metallic screen doors here and there, a stone chimney marking the outside end of the living room. Fifteen years ago the living room had been used only when relatives from other valley towns came to visit. Now it was panelled with knotty cedar, animal heads looking across at one another from the walls, and the Jacobsens sat there after all the evening chores were done, watching Spokane television in colour, and reading this week's paper, or perhaps having some toast and raspberry jam.

The rug was a pastel shade fairly close to that of the outside surface. The Jacobsens lived with it, though neither of them particularly liked it. One of them had, once, when it was new; the other never thought of offering an opinion, or holding one.

Characters

The Jacobsens did not discuss things. They spoke short sentences to one another in the course of a card game, or while deciding which re-run was more worth watching on the mammoth television set parked under a deer head on the west wall of the living room.

"We haven't seen this Carol show, have we?" suggested Mrs. Jacobsen. "I think it must have been on the night we played bridge with Stu and Ronnie."

"No, we saw it," said Mr. Jacobsen from behind his sixteen-page newspaper. "This is the one where her and Harvey are on the jet plane that gets hijacked to South America."

"Skyjacked."

"The same thing. But if you want to watch it again, go ahead."

"I can't remember a skyjack one."

"Go ahead. I'll probably fall asleep in the middle, anyway," said Mr. Jacobsen.

Art Jacobsen was tired every night. As soon as the after-supper card game was over, and his short legs were up on the aquamarine hassock, his eyes would begin to droop. He was sixty-one years old, and still working eleven hours a day in the orchard. Like most valley orchardists, he wore a shirt only during the early hours of the morning, when the dew was still on every leaf. His body was tanned and muscled, but it was getting more rectangular every year.

Audrey Jacobsen was ten years younger. She had only recently taken to colouring her hair, often a kind of brownish-red she mistakenly remembered from her youth. Her first husband used to tease her about having red hair, though it wasn't true. By the time that Ordie Michaels had died and Art Jacobsen had started courting her on rainy days, her hair was a good plain brown, usually under a kerchief.

She'd taken to wearing the kerchief, as all the women did, while sorting fruit at the Co-op packing house. By the time Donna was five, Audrey had assumed the habit of wearing it all the time, except when she went for drives with Art Jacobsen.

They had been watching Carol on television for five years now, and she didn't know whether she liked the show.

Point of View

It is not that I know all about the Jacobsens and Donna Michaels before I start telling you about them. I am what they call omniscient, all right, but there isn't any Jacobsen family until I commit them to this medium. I have some hazy ideas or images, rather, or their story, a sort of past and a present, I suppose, but really, for me the story is waiting somewhere in the future. Or I should say that I'm waiting for a time in the future when I will have the time to come to it, here. As a matter of fact, you don't have to, now, wait as long for it as I do.

So I am in the position ascribed to the narrator with the totally omniscient point of view. A know-it-all. Don't you believe it! "God-like." Don't you believe it!

For instance, I've been thinking about writing this story for two years. Just a month ago I began to imagine a woman visiting her mother and stepfather at their orchard home, and that common emotional violence later on. But I just got the names while I was writing the first parts of the story, and I didn't imagine the Jacobsen house near the lake—I thought it would be forty kilometres farther south.

Do I have to mention that there is something difficult to explain about a third-person omniscient narrative having all these "I's" in it? Point of view dictates distance. Well, I would like to keep you closer than your usual "god" will allow (except for people such as yourself, Leda) (no, that's not what I'm trying to do to you, reader: don't be so suspicious).

From up here I can see the Jacobsen house as a little square surrounded by trees that have nearly lost their blossoms and are just producing leaves. I have good eyes; I need them to see all that through the drifting jet contrail.

By the way, have you noticed that when the narrator speaks in the first person, he makes you the second person? When he speaks of others in the third person, you are perhaps standing beside him, only the parallax preventing your seeing exactly what he is seeing. That makes for a greater distance produced by the first person narrative. You must have noticed that.

Protagonist

Donna Michaels, an attractive honey-blonde in her early twenties, was about four kilometres from the Jacobsen house, driving along the lakeside road in her dented Morris Minor convertible. She has already gone through her rite of passage between innocent childhood and knowledgeable maturity, involving strong Freudian implications. Now she was driving through a warm valley evening, wishing that she had come a week ago, when the cherry blossoms were still at the beginning of their decline.

She had not been home during blossom time for seven years, and perhaps this more than anything else told her that she had really ceased to be a valley kid, that she was a coast person. Looking to her right she could see, even in the shadows made by the hills over the water, splotches of brown weeds under the surface of the lake. A part of her that still wanted to be a valley person was hurt by that.

She thought about taking a Valium before she got there, only two kilometres to go now. It was not really the time to appear. She should have arrived while Art was still out in the orchard, so she could have a calm talk with her mother. When Art was there, making his blustery remarks or criticisms about her language, her mother could be depended on to remain silent, just as she had always done during family hassles, just as she had done then.

"I love him, Donna. What am I supposed to do?" she had said.

"More than you love me?" That newcomer.

"I *chose* him."

That was the last time her mother had ever said anything so devastatingly open.

She got out of the car and took a Valium. One gets adept at swallowing them without water. She was mildly surprised that she was walking slowly toward the single little Ponderosa pine that used to be her going-to-be-alone place in the far corner of their orchard. It had perhaps grown four inches taller. Looking farther up, she could see Star Bright. She made a trivial wish and walked slowly back to the dusty car.

What a beautiful sight she was, with her long legs and summer dress, sunglasses perched on top of her short feathery blondish hair.

Symbolism

Donna got back into the dented Morris Minor, and before she let the clutch out, she unaccountably thought about the animal heads protruding from her stepfather's walls. The first time she had seen one, she had gone to the room next door, to see whether the elk's body stuck out from that side. What had ever been done with the bodies, she wondered now. Were they discarded, left on the forest floor for the delectation of the ants? Did the family eat them? She couldn't remember eating mountain goat or moose, and she had been a picky eater as a child.

She decided that whatever had been done with the torso and legs, Art was only really interested in the trophy. He talked about nature a lot, but he was quite comfortable under the stare of the big glass eyes.

When she was twelve, her dog Bridey passed away after a fit. Quickly, before he would have a chance to take her to the taxidermist, Donna put the heavy and limp body along with an adult's shovel into a wheelbarrow and pushed it for half an hour through the crumbling earth, to the Ponderosa. There she wasted no time looking at Bridey's fur and tight-closed eyes. She dug a hole and dropped her in and covered her up, without looking. She left no marker. She knew where Bridey was, and that was all that was necessary.

Now, she reflected, looking at the sagebrush growing around her tree, they probably knew, too, he probably saw the wheel tracks the next morning.

She let out the clutch and drove the last kilometre slowly, having pulled on the lights. Just in time, a mother quail and her five little ones raced in a line to the safety of the roadside weeds. She smiled as she imagined the mother there, counting them.

Then she was at the turn just before their driveway, where the truck and the new Toyota were parked in a sharp vee. People here along Rawleigh Road never pulled their drapes. Through the window she could see Mr. and Mrs. Jacobsen, an over-coloured Carol, and a deer she used to call Bambi, first childishly, then later to needle her stepfather.

Her car's wheels crunched over the driveway. Before she got out she did up her two top buttons.

Conflict

Donna had driven four hundred kilometres to be there, but she didn't want to go inside the house. Of course in a setting such as this, they would know that somebody had driven up the gravel driveway, and one of them, probably her mother, would be walking to the door at this moment.

Donna wanted to be with her mother, and especially because she never wrote letters home. She did not even imagine writing "Mrs. A. Jacobsen" on an envelope. She felt as if, yes, she still loved her mother, that strange older woman in polyester slacks, though they had not once spoken to each other on the telephone since Jacobsen had mounted her as his casual season's trophy. What ambiguity in the delivery of the thought. When it was accomplished, and all three knew, what depressing decisions and solitudes.

Donna could not stay in that family where her first love, her first-world face, lost all hope and fell in, decided to stay with the bringer of death. What polluted language in the formerly unchallenged Eden. Why? How, rather.

"But I chose him. I made my choice."

"Do you love him? Can you?"

"I chose him."

She was not a woman then, but she was not a valley girl, either. She left Dog Lake, she had to, and there was no question but the city on the coast, several ruinous jobs and some solitary education.

Now the door opened and it was Audrey who was illuminated by the porch light. Donna was momentarily ashamed with disappointment that her mother, Mrs. Michaels, was not the picture of a defeated lusterless farm wife, the sensitive buffeted by life, such as one expected to find in the Canadian novels she had been reading.

"Donna! For the Lord's sake! Why didn't you tell us you were coming? Come in, you rascal," the woman said, her arms outstretched as if offering the red knitting she had been doing while watching television.

Donna held her mother's elbows and kissed her nose as she felt the screen door bat against her rear. Her mother chattered with a little confusion as the pretty blonde deposited her purse and a book and something wrapped in a party paper on the telephone table.

"Well, well," said Art Jacobsen, looking up from his paper, his feet still stretched out on the hassock.

Dialogue

"I wish I'd gotten here while the blossoms were in full bloom," said Donna. It was the perfect little bit of business to get through the awkwardness of their surprise.

"Oh, we had a wonderful year for blossoms," said her mother. "When a breeze came up the whole valley smelled like a garden."

"It *is* a garden," said Donna, getting herself a cup of coffee from the pot on the stove. She came back through the arch into the living room, where her mother was still standing with the knitting in her hands. "At least that's how we coast people think of it."

Art shook his paper to a new page.

"It's not the blossoms that count. It's the bees."

"The workers, you mean," said Donna, a little edge on her voice. She sat down with her coffee, not looking at him.

"Yeah, the queen sits at home, getting fatter and fatter, while the workers bring her the honey," said Art, his eyes looking at a news photo of the local skeet-shooting champs.

"Have you had any supper, dear?" Audrey piped in.

"Yes, I stopped at the Princeton bus station café, for old times' sake," said Donna.

That was a nice shot. It was there that she had abandoned Art's truck that night, with the keys in the dash. She'd taken the bus to Vancouver with no baggage, not even clean underwear. Just two apples and her purse.

Art didn't say a word now.

"Well, well," said Audrey Jacobsen.

There was a silence. Even the knitting needles crossed and opened without a sound. It was pitch dark outside. A mirrored deer looked in from between two young Lombardy poplars.

"How are all your aches and pains, Mom?" Donna asked at last, idly looking at snapshots from a glass bowl on the table beside her chair. Carol was over, and Art raised his remote control and shot the set off.

"Oh, the osteopath in Penticton said I did something to my lower spine when I was a girl, and I can never expect to be a hundred percent."

"Does that mean you're not all there?" asked Art.

Flashback

When he seemed absolutely ready to give it up, give up on it, to settle for some costly talk then, she offered him a cigarette, which he took politely, and lit one herself. It was the only sort of occasion upon which she smoked, anything. They were always grateful, the talkers, when she by her gestures allowed them a certain comfort, a freedom from embarrassment.

"Thank you," he had said, and lay on his back beside her, carefully sharing the ashtray she kept on her belly.

"You needn't feel badly." Her voice was soft and sure, caring and casual, it seemed. "You might be surprised how often it happens. You had a lot to drink, I would imagine, it was only enough to make you think you wanted me. Happens quite a lot."

"No, that's not it. Well, it might be a little, but that's not really it. It's …"

She did not offer the interruption he was waiting for. She just smoked her cigarette. She butted it out in the ashtray, and handed the ashtray to him. So he had something to do with his free hand.

"It's just that you are about exactly the age of my daughter," he said.

"No kidding," she said, with a twiggy edge to her voice, and that was his first hint that it was time to go back to his hotel.

Foreshadowing

After he had left, she got the scissors and clipped her toenails. Having done five, she lay back and imagined the john walking back to his hotel. He did not seem like the taxi-taking kind.

She pictured him lying on her, brought by her to the margin of success. Then she yanked the scissors toward her, fetching a jolt as they sank into the flesh of his back. It was not an old movie on midnight television. The points of her scissors were just below the joining of her ribcage, forcing the skin a little.

I wonder whether I could just throw a few clothes into the car and drive to Montreal, she thought.

Maybe you could work your way across the country, she replied.

She clipped five toenails again. They were the same ones.

Plot

The spare bedroom of the Jacobsen house was also a kind of storeroom. It contained a gun rack in which one could find a pump-action shotgun, a .22 calibre repeater rifle, an old .303 that once belonged to the Canadian Army, a .44 handgun in a tooled holster, a 30-30 with a scope sight, and a collector's .30 calibre machine gun with a plugged barrel. This is where Donna was, taking off her light cardigan and shoes, finding the toothbrush and dental floss in the bottom of her big-city street bag, looking at herself, untanned, in the vanity mirror. A severed goat head looked over her shoulder.

Through two walls she could hear the Jacobsens disputing. Art's voice rose and rose, and at the end of a declarative sentence fragment it uttered the word "slut," followed by an exclamation point.

One would expect the ammunition to be locked up, and it was, in a cabinet with glass-panel doors. Donna shook the pillow out of one of the pillowcases, wrapped the pillowcase around her fist, and punched one of the glass panels three times, each time with greater force.

The male voice rose to the word "hell!" and stopped. A door banged against a wall, and heavy footsteps approached. Donna threw the pillow-case onto the bed beside her sweater. When Art propelled the bedroom door open, Donna was pointing a loaded shotgun at his head.

Art backed out of the bedroom and walked backward all the way to the living room. There he observed a slight movement of the dark holes he had wiped clean just the night before, and sat down in his favourite chair. He was on top of Audrey's knitting, but he felt convinced that he should not bring attention to such a minor problem.

Audrey Jacobsen, usually a chatterbox, found it hard to find the words she should say.

She said, "Donna…"

It was frightening that Donna did not say a word. Art looked depressed. He was a heavy man in his chair. Donna blew out her breath.

"For God's sake, girl, that's my husband!"

Donna did not breathe in.

"He's my husband, he's all I have!"

Donna turned a smooth quick arc, and shot her mother's face off.

Theme

Donna walked from the house and into the orchard, the shotgun still dangling. She had no shoes on. No one followed her, and she did not look behind. She was walking between two rows of cherry trees, so that when a quick hard breeze came around a rock outface it blew a snow of exhausted blossoms over her head.

Donna walked down the slope, not flinching when a clacking sprinkler spun slowly and soaked her dress from the waist down. It was really dark out now, and she could see the lights of the retirement village on the far side of the lake.

The gun had made a dreadful noise. But now the night life was speaking again, crickets nearby and frogs from down by the lake. They were calling each other to come and do it.

Donna walked till she came to the dirt road with the row of couch grass down the middle, and followed it till she arrived at her ponderosa. There she sat down with her back to its narrow trunk, and dropped the shotgun to the dry ground. The sky was filled with bright stars that seemed to have edges, and black behind them. One never saw anything like that from the streets in Vancouver. She thought of the universality speaking through her condition.

Nearby, her dog curled, waiting for her to signal something to her. But she ignored her, as she fought to remember what had happened in the last hour, or was it some years? An airline jet with powerful landing lights appeared from the other side of the hills and descended over the lake, heavily pulling back on its fall toward the airstrip at the end.

Now that her eyes were adjusted to the late spring darkness of the valley, she saw a bat flipping from direction to direction above her. She remembered the fear that it might get caught in your hair. Bats don't get caught in you hair.

I'm not very old, thought Donna, I'm not very old and here I am already. She picked up the shotgun and fired the other barrel, and threw it over the side of the hill.

Caprice

It was difficult to figure out how I might work the Okanagan Valley into the first volume of my so-called trilogy of historical novels, beginning with *Burning Water*. That one takes place near the end of the eighteenth century, and follows Captain George Vancouver's seafaring vessels up the coast of what would not be British Columbia for nearly another century. Looking back on it all these years later I kind of regret that I had the ship *Discovery* fly to Hudson's Bay instead of, say, Lake Okanagan.

The other two volumes take place largely in Kamloops and nearby towns and natural settings, but I did manage to work the Okanagan into both of those books. In *Caprice* my titular heroine rides her wonderful horse down to Arizona and back, looking for the USAmerican villain who had killed her brother. On the way back north to Kamloops she stops for a while in Fairview, the busy mining town on the flats just south of the future town of Oliver.

As a kid growing up in Oliver in the forties and fifties, I was fascinated with the old site of Fairview. It was one of the places that my friend Bill and I would visit, and sometimes I went there alone. There was only one building left, the old hoosegow (which was later taken into town and placed in the yard of the museum, formerly the Oliver police station); all the kids said that whoever made the building drove an enormous number of spikes into it, making it impossible to escape or demolish.

At Fairview we would find old medicine bottles and liquor bottles, women's button-up shoes, bedsprings, and so on. Every year the pickings would get slimmer, as collectors from out of town brought in metal detectors. But in the early sixties I came to town with my friend Lionel Kearns, and we found the front door of a Victorian kitchen stove.

Lionel's grandfather John ran one of the hotels and hotel bars in Fairview during its heyday. The most famous hotels (and bars) in town were the Teepee (fancifully named after its shape) and the Golden Gate, popularly known as the Bucket of Blood. But John Kearns bought it and thereafter it was called the Fish House, because the Kearnses were Irish Catholics and served fish on Fridays. In *Caprice* my heroine stays at the Fish House and has thoughtful conversations with Mr. Kearns. One of my favourite things about writing novels is that I get to put in people I know or more often characters from their books and others. For example, before heading back north to Canada, Caprice had talked with a lonely ranch widow first found in a novel by Louis L'Amour.

As for John Kearns—Lionel told me family lore had it that when it came to his bar he was his own best customer. Another thing I like to do in my novels is to put in little messages that only one or two persons will understand. For example, in this case I have Caprice calling Mr. Kearns "Tenny," which was in real life a childhood nickname laid on his grandson Lionel. I also describe him as "rug-headed," which derives from Shakespeare's *Richard II*, act 2, scene 1, in which Richard refers to his Irish foes as "rug-headed kerns." Years ago I used to refer to Lionel's hockey-playing son Frank as "Rughead."

The beautiful view of the Okanagan Valley tempts Caprice to forgo her quest for revenge and consider living in Fairview, but the plot needed development, so I put her back on her horse and sent her northward.

from Caprice

The beautiful black horse did not feel very lucky, and his rider was just about asleep when they came through Nighthawk again. They had nothing to declare. The horse had to watch for snakes himself, and there was more than one cactus adhering to the skin on his tired legs. A tumbleweed sped out of the flatland and fetched against his back legs, but he kept it down. Grasshoppers clacked across his face, and he did not flinch. He still had a sore haunch where he had brushed against an ocotillo a few months ago. She had got most of the tiny spines out, but there was still an ugly festering there.

She looked a little better. There was dust in the folds of her clothes and lightening in her dark red hair. Her nose was peeling less now as she had been pointing it north for a month or two. She was thin where she had been slender.

They did not want to make camp tonight. She was determined to rest in Fairview, and she wanted to give the black some oats and carrots. But would they make it? It was as if they had marshalled unlikely powers of endurance to reach the boundary, and now that they were back in the country they might collapse at any moment.

"*Poquito más de heroismo, Cabayo,*" she murmured, leaning forward even more on the saddle horn.

But they reached what she knew had to be Reed Creek, and she knew it was downhill now, that for a few seconds at a time they would be in shade. When they came into sight of the first miner's shack, the horse lifted his head at last and offered an intimate snort. She loved him for his generosity in the middle of pain. She sat with her back straight and her dusty braids falling straight behind her shoulders.

"*Tú eres mi alma, Negro,*" she said out loud, and his ears twitched. He saw the dry creek bed passing by his left, and he saw horse droppings in front of him on the wagon trail that had widened a little from the horse path higher up.

When they passed the big house where George Atwood directed the operations of Strathyre mill, a man with a swede saw stopped his work and raised his wide-brimmed hat. That was the way it was in Fairview. It was the first time she had seen that since they had left here in the late spring.

It was late in the afternoon now. The gold-pickers in the shafts were making their last loads. In an hour they would be joined by prospectors who congregated nightly at Moffat's saloon to discuss the situation and partake of the proprietor's famous good cheer. She rode down out of

Fairview: the Golden Gate Hotel, a.k.a. the Fish House.

the coulee and onto the grassy bench where the lower town had grown. In a few minutes she almost fell from her saddle at the front door of the hotel she had left more than a year ago.

It was a two-storey log and plank structure, or rather two of them attached, one set back ten feet from the other. Over the upper-storey windows of the forward half were the words "Golden Gate Hotel." That had always been its name on the registry, but for most of its short life it had been called the Bucket of Blood. Since John Kearns had taken it over, however, it was coming to be called simply "The Fish House."

Mr. Kearns was a devout Irish Catholic and Mrs. Kearns was a tolerable cook, so on Friday nights the Catholic miners and some others with a taste for something other than beef would gather at the Fish House and eat a lot of finny creatures pulled from Osoyoos Lake and the Okanagan River. Sometimes a man and his wife might put away a dozen little yellow perches. On the best days they would devour rainbow trout with butter and lemon. Freshwater clams were not popular, but there were satisfactory feeds of wide-mouth bass, and when the government man was away making his rounds in the Kootenays, some nice red inland-bound salmon.

There were a lot of hotels in Fairview, some just one-storey saloons with a few back rooms, others that had been mentioned in Vancouver newspapers. But the Bucket of Blood had three things going for it: it was farther than some from the stamp mills, there was fresh fish on Friday night, and it had a dance hall, where clean prospectors and shaven miners would go shake a leg on Saturday night.

Caprice was really happy to see John Kearns. This was partly because he was the hotel man and where there is a hotel man in a growing town there is a bath and bed, and partly because of the good talks she had had with him on her way south.

"Didn't find him, eh?" said John Kearns.

"I'll tell you all about it tomorrow morning," she said. "Right now I just want to get clean and go to sleep for fourteen hours, and then get clean again, and eat some pancakes, and then sit in your lobby out of the sun and look out the window at other people going to work. Can I have a room?"

Kearns ran a big hand through his thick curly rug of hair, and cleared his throat.

"You bet," he said. "But it'll take fifteen minutes to get it ready for you. Can you hang on that long?"

"Of course," she said. "Or rather, I hope so. I am going to see about my horse. Unless you have a nice bed with clean sheets for him."

"We've had a few guests in the digging trade who looked a lot like him."

"I recall that you have a first-rate stable, Mr. Kearns. I will be back in fifteen minutes."

When she came back around front there was a commotion in the street. Seven men and six children were watching as two other men were punching each other in the middle of the hard-mud street. Unlike most fights, this one did not feature swearing and shouting on the parts of the combatants. They simply pounded one another and shoved one another around in their inexpert way. When she came into sight, walking slowly on her long thin legs and carrying her whip, they stopped their flailing and smiled at her. If they had not already had their hats knocked off they would have lifted them.

It entered her mind that if this had been going on in one of the towns she had passed through in the past month or two, someone would have discharged a revolver by now.

When she entered the small lobby with its carpets and animal heads, she saw that Mr. Kearns was not looking out at the scrap, but rather counting some coins into the palm of an Indian man.

"Thank you, Tenny," said the latter.

"You don't have to thank me," said Mr. Kearns. "Just bring me some more of those critters with the speckles all over their backs."

"Can I have a bottle of firewater?"

"Piss off."

The Indian man smiled with big perfect teeth and walked out, rattling the coins in his fist.

"Sorry about the language, Miss. Didn't see you coming in."

"Mr. Kearns, what is going on out there in the street?"

"Fistfight. Dust-up."

"I can see that, and I am too weary for a lot of questions and few answers."

"Well, let me put it this way. Before you came there were going to be three loose beds here tonight. Now there's two. Those two gentlemen are discussing which one of 'em is going to get the last one, the other having been claimed by a pistolero from Mr. Atwood's claims in Nevada."

"I don't want to cause trouble, Mr. Kearns. You should have told me you were out of rooms."

"Not true, Miss. There is always room for you."

"But it is embarrassing and unpleasant to have men brawling in the street for the last bed, I mean when one is the cause of it."

The rug-headed man turned the register book and held out the elk-horn pen.

"When it gets close to the weekend we get filled up. It is normal for men to sock each other to get the last indoor sleep."

"That's rather unpleasant, isn't it?"

"It's a tradition," said Mr. Kearns. "Your hot water will be ready now. I'll have it sent up right away. See you in the morning."

"I'm so tired. Yes, I'll talk to you in the morning."

"You want fresh peaches with those pancakes?"

From up the hillside she could hear the rumble of heavy machinery at the Strathyre quartz mill as she sat near a window and read last week's *Okanagan Mining Review*, the first whole Canadian newspaper she had seen in more than a year. On the tablecloth in front of her were the remains of an elegant breakfast. Mr. Kearns had told his cook to work his skill to the edge, and Caprice had done justice to the cantaloupe and the trout and the pan-fried potatoes and the toast with gooseberry preserves, and the goat's milk and the three cups of French coffee. Mr. Kearns told her that her ebon friend at the stable was receiving the equine version of this service as well. It was the kind of welcome that

Fairview, looking southeast.

removed all doubt about motives. She knew that her host was going to give her a lecture afterward, but for the moment she was grateful for the night between clean sheets and the sunshine that was falling across the valley and glancing along the silver knife that a few minutes earlier had spread thick butter on perfect toast.

She allowed her fancy to play with the idea of staying in Fairview, of forgetting her bitter quest. The newspaper in her hands explained that Fairview would one day soon become "the leading city of the Okanagan Valley." She watched little Jimmy Kearns at another table, his head bent over a book, and imagined the school they would need here, imagined a cottage beside Reed Creek, lady's slippers and buttercups growing without urging in its yard. She smiled as she imagined work-dirty miners doffing their hats to a schoolmarm taller than most of their number.

But she was not a schoolteacher. Roy Smith was a schoolteacher. She was riding the grub line. She was what some people called a saddle tramp, but it was not a good idea to call her that to her face. She had spent more than a year meditating on death, and that is not a schoolteacher's occupation. Roy Smith would like her to be the wife of a schoolteacher, the mother of some of the children in his school one day. Mr. Kearns, she knew, was going to encourage peacefulness, too.

The beautiful tableland she was spending this day in, and the optimism in the faces of its people, could almost have persuaded her to leave accounts in the hands of the Provincial Police, or to forget her fate as nemesis. Except for the last word her brother had pronounced on the hard dirt of the Kc Ranch.

John Kearns had been watching her as she alternately scanned the thin newspaper and looked out the newly scrubbed window at the bright high morning. Now he signalled a small ex-cowboy to take her used dishes away, and approached her table himself. When she smiled at him he saw in her bright grey eyes that the exhaustion she had arrived with had now been succeeded by a kind of out-of-time languor. He sat down at her table and asked her how the trout had been.

"It was the best thing I have had in a year."

"It was probably the best one I have served in a year."

"I think that last night I was in such a haste that I said something about having been away only a month or two," she said, with a little wonder in her voice.

"Something like that. I did not think it was the time to disabuse you," he replied, friendliness in his tone.

"I was just thinking that I wish I lived here."

Kearns smiled.

> "His servants he with new acquist
> Of true experience from this great event
> With peace and consolation hath dismist
> And calm of mind, all passion spent."

She smiled his smile back at him.

"I have been wondering about peace and consolation a lot lately, Mr. Kearns. I know that here in the west poetry is a consolation to a lot of people who feel as if they have been exiled from the earth their families have assumed to be their right home. Even in the meanest little railhead in Arizona I found people spending their scant coin on travelling recitation shows and desert-eating opera companies."

"I am Irish," said John Kearns, "It is my lot in life to consume whisky, which I manage in some quantity, so that it has been said more than once that I am my own best customer. And to remember the words of the bards and minstrels."

"Some people would say that a scattering of mine shafts on a hillside of rocks and rattlers was a strange place to be reading poetry, Mr. Kearns."

His big open face with its roof of thick curly hair turned to gaze at her and offer a look of amusement. It was the look that a poet devises just before uttering his favourite lines.

"Ah, but I cannot read or write a word, my dear lady. I was brought up in the family tradition of illiteracy."

"You are fooling with me, sir. Since leaving Quebec I have not met a person, man of God or instructor of youth, who knows as many poetical words as you do."

"That is because I am blessed not only with a copious thirst but also with a tyrannical memory. I have had many a poem read to my ears, and what my ears have been assailed with my heart has engraved. Even while I try to disremember the Protestant self-assuredness of Mr. John Milton, the splendour of his versification settles in me like gold in a vein of quartz."

Like most poets who wander anonymous among people who know nothing of their other life, she was tempted on the one hand to tell him more about her publications, and determined on the other hand to guard her knowledge, believing that it is the reader's job to come to poetry. One should have friends of the regular person as well as admirers of the poet. One should not sacrifice one to the other. John Kearns knew her as a person who could recite the words that he would never hear from a prospector, and he knew that she would do more than repeat a verse. She would not tell him any more about her book. Later she would send him a copy on the stagecoach. It was pleasant to imagine his opening it, and giving it to Jimmy Kearns to read aloud.

"I am armed with more than complete steel—

The justice of my quarrel."

"Ah," said John Kearns, "are we then to trade passages from our wise and musical instructors?"

"It seems to me, sir, that you began such an undertaking," she said.

"You took as your subject justice," he replied, "but another person might look at the strain in your eyes last night and give your theme another name."

She smiled at him, and lifted her unbraided hair back over her shoulder. The light of the window played through the several dark shades of red there.

"I have heard that lecture from another man more than a year ago," she said.

"Heat not a furnace for your foe / That it do singe yourself."

There was something that arose from the middle of her warm and rested body that told her that this was more than a pleasant dream, this morning of the bright sun. The light on the tablecloth was certainly preferable to the dark cold ashes of another night's campfire. She had wakened more than a hundred times lying on the ground whose name she did not know, and she was capable of doing it a hundred times more. But waking with her bitterness at sunrise near a canyon creek had nothing to do with beauty. Sparring over English poetry with a man who was indisputably a friend should be more than a dream. It could be something a person might call a life.

"You are a kindly man, Mr. Kearns. And you are certainly right. Sometimes when I stop riding or thinking I look at myself and I do not see the woman I thought of growing up to be. I have not been able to write a single line of poetry in more than a year, not since I heard of my brother's death. I thought at first that it was because I could not be a poet again, had no right to be a poet again until that man is brought to justice."

"To vengeance."

"All right. I thought the bullet that stopped my brother's heart had also struck mine. But when I am able to see myself clear I know that I have poisoned my own well. I know that."

She was staring out the window now, at the empty boardwalk in front of the general store across the way. John Kearns left her to her silence for the space of a minute.

"Ride to Kamloops, Miss. Ride to your schoolteacher. Take the stage to Kamloops. Or take the train to Quebec. Your horse will thank you for returning him to the more civilized grass that was his home. Forget Frank Spencer. The Provincial Police will not forget him, I promise. If you are interested in justice, leave justice to them. Remember this country, and remember the talks you have had with me. Try to be more sensible in the things you choose to remember, will you, Miss?"

She turned from her gaze across the road and favoured him with a smile that almost transformed her freckled face.

"You are a true friend, Mr. Kearns. I will remember my talks with you more fondly than anything else I have known in the west."

She thought it should be more than a pleasant dream to sit in the morning sunlight and drink coffee where she could smell the new wood in a building at the centre of a community's faith and optimism.

"So you will go to Kamloops and forget Spencer?"

"No."

John Kearns uttered a sigh and rapped the knuckles of his enormous hand against the side of his curly head.

"Then come to the dance tomorrow night."

"I will. And if you are not too drunk, I will save a dance for you, my true friend. If Mrs. Kearns does not mind."

She had seen Mrs. Kearns entering the room with a fresh tablecloth.

"I certainly do not mind, Miss. But this night you had better get another night's sleep such as you got last night, for he is a dancin' devil, that Irishman," said Mrs. Kearns.

Her husband got to his feet, facing Caprice and placing his hand over his heart. Then with a futile attempt at an Irish accent he offered a final passage from the deathless anthology:

When you do dance, I wish you
A wave o' the sea, that you might ever do
Nothing but that.

Here's the press box atop the grandstand. There was a nice shaky view from up there.

Urban Snow

Urban Snow is in its way a typical Bowering book. It has nifty one-page poems, longer poems, sequences both short and long, and long radio poems. It reprints "Thea in Oliver" in a sequence about female persons in different sites. It has a couple of my homage sentence poems to friends who are being honoured in some occasion, thus real occasional poems.

When it comes to short lyrical poems, I think "Grizzle Boy" is pretty good. I like it for its music and images, of course, but I kept it for my so-called canon because of all the points at which it directs the reader momentarily to elsewheres that the terse voice has the sense not to wander. Still there are the words for things I love all through the four quadruplets.

The other poem "Oliver Community Park 1948" is part of one of my favourite sequences. The sequence is called "Yards," and is about baseball parks in which I had attended games. I stopped writing these poems when *Urban Snow* was published, right after "Candlestick Park 1990," and a good thing, too, because since that Giants-Cubs game I have been to more than a hundred yards.

I drive by the site of those 1948 ball games every time I go to visit my mother or my brothers. The old grey grandstand is not there now, and neither is the community hall on whose south wall the scoreboard was affixed. Adults don't play baseball there any more. They are all supervising wine tastings up and down the valley.

Dad in his Summerland basketball team uniform.

Grizzle Boy

How I miss my father,
crumbling crackers into tomato soup.
I see him doing that,
goofy smile and stern forehead.

I must have been a watching boy
all the time, to save up
all those scenes, my dad
and me, mountaintop, kitchen.

How can I miss a man
younger than I am now, grey whiskers?
Oh, you should see him
the way he stands like James Joyce

and him just an Okanagan boy,
thinking of basketball, not me.
I miss him fully, and long ago
we all thought we'd meet again.

Oliver Elks scoreboard on the community hall outside the
right-field fence.

Oliver Community Park 1948

Familiar sun
declined is hasting now with prone career
to the Ocean isles, and rising are some few bedraggled stars,

not to mention what I recall of my hometown
ball field, 1990, weather-grey wooden grandstand
that would crash like a giant accordion
if four strong infielders full of beer
lined up and gave it a good shove.

We took oranges to the ball field, later
used the skins to cup water from the tap.

Willy and I wandered the perimeter trying to sell
Orange Crush and peanuts in the shell.
Other Sundays we pursued foul balls
through the deep rattlesnake grass for Elks Club dimes.

Once, age fifteen, I hit a single
with the bases loaded, but went next week
for work out of town,
                    where I still am,
and that was my real career.

They don't play ball there now, television
and then golf courses arrived,
highways became easy to use, money dropped by.

The tall wooden grandstand with the roof
stood through four decades of winters,
forty years of family picnics elsewhere,
power boats on small green lakes.

                                    I went to
Quebec, I forgot the P. A. announcer's voice echoing
off the centre-field scoreboard.

The Rain Barrel

By the early nineties I had pretty well decided that my short fiction was not for mimetic purposes but for self-imposed problems to be solved. I mean, the question was going to be less "Can I get it true to life?" and more "What would happen if I tried this?" I would still "set" stories in the Okanagan, but it was going to be more openly an Okanagan of my invention. I wanted to write an imaginary valley with real fruit trees in it. Does that make sense?

Maybe I should point out that the dedication page for the volume reads: "These stories are dedicated to Southern Okanagan High School, which expelled me in grade twelve, so I could get something done outside."

The very short title story, printed in italics to set it apart, was written as an introduction to the collection. Reading it now for the first time in a while, I see that while Shakespeare's *Richard II* is quoted in *Caprice*, it is *Richard III* that is unnecessarily alluded to here. Remembering what I've just said about the Okanagan as setting, you might note that the rain barrel is an authentic reference to the valley, but you might also wonder whether you have to choose between God's head appearing in it as literal or psychological or mythic. That question was meant to be an introduction to the collection of stories that follow it.

Over the years I have perhaps archly described the poet H. D. as my poetry "mother," and I used to have dreams in which she was my mother or something like that. So I thought: well, H. D. got her pen name in the form of those initials from Ezra Pound, and my real mother would come to be referred to fondly by her initials P. B. in family talk. So I decided to combine them. In "Blithe Trees" I joined their biographies, placed them (her) in an Okanagan orchard, and told among other things, the story of my mother and D.H. Lawrence. (Years earlier I had written a piece in which my paternal grandfather and D.H. Lawrence once saw each other when they were young.) H.D., of course, had written on orchards in the Classical world, and both women had been basketball players when young. I think that if I were to try writing a novel about all this, I would go on finding more and more coincidences or associations. H.D. we know as a most poetical person. I tried as hard as I could to write some poems as H.D. (taking the job over from my mother?) or eventually as P.B., and the story ends with G.B. and *that* story. I like this story that no one seems to have read.

"Rhode Island Red" was written as an attempt to answer the famous question about the chicken and the road. Now every time I drive Highway 97 along a certain stretch between Osoyoos and Oliver I watch carefully for that bird, remembering there are two sides to every story.

Having reassembled a story about my mother and the valley, in "The Creature" I decided to reassemble a story about my daughter and the valley. In this one a horror story about something like the onset of death is shuffled with a story about the onset of life. The latter is a transcription of my diary's pages that record the moment-by-moment birthing of Thea Claire Bowering, who is now a woman with a published collection of stories in which her father is occasionally mentioned. But she makes them all up, you understand.

I think that if you were ever to take the time to read my stories chronologically, you might think that this collection is a real improvement over its predecessors. Anyway, usually I think that invention is more fun than reproduction, though we need them both. But then I remember that invention not only can make things appear but it can also make things disappear, as in the way "Blithe Trees" makes my father disappear, robbing me of what the Québécois call my *patrimoine* and what my wife, Jean, calls my lineage, leaving me to write a life.

The Rain Barrel

When I was eleven years old my parents and I spent a lot of the summer fruit season on a big orchard in Naramata. It was so big that it was called a fruit ranch. My uncle managed this place and lived in one of the houses on it. At the northeast corner of this house there was a rain barrel. It didn't rain very often in the valley, but you could depend on a deluge to damage the cherry crop, and maybe another terrific downpour in peach season. In between there might be an early morning shower from time to time.

But everyone who lived on an orchard ten miles from the nearest real town had a rain barrel. They knew where to put them to get nearly all the rain that hit the roof. Women liked to wash their hair in rainwater because the regular water in the valley was full of minerals. You couldn't make the softest soap lather up.

An eleven-year-old boy does two things with a rain barrel. On cloudy days he sticks his head in and yells for the marvellous echoes. On bright sunny valley days with puffy white clouds he looks at the reflections of the puffy white clouds. We should stay in the past tense. These were the two things he did in the days before boys watched television, which was slow to get to the valley, but which now controls the imagination there, with moving images of the mean streets of Detroit. And that person is a long way past eleven years old.

One day that boy was watching the puffy clouds slide over the surface of the water, when all of a sudden the reflected sky was filled with the huge shaggy head of God.

He turned and looked behind him. He looked above him. He decided to look in every direction. He could see tractor smoke rising from between the trees fifteen rows to the west, but no human beings.

He looked back into the rain barrel. There was God's face again, maybe closer than the clouds, maybe just bigger than the clouds.

Then he was in the water, face first. Grabbed by the ankle and tipped in. A prince struggling to get back out. In his kicking and underwater yelling he made it harder than it need be, but he got out, all wet in the good morning sun.

He looked around again, and saw his uncle with his normal friendly creased face and grin, carrying something that needed fixing. He was just coming out the kitchen door of his house.

The eleven-year-old boy looked carefully at his uncle's face. It did not at all resemble the reflected face of God. He looked at the water again. It was still rippling, so any reflection was just a little plane of chaos.

He decided to wait until the water became a simple mirror again. But a squall brought in dark low clouds from the east, and soon it was raining into the rain barrel. Next thing he knew his mother was telling him to get in out of the rain. What could I do? When I was eleven years old my mother's word was law.

Blithe Trees

"Haven't I told you a thousand times that it's better to be mysterious as far as your lineage goes?" she asked him.

She was trying on rings, silver, gold, old dull stones in settings from the olden days. She always told him that she could not tolerate metals on her skin. But a woman was expected to have rings, and to wear some of them.

"In these days, anyway," she said. "You want to be interesting. It is as if you have no name, isn't it? Odysseus said he had no name, and his son was given a beautiful beach at Antium. You have a name borrowed from me when necessary."

"That's what you always tell me," he said.

He was twelve years old. His voice and his limbs were changing, but he had no idea what they would change into, no model. His nose was a lot like P.B.'s, but what did his eyes resemble, or whose?

"Nameless, you claim a great heritage. That is certainly to be preferred over being son of a small-town mayor, or a shoe merchant, or a school choirmaster, wouldn't you say?"

She had never promised him anything, never told him that she would reveal his history when he was of age, never told him that he would one day stand face to face with a stranger in a mirror.

She was trying on her rings, at the open window of her sitting room. Outside the window the apricot tree was heavy with green fruit, and a breeze turned the leaves, silver and green, not silver, but a green notion of silver. He stared into the jewellery case, willing her to pick up the emerald.

"Who am I?" she asked, asked someone out the window. "I am your dam. I am a shameful presence in their midst, an unmarried artist. I am daughter of a great man. I am a seed pod carried by a careful stream. You see, I am many women, and all of them your mother. You have many mothers. What does it matter whether you have one father or a tradition?"

When she said artist he knew she meant poet. He knew nothing about such things. She offered now to rub the top of his crewcut head. He moved his head till her hand went back to the jewellery. She picked up the emerald.

"Well, that's nice," he grumbled. "You have a choice of things to be. I don't even get to tell my best friend what my real name is."

"Neither does he, dear. You will know what I mean in the years to come."

At least that was almost a promise.

She put the emerald back and closed the box. The scent of cedar departed through the window. He turned and went to his room, to his books.

In the middle of the Depression she broke her engagement with a famous young poet and left Philadelphia almost forever, but unlike her friends, she turned her back to the ocean and went westward. She left her father at the station in Philadelphia and sat beside a window for five days, watching all the countryside in her father's picture books drift by. She fetched up in an orchard that had been planted fifteen years before. She was twenty years old. Her friend was nineteen. Her friend's mother was forty-five.

They were an odd entourage in the valley full of fruit trees and undeveloped lake beaches. P.B. had no illusions about the neighbours and the people in town. She knew that these hard-working folk, as they probably liked to be called, would be talking about the three females newly in their midst. A beautiful girl, a tall gangly girl with bobbed hair, and a striking woman of a certain age. Three females with enough money, despite the Depression, to rent a cottage in a widower's orchard. And to operate a motor car.

A motor car is what Sandy's mother called it.

Sandy's mother was a very careful and very unreliable driver. She never got the Ford from their gravel driveway onto Highway 97 in less than five minutes, sometimes even getting out of the car and looking down the road both ways. Sandy, on the other hand, would have been terrific in a flivver at Atlantic City. That's what P.B. always thought. She had been to Atlantic City more than once in her life, or so she was told, and didn't remember anything except one memory she was always told about, a young man dipping something into a jar and taking it out to make rainbow bubbles float in a stream away from him.

P.B. never even wanted to try to drive the motor car. It was one of the very few new vehicles in the valley, and a mystery to her. Sandy might as well have been Phaeton and she one of his sisters, locomotion was that much a puzzle to her, a puzzle and a bit of a terror.

But neither was she devoted to their little cottage. In fact it was pretty, the sort of blossom-surrounded quaintness imagined by people in the cities back east. It was settled right in the middle of the young orchard, apricot trees on one side, taller cherry trees to the edge of the lawn in front, apple trees stretching up the slope behind the chicken pen in back, and dark prune trees on the fourth side. The tree blossoms followed one another in an orderly schedule, white cherries first, then the apricots and the prunes—finally the pink apples. When a light breeze swept through from the north, the air, even inside the house, was a river of perfume. The three women would bring chairs out onto the lawn, and sit, knitting and tatting, smoking white cigarettes that Sandy's mother made, five at a time, on a clever little machine. They hardly ever talked about the past, seldom about the famous young poet, never about the source of their money. They told stories about ancient Greece, or prose glosses of the recently translated Eddas, or inventions set behind the almost bare brown hills behind their orchard.

And P.B. walked there, because she could still walk strongly in those days, dressed in what the local people would have to call a costume, jodhpurs and scarves, wide-brimmed hats and wrappings around her ankles. Walked, this visitant, nearly six feet tall, among the ground cactus and the sagebrush, around ancient crumbling rocks left by glaciers, around greasewood showered with narrow dark leaves in the summer and standing as dark twisted branches in the winter, perfect, if she only knew, for sudden hot campfires such as any ambient gods would notice and appreciate. For she was, she thought, walking in search of gods or at least their messengers, looking for a poem that would owe nothing to Europe, nothing to the smoking cities of the east.

Once in that first year she saw a coyote, and later gave herself the gift of considering him a god or at least messenger. She knew nothing about the stories the valley's Indians told about coyotes. This animal stood across an open area of burnt couch grass, his tail toward her but his head turned to look. She took a few quick steps toward him (she assumed that the animal was male, as one did in those days, about animals, about poets), and he loped away a little, his rump rising with each easy jounce. She stopped and sat on a rock, taking off her hat and settling as best she could on the aged granite. The coyote faced her and sat, his tongue hanging out, a kind of grin on his face. She wondered for a long time what his grin reminded her of, and one morning she remembered the smile that was always, when he spoke to her, on the face of Andrew Gray the Scottish composer. And so poet and wild creature regarded each other. She spoke to him in her language.

"I thought you a dog, but you are too much the colour and shape of this place," she said. "I wondered were you a wolf, but you are not serious enough, are you?"

The coyote smiled. He ducked his head and leaped up and away.

"Yes, you remind me of someone," she said, not rising.

He reminded her too of herself, of course, and that may have been what she meant.

She had to walk in these low hills, climbing sometimes to the second bare brown bench, and other times struggling her way along the willow-sided river, had to make these excursions for almost a year before the first poems came.

And when they came they were not Greek, they were not European, they were not from the smoky cities of the east. But they were not regional descriptions of this dry sagebrush valley, either. Still, they were not eruptions of the human heart, and they were not expressions of the self-engaged soul. Those are some of the things they were not, but what were they? They were things no one had seen or heard in the past few centuries, so P. B. sometimes showed them to Sandy and her mother, but asked them not to talk about them, especially not to talk about the things they were not.

In the summer in this valley the air was hot and clean. When the sun went down the air cooled and the rocky cliffs that had baked all day gave off their heat, to the hand, to the nearby face. In the winter the air was cool and crisp and dry, so that puddles in the road would be a surface of thin ice with nothing underneath, a pleasure to crack with one's steps. In the winter Sandy would deliberately run the high narrow tires of the motor car through the crisp puddles.

In winter and in summer the air of the valley was clean and dry, and objects seen through the air were clear and sharp. P. B.'s short poems were like that. She was an outcast from the east, taken to walking in dry air. People here spoke of the blue of the valley, the sky bluest blue, the hills, the lakes, the air, blue. They said it was a Mediterranean blue.

> The speckled rock
> broken, thin salt
> drifts over a new surface.
>
> Sage, whipped round my ankles!
> Ah, wind!
> Ah, who are you,
> to meet me in this place?

She did not carry pen and paper to the hills or the river or the orchard. She found the poems there, perhaps, and brought them home with her to the stucco cottage and wrote them swiftly or slowly at the window table. If she saw a finch at the bird feeder she might let the bird into her poem. In that year of 1937 she wrote many poems at the window table, and carried others home that she never put to paper. She burned many poems in the spring of that year, and in the late autumn she consigned whole booklets of verses to the kitchen stove. Still, she saved numerous poems that people later would call hard and crisp, but they were never hard and only sometimes crisp. People did not know quite what they were. They were only vaguely aware of the absence of the things that they were not.

In the valley, or at least in the nearest village, there was nobody to show the poems to. So she showed some of them to her friend and her friend's mother, and that was it. Until she sent four of them to the famous young poet back east. She never considered sending them to her Moravian father, although she wrote letters to him once a month.

On the last Saturday morning of every month she wrote four pages to her father, making sure to tell him about the rocks and the clouds when there were some, about the birds and the foliage and the latest condition of the fruit trees. Then Sandy would back the "flivver" out of the faded wood garage and turn it around, and they would drive to the post office in the village. They had a box at the post office, though they could have had their letters and catalogues and newspapers left in the mailbox at the bottom end of their gravel driveway.

The valley was made of a little soft dirt on top of ancient crumbling rocks. Some of the rocks in the hills had old writing on them, runes rather, usually hidden with the thinnest possible cover of light grey lichen. Tall gangly P. B. found this writing, images of human beings, arrows, wild animals, other items lost to time; and she memorized them, so that when she returned to her peach-coloured cottage she could draw them on paper and send them to her brother. Never to her father. This she withheld from him. Her brother Ira had tried to live in the scant woods of Pennsylvania. He read books from Canada, about men who put on furs and cooked in pails filled with water made from melted snow.

She looked among the bulges of rock for a picture of her coyote or writing done by his friends, but never found them. This she understood to mean that it was left for her to make his portrait, with words. She never did. She hoped that this abstinence would bring him again to the faded brown bench where they had met. She did not see him for more than a year, though she found his spoor, she thought. She never wrote a poem about her coyote, but she wrote poems for him. These she sent to the famous young poet back east, and wondered whether he would ever know the identity of her muse.

One day at the post office in the village she found an envelope with British stamps on it. The famous young poet was in London, listening part of the time to Mr. Auden and Mr. Spender, subjectively screening out their social politics, and instructing the unknown younger poets who had never read any of the lesser-known poets of Italy and "Provawnce."

She was happy to be here in the ancient west. They had made the right decision. Here she would be instructed only as she required, or only as she was startled anew by the earth.

One day she bent her costumed lanky body and with her long fingers picked up a field mouse. She put it into the pocket of her peculiar long skirt and almost forgot it. From time to time on the way home she slid the ends of her fingers into the pocket and touched the rough fur of this creature. It did not offer to bite her. She felt as though the gods or at least their messengers had seen her passing a test that was not even offered to most of the hard-labouring people of this new place.

When she got home she did not go inside the cottage, but straight to the grey chopping block beside the wood pile. There she kneeled and took the mouse out of her pocket. It lay on the smooth wood, dead, its eye mercifully closed. A fat white worm protruded from its abdomen.

The next time they went to the post office in the village there were two letters from London. One said that the famous young poet had received her four poems and thought they were better than anything he had seen her do before she had left. The second letter said that they were great poetry, that they were better than anything he had seen from their generation, and that he wanted to see more.

She wanted to be placid, but she held the two envelopes to her chest on the way home, and she took out the letters and read them often over the following week. For a reason she did not understand or question, she did not give the letters to Sandy and her mother to read. She told them that the famous young poet was principally concerned about whether they, the frontierswoman, and he the Old Country aesthete, were still engaged. She said that his language was a little intemperate and that she was embarrassed to show his words to them.

So their life in the dry valley continued. Her father sent her the regular cheques that family affairs had regulated. Sandy's mother had probably the largest bank account in the village, and several accounts back east. Sandy took up watercolours, and was often to be seen somewhere among the trees or in the yard, capturing the low hills and the higher hills with long gentle brushstrokes. Sandy's mother wrote letters, took the sun that shone brightly every day, and spent hours at the stove, cooking badly.

P. B. continued her hikes, visiting places that had become important to her, and exploring new ground at least once a week. But she also grew interested in the work of the orchard. They rented their cottage from the orchardist who had lived in it until he had built a large house farther back off the highway.

The orchardist and his sons grew accustomed to working under her gaze. She generally sat a row away from them, on an upturned apple box, or she strolled about, appearing and reappearing while the men attended to the growing trees. In the late winter they came out with long pruners and lopped off small branches, while the youngest son, striped electrician's gloves on his hands, yanked the new suckers off the trunks.

"Time to prune the prunes," this boy said, more than once.

She watched them thin apples. When a man was finished with a tree of Jonathans there would be a carpet of the smallest green apples on the tromped grass under the tree, some in the furrows of the disked earth. She stayed out of the orchard when they were spraying. From her apricot window she watched them with their hoses, sending green poison up into the high branches, emerging from a day's work covered with the green stuff themselves, coughing as they trudged home for an early dinner. P.B. hated the odour of the spray, which stayed in the air for days, and which she could detect a month later when she held a green Macintosh apple to her nose. Some of the orchardists were experimenting with sprinkler systems, but the crew on this "fruit ranch," as these places were often called, still went to the place where the irrigation ditch was met by their syphons, and opened some little gates. P.B. liked to watch the first of the water find its way down the furrows between the trees, much of it sinking quickly into the dry earth. In late June the first crops were picked, the fat cherries from the tallest trees in the orchard, dark Bings and Lamberts and the yellow Royal Anns. The three women were told that they were welcome to all the fruit they could eat, and they loved cherry season. Every June, just before the cherries were to be picked, there would be a terrific electrical storm, and a downpour of warm rain that would collect on the cherries, swelling them and splitting them, dashing annual expectations of a bumper crop. The orchardist called this unhappy phenomenon the proof of the existence of God. P.B. liked him for having the patience to say such things.

But her favourite month was August, season of peaches and pears. She wrote a poem about the heat of August, the weight of pears and grapes, the rough god she knew was loose in the orchard. This poem would do much to make her famous for a while, before her poems and herself were forgotten except by her friends and the people she would meet when she worked in the village during the war. This poem, too, she sent to the famous young poet.

In cherry season of 1938 she received a letter from him, saying that he had sent her first four poems to the most important new poetry magazine in America, and that they would publish them. This letter, too, she did not show to Sandy and her mother. But in pear season the magazine itself arrived at the village post office, probably the first issue of that magazine ever to appear in the southern part of the valley, at

Pearl Bowering, high above Peachland.

least. There they were, a poem for her coyote, and the others. On the first page of the magazine were the words "Four Poems by P. B."

"Imagine this," said Sandy's mother, her happiness undisguisable. "And we may see you every day. We made the right decision in coming to this country."

But she would be gone in less than a year.

One September morning P. B. was not the only poet in the valley. She met him during one of her hikes. This sunny day the scent of ripening apples rose from the orchards that stretched as far as she could see, and the breeze that blew across the bench carried alternating perfumes of apples and sage. She was wearing her high boots because this was traditionally the season for rattlesnakes. They would doze in the sun, and wake in momentary confusion if you stepped near them. She kept her head down more than usual, so that by the time she saw him she was nearly in his arms.

Waking from her own preoccupation, she must have looked a little vexed. She was not used to encountering other people up here. Tall in her boots, she looked at him from above. He was sitting on a flat boulder, with a stone in one hand and some kind of tool in the other.

"My gosh, you're a tall one," were his first memorable words to her.

"What are you doing in my garden," she asked. She was bashful as always, but one way of handling bashfulness is to engage in vocal artifice.

He held up the stone and showed her the design on its flat side. It was a small seashell, or an insect such as one had never seen.

"This little fellow was nicely settled here quite some time before it became your garden," he said.

She did not like him, and she was attracted to him. He was very handsome, and this fact did not make her antipathy and his attraction any easier to reconcile. He spoke with the kind of British accent that one associates with tweed coats at inefficient country houses. In fact he was wearing a smooth old tweed coat at this first meeting, along with high laced boots and corduroy breeches. He wore no hat, a mad Englishman, she thought, and his hair was thick and curly. It looked as if he had brushed it at dawn, and it had been struggling to break free all morning.

When he got round to inquiring of her her name she said that it was Artemis.

"I must be dreaming," he said.

He was an archaeologist who was tired of Europe. Like her, he had come out here to be contrary. Holding to an original theory, as all famous archaeologists will, he was looking for something a Spaniard horseman might have dropped on the dry ground here while Robert Jenkins was exhibiting his severed ear at Parliament. So far the Spanish had to be considered meticulous about their equipment, but in the meantime, he was finding some interesting evidence of very old aboriginal habitation in the region.

"Very old is a phrase that we archaeologists are hospitable to," he said. When he smiled his military moustache spread across his face.

I am still pretty young, she thought.

But she fell for him anyway.

His name was Richard Morrison, of the Bristol Morrisons. He was once a teacher of antiquities at an important university, and an amateur poet. When he left pedagogy to become a freelance digger, he coincidentally became a more serious and successful poet. When P. B. met him he had published in all the best of the new magazines in Britain, and would soon see publication of his first book of verses. Not from one of the big houses, of course. He was a modern.

He took her as a student first, showing her what to look for under the lichen on rocks, how to see arrowheads in the tumble of stones at the river's edge. She began to comb her hair over her small ears because he remarked on their peculiar shape. She took him as a teacher, then as a friend. Then he took her as a lover. She persuaded him that she could not cook. He admired the poems she would show him, and he showed her his own. She did not mention that his poems were not quite as good as hers. After a while they mentioned the famous young poet, who was now living in Paris.

In April 1939 she married him in the little Anglican church in the village. In August Sandy and her mother returned to New York, and the couple took the stucco cottage in the orchard filled with peaches and pears. In September Richard Morrison went to England to join the Royal Fusiliers as a Lieutenant. Now P. B. had to walk four miles into the village, or depend on the orchardist or his younger sons for a ride in their smelly old truck. After she got her first letter with English stamps, she wrote a poem for her husband.

What are these trees to me
if you are taken away,
what are these dark stones
if you lie on wet earth?

In my garden
the rain beats on ripe apples,
small animals crouch underground,
what is the sun round edge of clouds
if Endymion be gone from the air?

Still she did not read the newspapers, and she did not tune the radio to the war news. When people in town or the family in the orchard raised as a subject the progress of the fighting she would not reply. Soon people began to treat her carefully. It was agreed among them that she had been offered too great a shock with what they called a "whirlwind" romance and a sudden loneliness. She read his letters and the poems in them, and she knew that any one of them might have been sealed and dispatched by a man now dead.

The boy played with the food she had prepared so inexpertly. He had never known any other cooking, save the meat and potatoes and carrots served at the local cafés. This was 1958, long before interesting restaurants were to come to the south end of the valley.

"Could Morrison have been my father?" he asked.

She was using her fork to pick up one little tooth of corn at a time. She smiled and pointed her fork at her son. "Could have?" she said, teasing him. "Are we talking just about could have? Well, let us say maybe he could have and maybe not."

"Did he ever see me, Morrison?"

"Or did *you* see *him*? I do not know whether he ever saw you. I do not know whether he bothered to look. But you have seen him, yes. When you were three years old, when we lived in Philadelphia."

The boy had stopped eating entirely, though there was food of some sort on his plate, and even on his fork.

"Morrison was a reporter in New York then."

"Not *reporter*," she said, as if instructing a pupil. "He was a correspondent. For the *Times*."

"The times, the times, the times," the boy mumbled, his chin on his chest. He used to mumble this way when he was younger, when his legs hung from the chair and his feet did not touch the floor.

In April 1940, P. B. was lying in the hospital of a small city slightly to the north. Morrison's daughter was born dead. She resembled a perfect new human being except for the curious lack of breath and heartbeat. The labour had gone on for more than twenty-four hours. P. B. was a strong tall woman who had played basketball for her high school in Philadelphia. But the little girl, whose kicks P. B. had felt in her enormous body, was never to take a breath of valley air.

P. B. stayed in the hospital for two weeks, and there was no one she knew who could visit her. If the orchardist had had a wife perhaps she would have asked to be driven up for a visit. The men were not the kind of people to visit in the hospital. Especially in such embarrassing circumstances, a young woman with full breasts and no child.

She had not made nor bought many baby's things, and had been given only a few gifts. That was good, somehow.

Her husband was somewhere in Africa. Her daughter was nowhere at all, unless there was a Limbo. She lay alone, on her side, looking out the hospital window at a cherry tree in full blossom.

For three years people in the village or south of it were surprised when they saw her, walking along the river, or trying to learn to drive the "flivver" that Sandy's mother had left behind. She would disappear from sight for months at a time, and rumours moved with the breeze up and down the tree-fruit highway. She had gone to Vancouver to become a character on the street. She was back where she came from, taking up the high-society life in New York and Boston. She had locked herself inside her house and was living on apricots and the wild asparagus that grew between the trees.

They did not see that she caught the train from time to time, when it stopped at the packing house behind the orchard where her cottage nestled. This was a fruit train that stopped at all the packing houses, but it always had one passenger car. It would meet the tracks that ran east and west through the city up north, and there P. B. would take her reserved roomette and settle in for the ride to the coast. There she met the train that travelled south to the bare hills of California. There she spent her days in labour over the rush of poems that came to her in those years, and some of her nights with a very famous British novelist, short story writer, and poet. He was, many people thought, a great novelist, and she never showed her fiction-writing to him, but she was the better poet.

He was B. P. Oliver, a name that struck terror into the souls of puritans all over the English-speaking world. He wrote shamelessly of the passions that made people's lives blossom suddenly and then wither. Where P. B. was reticent, and concentrated a life's yearning into eight short lines, Oliver exfoliated, repeated himself, blustered, explained. His photograph, with bushy beard and poorly tied neckware was active currency all over the world. P. B. laboured in secrecy. He trumpeted his humble beginnings, and made fun of her gentle background. She fell for him completely. Almost completely. She thought he was a fool or at least an ass. But she also thought she knew that he was a great man.

He had left Britain years earlier, and never expected to go back. He had wandered and domiciled on all the continents save Antarctica. He had been living in the United States for four years before he came north for his one trip to her stony home.

There he strode the hills in his woollen suit trousers, waving a stick in front of him, prepared for rattlesnakes.

"In Sicily I had golden snakes for companions. In India I stared down the king cobra. In Australia I found killer reptiles in the latrine," he said. "I am not likely to be cowed by these little fellows."

P.B. was happy that he never once saw her coyote. She did not know for a fact that she saw the same animal each time, but she liked to think so.

For he never did what the other did. She was very fond of that coyote for many reasons, she thought, but chief among them was his grin. The very famous British novelist did not smile, and he certainly never laughed. In San Francisco the Scottish Andrew Gray was writing music criticism, and dining whenever possible with them. Andrew Gray smiled whenever he spoke to her. He often laughed as Scotsmen are not supposed to laugh, and he often laughed at himself. But the very famous British novelist did not laugh, and certainly never at himself. That was perhaps the reason why so many others laughed at him, even while they were impressed by his onrushing paragraphs. Sometimes he moaned, sometimes even growled. Often he was given to long silences, though she knew that the paragraphs were expanding in his head. She took him to her bed in the little cottage with the blossoms at the windows, and there they were serious and not altogether successful.

For it was true that she did not smile either. It was a strange and ominous relationship, and she never spoke of what they did or what they said, years later when she cast him in one of her late unread novels. She spoke of the "fire-blue eyes in his burnt-out face," and gave him the name she had always wanted for herself, Nico. Nico Flame, she called him, so that anyone who read the novel would know who he was, but not what he was. Hardly anyone read the novel.

"That novelist, Oliver, was in this house?" asked the twelve-year-old. He was making scrambled eggs and toast for their late Saturday breakfast. She was in the front room, reading a month-old newspaper from England, in which she had turned first to the book pages. The brace for her leg was half-hidden behind her chair. Mother and son had to shout a little to be heard.

"He was here for one visit. He said the dry climate agreed with him. He had tuberculosis, you know."

He knew. He knew as much as he could. It was because she and her son lived without anyone else that he could ask things about his mother that most boys would not.

"And you saw him in California?"

"When I went to California we would see each other, certainly."

The eggs were ready. He made them with a little milk in them, and when they were done he shook pepper on them. He took the two plates into the front room. Scrambled eggs and slices of beefsteak tomatoes.

He handed her the ironed and slightly starched napkin that she liked to insist on. They did this every Saturday morning, before he walked into the village for the movie. He tried to slow down his eating so that he would not finish before she had made any headway.

"B. P. Oliver might have been my father?"

She finally took a forkful of egg, to provide her with a short silence. When she spoke it was with the mock-lecturing tone she favoured on such occasions.

"As you know, his writing is filled with energetic advice about living and making love and grasping what you can of passion, etcetera. But it is common knowledge that he never had any children. They may not have been able to put up with babies in the house."

The boy took their plates to the kitchen. When he returned he stood behind his mother's chair. Her hair was done up the way Greek goddesses have theirs done in the books they both pored over.

"But," he said, "in terms of time, in terms of time—"

"Time," she whispered, She was looking out the window. Her hands were on the arms of her chair. Bright sunlight faded the carpet, at least temporarily. "Time, time, time, time."

"It's possible," said the boy.

"Tell yourself," she said, "you are the child of time."

She could not remember quite what it was like to be pregnant, waiting for the baby, waiting for it to become visible, waiting for her to be completely composed and separate and regardable. It was as if the stillborn child was not and then had not been. Now she spent a longer time making a book. She watched for the shaggy god she knew was in the apple trees. She thought she saw an angel in the mist of a bright morning's sun-shower. The poems came steadily but they were not all poems for the book. The book grew and the famous young poet, now back from Occupied France, back in London, was writing to her and urging a manuscript. So she spoke to the blue eyes in San Francisco, and she wrote a letter to Morrison, a soldier labouring in some theatre of war, a letter which was never to be answered, and she argued with the famous young poet in London, till there was nowhere else to turn, nothing else that she could do. She completed the book, she typed the manuscript, starting with the first four poems. In Europe and Asia and Africa people were dying in explosions as war machines roared through their villages and cities. How could a woman in an orchard in the only quiet part of the planet complete a book of poems?

> The shadows of these branches
> are twisted
> after many a wind, after
> many a cold winter.

> The apples are sweet
> to the powerful teeth, the news
> does not sour them, death
> in your far country
> does not sour them.

> Where the great sea foams
> and angry men
> flail it with chains
> these shadows are white.

As her body had once given up flesh that became other and was put away soon, now her hands delivered the manuscript. She mailed it to London, and the people there told her that if the printer in Plymouth could procure the paper, the book would be published in 1943. During her walks in the orchard, along the river, or in the hills, she often murmured the name of the printer in Plymouth.

She was filled with aspiration. She grew sweeter while waiting to see this book. She paid the rent on her cottage, and she entered the community. She overcame her bashfulness, she did her hair in braids piled on top of her head, and volunteered for every war project in and around the village. She drove the "flivver" as well as she could, visiting people who might buy war savings bonds or need to know where to send their scrap metal.

Metal fell on the shelters of warriors elsewhere.

She was consumed by aspiration. Or it was consumed by her. She read all her most dear texts. "And I took the little book out of the angel's hand, and ate it up; and it was in my mouth sweet as honey: and as soon as I had eaten it, my belly was bitter." She woke each day a new person and each was filled with aspiration in her own way. She longed for this book from England that would have to be carried by fearful sailors on the North Atlantic convoy.

One day late in 1943 she drove the "flivver" over wet asphalt into the village, to mail her letters to Sandy and to Andrew Gray, and there was a box for her at the post office. She placed it in the trunk of her car and continued all day to aspire while she performed her duties to the community, to the "war effort." She drove back home in the falling darkness, and carefully, slowly, put away the vehicle, spread food for tomorrow's birds, brought in some firewood from the shed. Then she put away her coat and hat and gloves. She made herself a pot of tea and some toast with damson plum preserves. Then she fetched the sewing scissors and cut the twine on the package. She put the English stamps in the envelope in which she saved stamps for the youngest son of the orchardist. Then she took some tea and a bite of toast. And then she unwrapped the books.

Pearl Bowering, known in our family as P. B.

There were twelve copies, plain and beautiful, with the two words of the title and the two letters of the poet's name in clear black type on a dust jacket the colour of August sagebrush.

She held her first actual book in her long fingers. And watched it fade. It faded. This was attainment, but it was not hers. She was not disappointed. It was just that this was not her aspiration—it belonged to someone else, to someone she had been a year ago, and then six months ago, and then perhaps yesterday. She would put the book on the shelf. There would be copies on those tables in London and San Francisco and somewhere in Africa. She would leave one copy for a while on the table beside the apricot window. It was someone else's beautiful book.

She was not disappointed. How could she be disappointed in some-one else's book? Now someone else had had one child, nearly, almost certainly, and one book, poems that she herself knew well. She looked on the last page and saw the name of the printer in Plymouth, and then put the book on the table. The other copies she placed on a shelf.

He visited her on her seventy-fifth birthday. There was no family other than the two of them, and Claire, but there were several friends and their husbands. None of these friends had ever really read any poetry. They met each other to play bridge and tell stories, to recall events from a pioneer valley, to smoke forbidden cigarettes on the back step.

He flew all the way from London to be with her on her seventy-fifth birthday. She was wearing a birthday costume, something that spoke of the Middle East in the Middle Ages. She was still very tall, and not bent at all. It was the first time he had been in the cottage for a decade.

"These walls are still standing," he said.

"Clever boy," she said.

He winked at her while she walked with her slight limp, away to talk to "the girls," as she condescended to allow herself to call them. He went outside with Claire for a stroll through the orchard, looking for some trees that might have been there forty years before. Some of the orchard had been removed to make way for ground crops. Most of the acreage had been converted to miniature trees, an economic decision made through much of the valley during the years when the financial panic there was just beginning. Around his mother's cottage there were still the old yard trees, but he was looking for a stand, old twisted branches where a god might rest himself. He found a few old cherry trees still acting as a windbreak along the highway. But he had to settle, he told himself, for a secular fruit ranch.

He stayed with them for two weeks, and allowed the very image of London to sink below the horizon. Before he left he asked her seriously for some new poems. She said she had not been writing anything since "retirement age," but she did put a small book into his coat pocket. He had had no idea that there was a new book. He would read it on the plane. He hoped dearly that the poems would be perfect.

On the day that her second book arrived at the post office, there was also a letter from Ottawa. She knew what it was before she opened it. She saw Morrison's shattered body on a stretcher, carried as fast as they could manage by two soldiers in steel caps, objects exploding in the background. She saw his eyes become dull. She listened to hear whether he spoke anything of her.

But it was her brother. In a place called Anzio. That night she looked it up. It was a fine sandy beach. She remembered being there when they were children, learning to count: *uno, due, tre, quattro.*

Ira. When they were children she called him Chip.

She thought she could write a poem for him. But she did not. She read the encyclopaedia. For a while she stopped reading the newspaper. She read about Italy in the encyclopaedia. Sandy's mother's encyclopaedia.

When they were nine and ten, they went to hear the children's choir in Saint Mark's. The children sang Christmas songs they knew and Italian songs that only sounded familiar. The cardinal arrived and the children beamed as they were taught to do. Officious nuns scurried around backstage, where Chip had found a place to stand, nuns pushing children into place, silencing little girls who had not made a sound between songs. The cardinal smiled, a gift out of his high office. Everyone did as they were supposed to do. The children sang "*Adeste Fidelis*," and it was perfect, it filled the old brown bulby edifice, and then everyone went outside into the square.

It was snowing! Children broke ranks and raced about in the provisionary snow, making little snowballs and hurling them awkwardly at one another. P. B. and Chip stayed close to their parents and watched with gratefulness. They thought, despite what their father said, that there might be a God, in Italy at least.

Uno, due, tre.

She put one copy of the new book on the table beside the apricot window, and the rest on the shelf with the six copies that remained of her first book. The cover was elegant, simple, the colour of dry meadow grass. It was difficult to believe that someone might be reading it in a shadowed room in London, in Philadelphia.

Next day in the village post office she received a blue envelope with British stamps on it. Inside was a letter from Morrison's lawyer. Morrison wished to inform her that he was initiating procedures that would make their separation legal and prepare the way for their divorce.

That made two pieces of mail from England on consecutive days.

The letter did not say where her husband was now. Her last letter from him had been written on the south coast of the Mediterranean Sea. She presumed that he had crossed from there to Italy, but were the British in Italy with the Yanks and the Canadians? Sometimes she imagined Morrison dead on the fine sand of Anzio. Other times she imagined him with a swagger stick and little objects on his shoulders, strutting in front of younger soldiers standing in rows, like a little orchard made of scratchy brown wool. Sometimes she pictured him entering a doorway with a thin dark girl, and then she stopped imagining him.

When they were nine and ten she and Chip visited Nero's Villa at Anzio, at Antium. They saw the great statue of Apollo Belvedere, their mother said. They asked her whether it was the real one, the first one, but she did not tell them. Was Circe ever here, P.B. asked her Mennonite mother.

When P.B. began to read the newspapers again, she became fascinated with the maps. Every week in the newspapers the map of Europe and the map of Asia changed. In Europe the black part where the Germans still ruled grew smaller, shrinking from all sides. The white and grey areas came closer together, and large curved arrows showed the latest movements of the Americans and Canadians and British, eastward and northward. The arrows from the east had hammers and sickles beside them. In Asia the islands were sources of the curved arrows, or their targets. The black islands grew fewer. In the newspapers the changes were good news. The generals were exuberant. History was moving in the right direction. On the ground in the black areas there were many broken buildings, and under the weight of the broken buildings there were young girls with bare legs. P.B. continued to knit and to collect metal. She wrote letters to soldiers she did not know. That was what they called the "war effort." She did not write as if she were a poet. She did not mention the things she was mentioning in her poems. She did not mention, either, her brother or her husband.

And in the last year of the war she received a letter from her mother. Her father, whom she had left on the station platform in Philadelphia was gone, gone in a month of good news. His Moravian funeral had passed while the letter was being carried westward. There was no reason to go to Philadelphia.

A week later she received a letter from Sandy and Sandy's mother. They said that the funeral was quiet. They said that there was a piece in the newspapers in Philadelphia, on the middle pages, after the news about Europe and Asia.

P.B. climbed to the second bench above the valley floor, and walked and sat and looked at the bright sun on the brown grass. She did not know that she was looking at the grass, but when she brought her mind back to looking from her grey eyes, she saw that she was looking at the coyote. It was looking at her, its tongue hanging far out one side of its jaws, its grin. Was he, on these occasions, the visitor, or was she? She stared and stared, and when again she returned to looking from her eyes, the coyote was not there.

When the black area was no bigger than a city block and the war was folded into history in Europe, she was in San Francisco. The very famous Mr. Oliver was in Mexico for the moment, but the smiling Mr. Gray had a cottage in Berkeley.

"I don't suppose that my father could have been Count Zizendorf," the boy shouted from the kitchen, where he was drying the day's dishes.

"Don't be cheeky," she said. "It does not become you. You are, remember, a miracle boy."

He put away the tea towel and walked as any twelve-year-old might walk, into the little sitting room. He was, as he often was, eating a peach. With a look alone she indicated that he should not eat it over any furniture or carpet. He held his head and the peach out the open window.

"Oh? At school I am your normal C-plus," he said, juice on his face.

"To my everlasting sorrow."

"What were you?"

"About a C-plus."

"Some miracle," he said.

He was going to be quite tall when he grew up, she could see. At twelve years he had not yet developed the clumsiness that plagued her all through her school years, as she grew to stand taller than her teachers and yet felt that she held nothing in her head. All through school she read a book she had found in the attic of an abandoned house, *Between Two Worlds* by a man named Philo. She had thought it would be something like H. G. Wells, but it was something else. She knew, because she had found it so strangely, that none of her classmates and none of her teachers would know about it. Then they would never read the books she would write while they were living in their houses.

"Perhaps miracle is too sentimental a word," she said, and he could see that now she was serious again.

So he waited for a while, reached his arm fully outside and with a backhand motion threw the wet peach pit across the lawn into the grass of the orchard. Her new book, a kind of little novel, perhaps, was lying on the round table. He saw the permission in her eyes and looked at a few pages.

"Maybe you could tell me what nationality I am," he said. "I mean we are always filling out these forms, and they want to know what nationality."

"What do you write?"

"Canadian, like everyone else, just about."

"All right then," she said.

"But what am I really?"

"I don't know," she said. Not because she didn't know where he had been born. Not because she didn't know well enough who his father was.

"Is Claire my father?" he asked.

"Shut up," she said.

The sun shone warmly in Berkeley, but looking west across the bay she could see clouds roll over the city, roll toward her, and stop halfway across the still new bridge. Over there the people wore coats and tried to hurry up and down the steep streets. In Berkeley P. B. sat in a garden with a fortunate kumquat tree and read Euripides and wrote a few lines of poetry. Every second day she went to the university swimming pool and laid her long body in the water, swimming two more lengths each time.

With Andrew Gray she went to concerts across the bay and at the university. In the pool she would remember the music and strike out at the water in front of her while attending to the rhythm and the melody inside her. She found herself swimming beside a young woman, a girl with hair so short that one could see the perfect shape of her skull. They swam, and afterward, they walked together down Shattuck, sometimes stopping for lemonade, for tea. The girl's name was Claire, and her last name was well known in the financial district across the bay. P. B. waited a month, and then gave her a book of Euripides.

That was one of the three important things that happened while P. B. was in California that year, just after the war. B. P. Oliver came back from Mexico and was sometimes around, but that was not as important as it might have been. The second important thing was that P. B. again began to carry life inside her. At the pool she was amused and a little alarmed to see her belly gradually fill out.

Her brother was dead. Her father was dead. Her daughter was dead. Her husband was gone. Sandy was in Philadelphia, with a husband who belonged to clubs.

P. B. did not want to go through it all again. Better to tear it out of her now and fill her with drugs. But she went to the pool every second day, and watched herself, if it was herself, grow. Young Claire massaged her back before they swam. It was very helpful. Where did she learn that?

Then there was the third important thing that happened to her there in California. A poliovirus entered her body by way of her throat. From her alimentary tract it was absorbed into her blood and lymphatics, whence it was widely disseminated and ultimately reached her central nervous system.

She could not go to the pool any more. She lay in bed and tried to read, but her fever would not allow Euripides. She had a sore throat, a headache, nausea, and then aching legs. So they knew what it was. The university doctor asked her whether she were pregnant, and he said that pregnant women were especially vulnerable. I have always, she tried to say, been vulnerable. But she fell, all day long, into and out of a sleep that brought her restlessness for this moment to a relief. When she opened her eyes she thought she saw the face of Claire, here in the house. It was Claire, she thought, who moved her legs for her.

"My daughter?" she whispered. And the three men did not know what she meant.

"Do you think there is a Limbo?" she asked once, when she could open her eyes and speak a sentence. But no one answered her.

Take me to the valley, she heard herself say. But she did not know for certain whether she had said it aloud. In the hospital she looked out the window and saw a tree. It may have been a cherry tree. It may not. Claire's hair was very short, and it had the colour of someone she remembered. Claire removed her white mask and smiled for her, and it was the only genuine smile among them all.

Now she was in the same hospital room she had been in before, or she was not, and she would lose her daughter again. She did not want to see her this time. She could not feel her own legs now, but Claire moved them for her. Claire massaged her back.

Can you drive a motor car, she asked Claire one day late in 1946. Can you find the eggs the hens hide in the tall grass? *Uno, due, tre...*

So somewhere he was born. He would never see his birth certificate. He would grow up in the valley and move away. His mother gave him a name out of Latin, but he would move away and call himself G.B. and write poems. Why not? In fact he would write some of hers when he wrote a story about her life. He would think he was writing some of hers.

Rhode Island Red

Trust me, this will take only a fraction of the time it would take to write and read a novel, but there will be order somewhere here, faint order, human traces anyway.

If you were not in the southern Okanagan Valley in the fifties you will not be able to picture the scene I am picturing. But you can say this on the other hand, that no matter how well we think we are remembering scenes of thirty years ago, say, whenever we are given the opportunity to check those memories, we are invariably wrong, sometimes a long way off.

So I will have to do a little description, I guess, at least to get this going. The consolation will be that we will no longer have to listen to the voice delivering the goods in sentences that start with the first person singular pronoun. I like pronouns, but that one is not my favourite. Description, then. But be aware, won't you, that description will not bring you the authentic look or feel of the place, either.

We are three miles, because they still used miles then, south of the village of Lawrence. Lawrence could have been called a town, but the people who lived there persisted in calling it a village because it was cheaper when it came to taxes. No one could tell you how that worked, but everyone seemed to think that it made good sense.

Three miles south of Lawrence, let us say, in November. The orchards are just beginning to turn skeletal, the season's fruit picking finished weeks ago. Just across Highway 97 there is a funny-looking apple tree. It owns perhaps only seven dry curled brown leaves, but there are apples hanging all over it. These are overripe apples, brown and wrinkled. If the orchardist working on his tractor up by the house were to drive down here and bump the tree's trunk with the front of his machine, he would find himself in a rain of apples that were useless except to the health of the soil covered right now with slick leaves.

He would probably also notice the chicken hurling its head at the pebbly ground beside the blacktop, and carry it under his arm back up the dirt road to the home yard.

There is no fence between this orchard and the highway. Fences are only a nuisance around the kind of farm on which workers are always moving ladders or trailers covered with props or empty boxes. As every orchardist along the road has said at least once, you don't need a fence to keep apple trees in, and any fruit thieves that come in uninvited at night are going to have to get used to rock salt in the ass. The kids around Lawrence figured that every orchardist had a shotgun loaded with rock salt or worse standing by the back porch door with the baseball bats.

Most families had chickens in their yards in those days. Even in town, where people would make little chicken runs out of chicken wire, with a roof of chicken wire to keep large dogs out or to keep chickens in. It seemed normal to the narrator of this story, for instance, to keep chickens in the yard. When he was a kid in the South Okanagan in the forties he had to feed the family chickens. That was enjoyable, whether throwing grain on the ground for those flailing heads, or dumping the slop and watching them spear the corn cobs.

This chicken was a Rhode Island Red, a general-purpose breed created in the United States of America. It had a rectangular body and brown feathers of the shade called by parents red. By descent it had come from distant forebears in the jungles of Malaya. There were no roads through the jungles of Malaya in those days.

One time the narrator of this story planted some of the wheat that he normally would have fed as grain to his family's own Rhode Island Reds, and it grew. When the wheat plants were about three feet in height his younger sister pulled them out of the ground and threw them into the chicken coop. He still wonders today what made his sister think of doing that. The orchard in which their house stood contained lots of long grass, so she must have understood something about "wheat" when she ripped up his experiment to feed it to the chickens. Something about language. If he were to ask her now she would just treat it as an old family joke. Why did the sister pull the wheat?

These families in the South Okanagan kept chickens for eggs and for chicken meat. That is why the Rhode Island Red was so popular. It produced lots of meat, and brown eggs, thought by superstitious rurals to be superior to white eggs in the matter of nutrition. White eggs were for city folks who also betrayed their personal biology with white sugar and white bread.

The male sperm lives in the hen's oviduct for two to three weeks. Yolks originate in the ovary and grow to four centimetres in diameter, after which they are released into the oviduct, where the sperm is waiting. Whenever we found a red dot in an egg we said "Aha!" In the oviduct the egg also picks up the thick white and some shell membrane. Then it heads for the uterus where the thin white and the hard shell are added. The making of an egg takes twenty-four hours. Orchard moms are proud of hens that lay an egg every day. They are amused by the biddies that hide them in the yard instead of leaving them in the coop.

Now this one Rhode Island Red pecking away at pebbles and organisms at the edge of Highway 97. We certainly, I would think, cannot call her (or him if it is a capon) a central character in this little fiction. A figure at the middle of things, perhaps, but not a central character. A chicken does not have character. Unless you want to ascribe character to this Red's pecking and wandering away from the rest of the birds around the house, all the way down the dirt road to this shallow ditch beside Highway 97.

It is nowadays simply Highway 97, and not too much different from its condition in the late fifties. But in those days it was both Highway 97 and Highway 3, the alternative Trans-Canada. The two numbers, adding up as they did, really satisfied a teenage boy who lived in and around Lawrence, but he does not appear in this story. There is a human being, you will remember, sitting on a tractor, doing something of value up near the yellow stucco house, where the rest of the Rhode Island Reds and the bantams were.

If this fowl were a central character, as it might have been were the story a fable, it would have to be set down in a significant setting for the unrolling of the narrative. No, one supposes that fables do not have characters, but only fictions. Though Aesop's fables, for instance, are told in an attempt to mould character in their listeners, one can hardly ascribe character to, say, a grape-eating fox. If one were supposed to think about him in terms of character, a child might ask, why does this fox desire to eat grapes, especially grapes that are out of reach?

In any case, even though we refuse character to the young hen in this instance, we can say a few things about the nature of the setting she had pecked her way into. The most salient because unusual feature, as far as she was concerned, was the highway. It was a normal western asphalt or tar macadam road, what is called in the trade a flexible surface. Gravel of fairly consistent size is covered with hot bituminous material that penetrates the spaces between the little stones and then cools and hardens. If you are a quick driver you can just see a ribbon, as they say, of grey, or if it is the first month of a new highway, a ribbon of black. If your local member of the legislature is in the government's cabinet you will see more black than do people in other places. If you are a kid walking along the highway you can see the stones in the mix, and you have always wondered how many of them were Indian arrowheads. If you are a chicken pecking seeds and gizzard gravel into your interior, you will never get a pebble out of that hardly flexible surface.

There was a quick driver a few miles south, just passing Dead Man's Lake, heading north, probably going to the Co-op packing house in Lawrence.

He was driving a truck cab in front of a big empty trailer that was equipped with a refrigeration unit, which could be seen from outside, a big square item on the top of the front of the trailer. The doors were open on the trailer, so one knew that the refrigeration was turned off right now. If the truck went by you slowly enough and you were on one side of the road you would be able to see the other side of the road for part of a second right through the trailer. At the Co-op there would be some men and lads in cold storage ready to load the trailer of the truck with boxes of Spartan apples. Then the refrigeration would be turned on and the truck would head to a large city grocery store chain whose name could be understood by anyone who could read now that the doors on the trailer were slid shut.

This truck was proceeding northward at about fifty miles an hour, which was the speed limit at that time as long as the road was straight, which was not often the case. Its driver was an old army veteran named Stiffy. He lived in the city where the grocery store chain was located, but he spent a majority of his days in the cab of his truck, trying to catch small-town radio stations on his radio, stopping at roadside cafés where other rigs were stilled. He had had a conversation at Rhoda's Truck Stop in Castlegar this morning.

"Stiffy. How's it hanging, you old bugger?"

"Can't complain, Buddy. Can't complain."

The other driver's name was not Buddy. Stiffy called him Buddy because he couldn't remember his name, if he had ever known it. He called most men Buddy.

"I think I'm getting too old for this line of work," said the man.

"Know what you mean."

"No future in it either."

"Gettin' to be near time to pack it in and take it easy. Find out what my old lady does all day."

"Wouldn't know what to do with myself."

"Hah, I know what you do with yourself six or eight times a day, you old bugger."

"No, really. Guy owns the old bowling alley in Coleman. Been thinking of moving there, buy him out, live off the fat of the land."

"Oh yeah, bowling is getting more popular every day, they say."

"You know anyone goes bowling?

"You know anyone wants to buy a Kenworth, one-quarter paid for?"

That was the conversation at Rhoda's, or most of it. During all that talk the driver we are interested in, if that is not an overstatement, was spooning up some chicken soup and biting at a grilled cheese sandwich.

He often ate those things at Rhoda's, and something very much like that at the Orchard Cafe in Lawrence.

Now he was about ten miles south of Lawrence, braking behind a farmer in a rusty pickup truck halfway down Graveyard Hill.

In the high insect season trucks like that, and other traffic as well, brought about the demise of countless insects, fruit flies, grasshoppers, the black and yellow caterpillars that travelled the highway in huge groups. It was not high insect season now, but there were still some grasshoppers, those fleecy ones with wings that allowed them to fly in awkward trajectories. Despite the wings there were some dead grasshoppers on the macadam, perhaps a head squashed flat but a thorax still complete. The chicken in question was out on Highway 97, looking for body parts of grasshoppers.

There is a well-known benefit to this kind of diet. If you get your eggs from some large city grocery store chain you are likely to find, on opening them, that the yolks are pale yellow. If you boil them before eating them, you probably notice that the shells crack in the hot water. Those are eggs produced by chickens who are kept all their lives in the company of other chickens in small cages over conveyor belts. If you have your own chickens, and if they are allowed to forage, to eat bits of garbage and insects, their eggs will have tough shells and dark yellow or even orange yolks. They will taste a lot better than the grocery chain eggs. It won't matter whether they are white or brown; they will be higher in nutrition than those city eggs.

Stiffy's truck was no longer stuck behind the farmer's pickup. The farmer had become nervous about the sheer metallic weight behind him, and pulled off the road, without signalling. Now there was a 1949 Pontiac sedan behind Stiffy's tractor-trailer. Inside the Pontiac were four members of the Koenig family, Mr. Koenig with his sunburnt face and gas-station hat, and three of his teenaged children. The children were not in school because Mr. Koenig was taking them into Lawrence to get their shots. At the beginning of the school year in September there had been a nurse at the school giving out shots, but the Koenig teenagers had not been in school. They had been picking apples as fast as they could till it got dark in their father's orchard. Now there was not an apple at the Koenig orchard except for the boxes of Spartans in the Koenig basement. Eighteen boxes of Spartans, and one box of Romes.

The Koenig kids did not care if they missed their shots. But there was a family in the orchard next to the Koenigs which had a son in an iron lung at the coast. Mr. Koenig hated to think about him.

Two of the Koenig kids were in the back seat. One, the oldest and strongest, was in the front seat beside his father. His face was not as red as his father's. He had been born in this valley.

This is the sort of thing the Koenig teenagers were saying:

"Murray told me the needle is yay long."

"Oh sure, did he tell you it's square?"

"What the hell do you know? When the doc says roll up your left sleeve, you always have to get some help from me."

"Listen, if you weren't a girl I'd bash your teeth in."

"Just try it, jerk."

"Knock it off," said Mr. Koenig.

The road was never straight for longer than a few hundred feet. It looked as if they were going to have to follow the big truck all the way into Lawrence. Maybe they could pass him around the Acre Lots, but by then they were just as good as in town anyway.

Trust me, we are nearly there, and you will admit, I think, that there is some kind of order here. Human traces and some poultry thrown in. That's a bad choice of verb. Let's say some poultry added.

The poultry in question was now two thirds of the way across Highway 97, trying unsuccessfully to back up and scratch at the surface, but finding better luck with its plunging head. There had not been any traffic for five minutes. That was unusual for that part of Highway 97 even in the fifties. People near the road could not help noticing, when that happened from time to time, a feeling of peculiarity, as if the location were being *prepared* for something. Now that the tractor was just sitting up there beside the house, you could hear the telephone wires singing above your head.

Then Stiffy's truck appeared both to ear and eye. Its tires played a high note that would not descend. Stiffy saw the Rhode Island Red, saw it lift its head and fall momentarily on its tail as it turned to run back to its home side of the macadam, saw it disappear under the front of his machine. He did not see what a witness, had there been one, might have seen. The blur of red-brown feathers emerged behind the truck's long trailer, the living chicken picked up by the wake of hot wind and thrown high in an awkward arc into the air. It did not sail, nor did it soar. It was a roundish bird in the low sky, not flying but certainly falling now, and as it did along came the Pontiac sedan. Mr. Koenig knew that it was a chicken. He even knew it was a Rhode Island Red. He had no idea how it had got where it was, hurtling toward the windshield of his car. He jigged the car slightly to the right, but the course of the hen was eccentric, and it became a smash of feathers and blood and claws and noise in front of his face where the glass became a white star. The car with four Koenigs in it was still moving to the right, and now the front right tire crunched into roadside gravel. Then the car went straight as the road went straight for a little while but in another direction. The Pontiac, having travelled for a moment at fifty miles an hour through long grass, stopped all at once against a leafless apple tree. If it had been the tree just to the left, the car would have been deluged with brown fermented apples.

All this made a noise. Stiffy, a half mile north in the cab of his Kenworth, didn't hear any of it. But the orchardist and his wife did. It would not be long till they were both out of the house. Today they, like other people in the Lawrence vicinity, would be finding out what had happened. Tomorrow they would be thinking about why. Then they would talk about this event for a long time. Many of them would mention it in letters. As later events intervened they would sometimes ask each other questions about this one.

The Creature

When he was a boy, and growing up in a valley town with no traffic lights or curbs, the creature had always been seen in a black cape, legs wide, head down, on the edge of the roof of a tall apartment or office building, rain behind him, though in that little town it hardly ever rained. It rained once just before the orchardists could get the cherries picked without splits in their skin, and once again around the Labour Day weekend. He probably stank, the creature, stank of foul long-dead flesh and strained minerals and the torture of steel. But he had always held his breath hard when it was around. When it stood for a moment, for instance, in his bedroom the night after the day when his only older cousin died. When it looked over the shoulder of the fat soft anaesthetist during that first operation in grade six.

It had no voice at all; it would not speak. It would have been less frightening to a kid if it had spoken, even if it had had a voice that shook out of an echo chamber, even if it had an accent like something out of giant dark stony mountain crags in some sort of Europe-Asia snow-bound night of unrelenting wind. It did not speak at all, nor make any other sound. You did not see it move from place to place. You did not see it arrive or depart. It was there and then it was not. It was not a skull-face. It was not a putrid eyeball fleshface. It did not laugh like an animal.

It was not a hyena, and he was not in Africa, and none of his wounds was physical, and he was not in bed. It was very familiar. He had known it long ago, when his memory was intact, when he had not riddled his memory by using it. He had written about it in other shapes, but now that it was here again after all this while, he knew that all that writing was incorrect. Decent, but incorrect.

"You are obsessed on the subject," she had said. "Ever since I first knew you, you have been obsessed with it."

"In my writing?"

"In your writing and in your life."

"It is the great subject, I suppose."

"I have never met anyone who spends so much of his time thinking about it," she said.

Very well. He would think about life. Because now that it was here again for sure, he did not like to think about it, really. It had been one thing to grin as he titled a book after it, but now that it was here he did not love it. He did not like it.

Very well, then. He would think about life, the coming of life.

> She felt the urge to push, and that called for rapid panting, as the course taught her, and you could see the baby turn around, opening the cervix. Earlier, pushing on her tailbone during contractions, I could feel the baby's head in my palm.

In his memories of childhood, layered with the writing he had done about childhood, the kid was afraid of the creature. He knew it did not exist, not like that, not as a creature, but he was afraid of it. Now he was not afraid of it. But he hated it. He was depressed, he would say, if he had to go for a word like that.

Because it was there. He could not see it but it was there. It was not just something in his head, either. It was so damned sad, if something about yourself could be sad.

If he could have been in a different place. No, if his life were not about the damned things it is about, he would not have to know about the nearness of the creature. It was not a creature.

> From the time the baby got turned around the right way, things went much faster and the mother was now in control. We were in the delivery room, and I didn't know that it was anything more than just the place for the local injection.

Someone looking from the distance of say a few houses down the block might say that he had not really ruined all those lives. So people cried some tears and moved to other cities, and made impossible telephone calls. Maybe some of them will not be living together after all these years. That is regular business in this neighbourhood. Who do you think you are to get that mixed up with death?

> Finally the doctor put his fingers in and let her push a little, and I heard the lip go over with a wet sound. Then she started pushing, her face going red in her determination, and I was as busy as could be, putting moisture to her mouth, lifting her with my hands.

She probably thought, at times anyway, that he liked it. He did not like it. When it was at its worst he thought he would do anything to get out of its whereabouts. Figure that one out. Death would be, if you really did it, the sure way of getting away from the problem of death. There'll be no more dying then. No more slow glide of silk slip up the outside thigh, either.

No, he didn't like it, ever.

He could never understand, or never quite believe those young people when he was young who said that they did not mind death, it was just the idea of being old they didn't like. He had always said that he wanted to live forever, and then that he would like to live as long as he could.

Now he was not sure it was worth it. He had read about depression. He had read about clinical depression, or at least heard the word. To tell the truth, he had not read much about depression. But he had heard about it. It was something that often came just before death, sometimes theirs, sometimes yours.

> Another young nurse looked at her watch and listened with a stethoscope to the baby's heart. 150. 160. 160. Nurse Olafson said that the highest pulse came when the baby's head was between vertebrae.

The doctor came back from his cigarette and sat with his face in the right place. He looked like a painter on his stool, stopping to reflect over the canvas between contractions.

It did not make a sound but he knew it was there. He did not locate it, not behind him, as in the cartoons, or in any particular direction. He did not know how close it was but it was close. It did not stink. It did not cast a shadow. But he knew it was there. It was present. It was *with him*.

It was worse than any words about it. Therefore he should keep trying to describe it. When he was a kid he would lie awake at night in his room, afraid of what was there. It was not death. It was not a creature. But everything seemed too close and at the same time too far away. There was a relentless buzzing, or something like buzzing, grinding, drilling, but not a sound, a drilling presence of something. He would finally have to shout, hoping that shouting would break it. His mother came and asked him what was the matter, and he tried to tell her.

"It is nothing. There is nothing here," she said.

There was something wrong with his brain. Not his mind. That would be all right because he could deny that. But there was something wrong with his brain. Then he knew that his mother used to be able to do things but now she could no longer do something, and he was there by himself. Not a grown-up. A kid with a brain you could not fix or trade. You keep the one you are born with. Well, it could scare you to death, or you could make it romantic.

During the next pushes I can see not only the slit of grey hairy head, but now the whole pelvic floor bulging with the shape of the little head, and everyone is cheering. On the next contraction the doctor is holding the forceps with one hand, elbows up, cotton swabs in there with the newly arriven.

He tended to look back on his childhood as a childhood unlike the ones claimed by his friends. That is, it was spent in a small town surrounded by orchards and hills, where with topical variations people lived in families much like those presented in schoolbooks and advertising and later on in television. It was not a disturbing childhood then. That was the right word for that absence—disturbing.

Once, though, when he was around ten years old he was out later than usual on a Saturday night. He had probably just been to the movie and now he was down by the river a block below the movie house. He was never allowed to swim in the river. He could swim at the village pool or out at the lake, but never in the river. Some people did swim in the river, but they were the same tough kids who smoked in the school lavatories.

He was doing his usual lone sensitive kid act at the edge of the river, now, not hiding, particularly, not spying for certain. Not spying as he always meant to do on the strange people from somewhere else who lived for short periods of time during the summer in the little row of whitewashed shacks down by the river. In that town your standing was represented by the distance you lived from the river. If you lived near the river nobody knew your name, or if they did it was a name that had been around town for a long time, and so exceptions could be made for history.

Now this Saturday night two people he did not know appeared between the shacks and the river. The river was green and opaque, and it ran swiftly with little folds in the water. Really it was a brown kind of green.

They must have been people, the kind of people who lived in those shacks. The man was wearing an old purplish-blue suit, and she was wearing a dress and white high-heeled shoes. They were holding hands, with their arms touching shoulder to wrist, and walking toward the river. When they got to the river they continued to walk, and he, the kid by the water, unseen or ignored by them, watched. He was always watching things, but he was not often this lucky. Now he did not think it was lucky.

Because they were still walking into the river, and the sides went down quickly, and the water tugged at you quickly, so that your parents did not want you to go into that river. But now here were these two in their clothes in the water. The river was pushing on her dress, lifting its skirt to the turning surface of the water. They continued to walk and now there were just their shoulders and heads and then their heads, and he, the kid, may have turned to look elsewhere for a moment, but if he did, when he turned back again those two people were entirely gone. There was a little chance that they had come back out of the water. But no, there was no chance of that. If he had looked away he had not looked away that long. If they had walked back out it would have to be on this side of the river, but it would probably be a long way downstream. So maybe they did come back out.

Anyway, he was not sure of what he had seen. No one in his family did peculiar things, so he was not aware of what a lot of things might be. Was it religion? Was it death? Drink? Madness? It was something that was scary and beyond him. But it was something he would grow to know. If he grew up and left this valley he would know what it was. That was even more scary.

> The nurse on the right poked in the pit and I looked back to see that tiny wet head coming out between the two big spoons, which are then dropped. I saw the bones rippling apart in the head, and before we knew it, out came the body, comely shape hanging light purple now from the doctor's hand, thick twisty soft cord dangling—this call's for you—"It's a girl!" all the female voices say, as they often do, I suppose.
> "Oh Baby!" said its mother.
> Love was blazing out of all my senses, to both figures now on the gurney. Then I was laughing. Then I remembered that in all that hurry of images there were two that one had better remember. Immediately on coming out the little creature being turned, though she did not know it, upside down, made a tiny cry. And before that, the most beautiful thing, its little head, amazingly little head, turned by itself, toward its mother's left thigh. Its mother just pushed her out!

He had learned a lot of things since getting out of the valley. Some of them were about mortality and some were not. But then eventually all of them were about mortality. Every morning when he woke he said either aloud or in his head, "Another seven hours closer to the grave."

"Time is qualitative," a woman said to him once.

"Everything you have ever done?"

"Yes?"

"Doesn't matter what quality it was. It *was*. It's gone. Irretrievable."

"You are not the kind of man I want to spend my quality time with," she said. And she didn't.

The thoughts he had every day had made him this sort of person: if he saw an ant on the sidewalk he went out of his path to avoid stepping on it. Still, he ate slippery, bubbling hamburgers, the brown fat running off his wrists.

When he was a very young man he always said, even to himself, that he would die before he was thirty. Then he said he would die when he was thirty. That was romance. He skulked around in a soiled raincoat and ankle-high black running shoes. He did this while other people were wearing things with buckles on them. Three-voice folksinging groups were popular.

> *The last things to remain purple were her feet. She lay there with her eyes wide open. I saw her whole chin trembling. It must have been shock. They were squirting her and wiping her and putting drops into her eyes, and listening over and over to her heart.*
>
> *I was original and sophisticated in my oral response to the event.*
>
> *"Oh wow!" I said.*

So you see, I can write about life.

He never for a moment thought the creature would depart, would despair of making any headway here.

He got up from the scarred and lopsided chair at his desk and went into the kitchen to get a cup of coffee, he hoped, from the newest in a long line of imported coffee machines. His daughter was sitting at the kitchen table, fingers in the hair at the sides of her cranium, elbows on the tabletop at either side of the fat book she was bent over.

"That's what we like to see," he said, looking through the sink for a decent coffee cup. "Honest study."

She was nineteen years old. In reply to his habitual remark she read from the fat book:

How gladly would I meet
Mortality, my sentence, and be earth
Insensible! how glad would lay me down
As in my mother's lap!

"You haven't got that close to your mother in half a dozen years," he said.

"I was reading from literature," she said, lifting her face now. It was beautiful and at the same time deeply familiar. Her upper lip curled back a little, and moist teeth showed. "*Paradise Lost*," she said.

"Of course."

"Book Ten."

"Who is saying that?"

"We all are."

She had been hinting suicidal feelings at him since she was fifteen. Now she was a university student. That made it more difficult, if not harder. In literature there is lots of suicide, and university students are very fond of it. They don't know about the creature, but they know about suicide in literature and around the table.

"Do you ever feel," he said, "as if there is someone nearby but you can't tell where he is, and he makes you very discouraged?"

"Yeah, you, Dad."

"Thanks. No, I mean it. A creature."

"You're weird, Dad. Whacko. Creatures, eh?"

"The last things to remain purple were the feet," he said.

"Get out of my face, Dad. I have some fatal thinking to do."

Indoors or outdoors, it didn't matter. The creature was not affected by weather or environment or time of day or night.

What did it feel like, exactly? Other people were always asking what things are "like," and that makes some sense, because we have to gauge new experiences against old ones. People also wanted you to put out some abstract words, as if feelings are more expressible in abstract terms than objects are. What did it feel like, approximately?

Disappointment. I mean you thought you were going to escape, and as in the dream it caught you before your last step to freedom. Heaviness. Sad. I have said that before. Sad. As if for yourself from somewhere outside. Something like the paralysis of shock. You can move, make the usual moves, but how can you, how do you?

There is the bunny. When the hawk has been chasing him, and he has figured out that he is not in the end going to get away, he stops and resigns himself, hunches still, and perhaps, people in the country say, dies before the hawk can use his talons and beak. The hawk has always been there, but just now decided to move in. He is the bunny's creature.

But look at bunnies, how fast they make more of them.

My daughter, my daughter. When I said that phrase I felt new at it, as if I had won the right to use it now. There was a kind of easy resignation in joining all the people called Dad. Okay, I will not fight and holler against that business, and I will say "my daughter."

She was on the deteriorating sundeck of the house I or we had bought, yes, but I am not thinking of that weakness, that instance right now. I should be, because I have given him a place to stand and look in through the window. She was in her green walker, a kind of chair set in the middle of a table with rollers at the bottoms of its legs. She zoomed back and forth on the sundeck in the sun, saying, "Da da da da," which was her word for every emotion.

I was mowing the square lawn in the little back yard. When I bumped the rusty mower against the trunk of the apple tree a thousand blossoms fell down on me. For a second the place smelled sweet.

ALEXANDER HARE.
One of the Desperadoes of British Columbia.
PHOTO BY J. UREN.

ALLEN McLEAN.
One of the Desperadoes of British Columbia.
PHOTO BY J. UREN.

ARCHIE McLEAN.
One of the Desperadoes of British Columbia.
PHOTO BY J. UREN.

CHARLEY McLEAN.
One of the Desperadoes of British Columbia.
PHOTO BY J. UREN.

The Wild McLeans, late 1870s.

Shoot!

My original plan for the third novel in my trilogy was to set the story a century after *Caprice*, which was set a century after *Burning Water*. And as *Burning Water* had been set mainly on the sea, and *Caprice* decidedly on land, so the third book would be set in the air. I was sort of planning to make the main figures First Nations pilots flying in the north of British Columbia around the 1990s.

But the story of the McLean brothers had been bothering me since my childhood, and I had to get inside it and make some of it up, while telling readers who hadn't known it that we hanged teenagers who were the children of First Nations women forced into subservience by white men with rural power, the latter representing white men with Imperial power.

As in the earlier novel (whose story occurs a decade later than this one), most of the narrative takes place in the Kamloops area I love writing about. But the Okanagan finds its way into the story and the figures find their way into the Okanagan. Early in the book we hear about the Okanagan people who found their way up to Douglas Lake, and we hear from Mourning Dove, the wonderful Okanagan storyteller and labour activist from Omak and Fairview. She was a real person, and someone should write a novel about her. The McLeans were real people, too, but there is no evidence I know about that they ever pursued their activities south of the Medicine Line. I just made that up.

The only Okanagan Valley scene in the book has the narrator discover the bones of a First Nations child who had been buried at the bottom of a shale slide. A lot of that scene is, as they say, based on real life. It also seems to suggest a kind of symbolic mythic association difficult to pin down, doesn't it?

Looking heroic over Gallagher Lake. Bill took this photo.

A Thin Bone

All through my childhood and whatever it is that comes later, I spent a lot of time alone in the valley and especially the hills.

There were certain things I liked to do over and over again when I was alone in the hills. I liked to lift and peel moss off big rocks. I liked scaling cliffs. I often buried things I had brought with me, a baseball, a hunting knife, an old locket. Burying things here and there you didn't mention to anyone, especially your parents, because they would have asked useless questions. When the irrigation ditch was drained for the winter I often walked a few miles down its length and discovered things that had been underwater all summer. These things were generally wrapped in green slimy stuff. Once I found a small pistol. Once I found a necklace made of Dutch coins.

I really liked running rock slides. These were usually made of old shale with thin hard algae on it. The pieces were usually more or less flat, from as big as you to as big as your foot, and in their millions formed huge fan shapes. You had to go a little faster than the sliding rocks. You had to take a giant step before you knew which rock you were going to step onto. You had to go faster and faster. The only part I didn't like was at the end. By the time you reached the bottom you were really going, and when you took a step onto unmoving ground, you were pretty sure to bang your knees really hard or you would pitch forward onto your face, or your head if you managed to roll, and find a space between single rocks and cactuses and so on. You never thought about that part when you were standing near the top of the slide, looking out at the beautiful valley and getting ready to step into space.

One time I was catching my breath at the bottom of a slide, sitting on the brown grass and looking up at the shale. The afternoon sun made a million shadows. I was trying to recreate my downward path. Sometimes you came down on a slalom route. I always thought you should be able to see your track, but the dark grey rocks just looked millions of years old.

Near the bottom of the slide, where bushes and grass gathered between the last rocks, was a funny shape, a not quite natural heap of stones, flat on top of flat. I started removing rocks, tossing the pieces of shale to left and right.

More rocks were falling into the space I was making, so I had more to do than I had thought I would. If I had to do this much work at home, I would have had to make up a game to pass the time. Here I was just reshaping the end of a shale fan.

Then I saw a thin bone.

I picked the rocks out carefully now, and saw more bones. I saw a skull, separated from the other bones, which seemed to be in what was once a kind of little circle. The skull was pretty small in my hands. It was a human skull and it was brown like something from under the earth. I put it back as close to where I had found it as I could.

I saw a shape and picked it up and scraped it. It was a medium-sized seashell. I had not seen many seashells then, except the ones some people used for ashtrays. I put the shell back with the thin bones.

Then I put pieces of shale back. I figured out how to place the first ones so that the skull and the thin bones and the shell would not have rocks lying right on top of them. I worked another hour in the hot afternoon sun, building a pile of stones. This time they would look just like the natural end of a rock slide.

Bowering's B. C.

The title was not my idea, but I have grown to like it all right. I'll bet that Cynthia Good thought of it. She was the chief editor at Viking/Penguin in Toronto at the time. When my second history book came out, she was the publisher at Viking/Penguin. When my third was published, she was the president. Then she opted for a glitzy academic career and I headed for the smaller literary presses.

I really like Cynthia Good. Every time she would propose a book to me I would say no about fifty times, explaining that my B. A. in history was questionable. She may have pointed out that my M. A. in English was nothing to write home about either. But I had been writing historical novels set in what would become British Columbia, and Viking/Penguin had been publishing some of them. How about getting off the historical-fiction pot and writing real fiction, she asked, making it sound like an actual question.

I did a lot of real historical research for those novels, I pointed out. Then somehow she tricked me into doing what they call popular history. Well, bpNichol once pointed out that my stories read like essays and my essays read like stories. To honour him and alleviate the drudgery of non-fiction, I think I may have slipped a little invention into the history books. I never got into big trouble for that.

Some overly strict readers might complain that Rock Creek is not really part of the Okanagan region but rather what is called the Boundary country. But when I was a kid, students from Rock Creek were bused to Oliver for high school, and all summer in 1951 my father went in a carload of men to work on the Rock Creek Canyon Bridge. At 299 feet, it was rumoured to be the highest bridge over a canyon anywhere in the Commonwealth, and my father worked as what they called a carpenter. One thing he had to do was hang on under the bridge, and strip the wooden forms from the hardened concrete. It was a hot summer in Boundary country. Oh, and the bridge is as close to Osoyoos as it is to Rock Creek.

The other mining town, Fairview, acted as a resting stop for my vengeful heroine Caprice in the novel of the same name. I am still waiting for someone to write the Fairview novel. While waiting, I would recommend William Phillips's 2010 movie *Gunless*, a western comedy filmed a few kilometres south of Fairview.

The En'owkin Centre has moved from its location in downtown Penticton to a bigger and more modern complex across the river canal in the Penticton Okanagan Reserve. It is a wonderful school and meeting place to visit, and a good place to convene if you are some of the people trying to figure out a way to get the provincial government to understand the wisdom of backing a national park in the South Okanagan.

Rock Creek

Amateur gold miners are like amateur gamblers, in that they dream of a quick lucky hit that will soon have them in silk trousers. But veteran gold miners are unlike professional gamblers, in that they have to get used to looking for thirty cents in a muddy pan and sleeping in a tent pitched on ground scraped free of snow. All over the southern interior of British Columbia in the late fifties, there were amateur and veteran gold miners crouched over creeks, doing simple arithmetic. Gold was found in the Similkameen River late in 1859, and soon afterward at Rock Creek, just north of the border and just east of the Okanagan Valley. By the summer of 1860 the Rock Creek strike was beginning to look like a precarious bonanza.

As usual Governor Douglas was concerned about U.S. ruffians. He urged the Fraser River boys to go to the Boundary country and set stakes. Then he decided to ride the newly finished Dewdney Trail himself. When he got to Rock Creek in September he found a town with twenty buildings and five hundred human beings from Canada and the United States and Europe. He announced a meeting at which he would address the locals. No one wanted to hear the politician from the Island. His supernumeraries talked up the meeting, which was rescheduled to take place at night in the saloon, and eventually the miners attended and listened without rudeness. Douglas told them that he was impressed with their industry and lawfulness, and advised them that they were subject to British law, though the boundary was a short walk away. He told them that this law included the concept of duties on imported goods. Then he appointed Captain William Cox as the local gold commissioner and border supervisor. When Douglas rode back to his capital, he was pretty happy about the progress of civilization in the gold fields of his colony.

Captain Cox was not a stickler for London-style jurisprudence. When two disputatious miners vied for the same piece of dirt, he had them run a foot race to decide the claim. When a young Englishman was caught stealing from a flume, he was sentenced to five minutes of gathering his stuff, and ten minutes of getting out of town, which included settling his debts. On a more serious note, Cox reported the lynching of an Indian man who had apparently killed a French miner. Fifty miners had ridden into Washington Territory to retrieve the man and persuade the Okanogan Indians to hand him over. Then they hanged him from a pine tree. Captain Cox, government gold man and border guard, wrote that he did not see the hanging, therefore could do nothing about it.

Like other gold towns along the border, Rock Creek blossomed for a year or so, and then settled into village life as the news of the Cariboo rush spread southward. For the first half of the 1860s the miners left their sluices and rode north. Others rode through. The bartenders and whores sighed and packed their valises again.

Captain Cox was an invention by Governor Douglas. In the free-wheeling United States there was no such thing as a gold magistrate. Douglas got many of his ideas from the gold acts passed in Australia and New Zealand, and applied them in his governments' Gold Fields Act of 1859. But the notion of gold commissioners was his. As he saw the influx of miners to more and more areas of his mainland colony, and as he saw that London would not provide him with as many policemen as he might have wanted to have, he began to appoint young Englishmen and Anglo-Irish to oversee operations at all the new mining sites. These fellows would see that the miners held proper licences and register their claims, and that there was no skulduggery among the local mining boards. They were also made magistrates and justices of the peace; they had to settle disputes and impose fines. They had a lot of other jobs as well, being land commissioners and Indian agents and tax collectors and jailers. Most of them also took advantage of their placements to open businesses in their spare time.

En'owkin

Native militancy made daily newspaper items through the 1970s. Hand-painted signs appeared at the gates of reserves, to remind drivers that they were about to drive onto Native land. Sometimes taking their models from the American Indian Movement, young Natives put on feathers and made themselves highly visible at municipal meetings. In 1975 at Penticton, Native people from the Penticton Okanagan Reserve and elsewhere occupied the local office of the Department of Indian Affairs. Their message was that they pretty well understood how to address problems of housing and welfare and education. They told reporters and politicians that they wanted to be directors rather than clients.

When the people closed down the Indian Affairs office, they looked around and saw that coming together as a community suggested two things: as Okanagan Natives they could make an impact on the surrounding non-Native world, and they could tap ancient social ways to improve their own sense of power and pride. They could make it manifest that surviving Okanagan traditions did not have to be viewed as something that had to disappear if people wanted to get ahead in the world.

The Okanagan elders from bands all up and down the Canadian side of the valley met with the politicized young, and held conferences about their future. They decided that the highest priority would be given to education, not just for the young but for people of every age, and not just in subjects that would help Natives make way in the non-Native world, but in subjects that would make them aware of both versions of their own history. Thus was born the idea for the En'owkin Centre.

"En'owkin" is a stately word in Okanagan, and is not easily translated into English. But it refers to a process of consultation whereby people come together and figure out how to overcome problems, not by debate but, as the Okanagan writer Jeanette Armstrong says, by exchanging views to find out how the community thinks. The En'owkin Centre is in the middle of Penticton. It is a good place, because the name of the city means something like "the place where people can live the year round."

The En'owkin Centre is a school and a resource centre, a social gathering place and a publishing house. It began as a place to gather Okanagan minds, but is now a campus for students and teachers from aboriginal communities across Canada. Jeanette Armstrong, the great-niece of Mourning Dove, is a director of the school of writing and visual arts, which has an association with the University of Victoria. The writer Beth Cuthand is a Cree from Saskatchewan, and teaches poetry and life writing. Greg Younging is a Cree from Manitoba, and was long-time manager of Theytus Books, the En'owkin publishing house. Since 1980 Theytus has published fiction and poetry and history books, and since 1990 the journal *Gatherings* which is subtitled *The En'owkin Journal of First North American Peoples*, and is an invaluable source for the writings of Native people across the country.

Jeanette Armstrong edited a book called *The Native Creative Process*, which describes the difference between Indian and non-Indian art. The school conducts courses in the Okanagan language. The students and faculty and staff are all Native people. It is different in every way from the residential schools. Students who have had unpleasant experience at other schools are offered a sense of safety in which they can explore their personal, spiritual, and political selves and culture. Their parents or grandparents may have been taken to a residential school, where they were punished for speaking their parents' language, or practising their home community's spiritual traditions.

In describing the militancy that would lead to the creation of the centre, Jeanette Armstrong said that the founders were saying to the larger society: "We're not going to be you, so get used to it."

Blonds on Bikes

Blonds on Bikes contains one long poem along with some shorter pieces. The title poem was almost modelled on one of Jack Kerouac's blues sequences. For fifty-six straight days in 1995, days spent in Denmark and Germany, I riffed a page a day, fast as I could go, keeping a beat that kept trying to shift. Nothing very Okanagan about that.

Of the other sequences and a few lyrics, only two items are really and clearly Okanagan in substance, one being "The Poems of P.B." These three little poems are also to be found in the short story titled "Blithe Trees" (see my earlier note on *The Rain Barrel*).

The little lyric "Fall Bird" carries quite a bit of weight for its size. On the simple Canadian-observation-poem side, one sees that it was sketched or inscribed in Oliver on October 12, 1991. But in the first line we see a kind of John Skelton move, as the little late bird is called a "fellow," thus suggesting, if not an identification of speaker and spoken-to, at least a fellowship. Then the speaker (and I will admit that he sounds a lot like me) contrasts that association with the estrangement between him and the human beings who stay put throughout the year.

So we hear what I have often felt, the old feeling that the South Okanagan is my body's natural *locus*, along with the awareness that I am a kind of ghost there when I make my semi-annual visits.

Fall Bird

Last little fellow
of the year, cold
edge on clouds, the rest
have flown south,
he didn't notice, who's
to talk to, all the people
I see are too busy
with their own lives,
they live here all year,
you better get going
even if you don't
know where.

Oliver
12/10/91

His Life, a Poem

The structure of this book-length poem ensured that it would have lots of Okanagan references. It is based on my diary, which I started keeping in 1958. The poem was handwritten in a nice Italian ledger that was given to me in 1978. I started writing the poem in 1988. I finished the first draft in 1998.

I decided that I could get an unplanned biography of sorts, of the poet, in the third person, by heaven knows whom, his friend George, possibly. In other words, one needed a way to avoid writing "My Life," just as one had been trying so diligently not to "write what one knows." Could one encounter the unexpected in a diary? Dear me!

I decided that I would find the entries for every equinox and every solstice, and derive a poem from whatever I found there. But how to avoid the other trap of narrative? I would not use the diary in chronological order, but open the volumes at random. In order not to remember where I had last gone, I would write only one entry a month. So you see no deterministic order but a happy choice that had me finish the trip in exactly a decade, thirty years of a life caught in 120 pages of poetry, written spatially rather than timewise, if you see my meaning.

There is a thorough description of the poem's composition in *How I Wrote Certain of My Books*, published by Mansfield Press in 2011.

Curiously, if I were an innocent reader of this book, I would read it chronologically to see how the relationship of figure and ground develops. You never know. Here are some poems that show that relationship.

Winter 1958. Oliver

A legend
beginning to fade,
a noisy family
in a town without snow.

He can't flick his ashes in the fireplace.
It is a new electric heater.
You have entered the hill-straits—
a sea treads upon the hill-slopes.
There is nothing exactly
to do all day.
And yesterday went with the ice.

Winter 1959. Oliver

He and Willy had a few beers
at the Oliver Hotel. Then they drove
Windy Bone and the other Indian to their horses.

What note shall we pitch?
We have a song,
on the bank we share our arrows;
the loosed string tells our note.

Sally is working nights and he is working days.
They haven't seen one another for a long time.
Apparently a man died in her arms last night.

No coffee or poetry for him any more.
No more buzzing words in his ear.

Willy wondered whether they would see them
    leave. But Windy
wanted them to ride their horses in the crisp moon.

No, they said, thank you, Windy, but no.

Summer 1961. Oliver

The sun is down, he stands
fully awake
            and wonders what sleep is

in this vapidity, no .one
living in his hometown desires

anything but the new television,
they wish to see no further

than a man on a horse, a man
with a gun, a father who after all

did know best.
                He, on the other hand,
knows nothing, he's twenty-five, he

was the only person in the house
who watched *The Human Voice* of

Cocteau last night. He's writing a novel,
he thinks, no one else does, but

he only watches the ball game, he
keeps score and announces the hitters.

He likes the word "cerebral," he
uses it while characterizing his townspeople.

"Spring"† 1962. Oliver

Unable to stop the jangle in his heart,
he carries home from the small familiar post office
two fat letters from his darling today,
three in two days, oh wings,

alas he has them not, not
swift, a bird,
set of God
among the bird-flocks!

Her letters come to him in the desert
from a non-existent place, words
out of nowhere near the green sea.

She barely exists while he loses
these precious summer days away from her,

¡que lástima!
          and what an empty sky.

But he is home, and who is this
inside him now, hurting his body inside,
echoing the pain where wings would be?

†An error. Actually summer.

Winter 1963. Oliver

Pry apart the timid souls
he said, driving 450 miles

of frozen roads, the Rockies
behind them now, A

weeping for the young dog
dead at the vet's, a likely

incompetent. Here the new
puppies help her, and here

family banality and snow, what
a relief, calamity beyond belief.

But tobogganing on the old
golf course, his father behind,

they set a record pace, and jumped
into somersault, into snow crash,

dad flying over him, fetched
his ear a wallop with his boot,

the other people laughing their
heads off at the top of the hill.

Spring 1971. Oliver

Horsing around like a man, he grew excited
driving into the Valley, Valley folk
love capital Vees, Tenney in the car,
out of the car, they can walk
without coats, a little ice on the lakes.

Home was never sickness as other places
were, yesterday they all looked
at his grade two house in Greenwood, fresh
bushes behind it. Here he meets his
sister-in-law and niece, one of whom

promptly and silently pees in his lap.
His dad went curling and he observed,
and then placed Tenney on the midnight bus.
It is plainly ordinary in his mountain
fastness, he walked to his brother's place

giving thought to buying a pre-fab house.

Winter 1978. Kaleden

He washed and dried her hair and now
she looks gorgeous,

a seven-year-old daughter,
Okanagan light through blonde:

she got off the Greyhound,

        a suitcase in her hand,
        her back straight,
        pure food in her stomach,
        no buzz in her voice.

The Dutch in front of them
were thankful to have seen

        mountains full of snow,
        a road black tires make
        every minute of the way.

Here over this dark lake
the dainty dogs scamper indoors,

the little girl waits
till they bound into her lap.

Fall 1983. Oliver

Home town is the still
centre he's been getting away from
all these widening circles, these

men, John the director and
Doug the camera man and somebody
younger the sound man.

Roy the friend the consultant
and Pearl the mom. A simple
little movie, the orchard, the

ballpark, the dried mud, the
late slanting sunlight, the nouns
a little place is made of. A kid

never did come back to be filmed,
just this middle-aged man, all
excited, as if *he* were the kid,

as if he had brought those
tender stinking wings
to earth.

George Harry, Jabez Harry, and Ewart Harry in Oliver, circa 1955.

A Magpie Life

In the latter half of my life I got interested in writing memoirs, especially if I could write short pieces and gather them according to subjects. Sometimes, as in *Cars*, the book as project would be invented beforehand; in a book such as *A Magpie Life* I would work more the way that bird does. The book is subtitled *Growing a Writer*, and that is its narrative focus, if we may use such an ambitious term.

Contemporary Authors is an outfit in the United States that publishes big volumes for libraries and charges a lot of money for them. Some of these volumes collect essays and reviews about writers from around the world, and others are devoted to autobiographical essays. When I was approached I decided to write my essay in alphabetical order, and called it "Alphabiography." The fifth entry is "Ewart Bowering," and is about my father. He shows up again in another essay "Deking Dad," the story of the sneaky way I became a sportswriter. It was written for *In 2 Print*, Jean Baird's arts magazine for high school kids, in which I was lucky enough to be featured. I thought it made sense to explain how I became a teenage writer.

Late in the twentieth century I wrote a novel, *Shoot!*, that took place late in the nineteenth century. In the earlier novel, *Burning Water*, which takes place late in the eighteenth century, I included as narrative some of the stuff that the novelist was doing and thinking while writing the story. For *Shoot!* I did what other novelists have done, kept a journal connected to the writing of the novel. Even though the main story takes place in Shuswap country, the writer grew up among hills just to their south. Unfriendly critics have sometimes admonished me for parachuting into my narrative; I could not resist calling my diary of a novel "Parashoot!"

Ewart

Ewart Bowering was my father, and he died on March 12, 1975. His funeral was held at the United Church in Oliver, on the Ides of March. I held my mother's hand and my sister's hand, hard. We were in the front row, privileged and vulnerable. I thought I heard his voice saying, "It's all right."

He was just my father, but now I have come to know and to admit that he is a kind of hero to me, a standard against which I measure my behaviour. When I was younger I maintained this story—that he was a very smart and promising man who settled for less because it was the Depression. He was smarter than all his brothers and sisters but he always got along with them well, playing bridge, working summers in the orchard.

He was a preacher's son and an athlete. I have his small-town newspaper clippings in which he is usually the best player in the basketball game, or he got two singles in the baseball game. I have his first school inspector's reports, in which he is praised for his dedication and chided for his shortcomings as a disciplinarian. He had blue eyes and a straight nose. He was just about six feet tall and handsome. My mother was a schoolgirl athlete from a hillbilly family and she snagged him.

He was a quiet man who paid a lot of attention to his community. He coached young people's basketball teams and softball teams. He was secretary-treasurer of the Elks Club but he seldom had a drink; he organized their Save the Children fund. He worked on the committee to get the new hospital in Oliver. He started the fire every morning. He never drove over the speed limit. He wrote sports reports for the small-town newspapers when he got to be too old to play them. He took off

My father appears to be reading Revelations.
He was a preacher's son but I never saw him
in church except at funerals and weddings.

his shirt and in his undershirt built our house. He didn't like it when people said "nucular" or made plurals out of apostrophes.

He was the chemistry teacher at Southern Okanagan High School. I had to take a senior science course to graduate, so I took chemistry. I got fifty-six percent in chemistry. At school I called him Sir and he called me Bowering. After his funeral we went to the desert cemetery up Fairview Road in Oliver, and I broke away from the cluster of family and put my lips to his casket. I was surprised at myself.

Deking Dad

Is it just me, or have you noticed this, too? It seems as if every time successful writers or artists write magazine pieces or undergo interviews or give conference talks full of advice for young writers or artists, they like to recall being antisocial troublemakers when they were kids. Somehow being an antisocial troublemaker is a good sign that you are going to grow up to be a successful writer or artist.

My old friend the successful writer Susan Musgrave confessed to a misspent youth in an article in *In 2 Print*. In high school she necked with her boyfriend in biology class, forged notes from her parents, and dropped some mind-expanding drugs on the beach. Heck, I knew someone who did all those things, too, except that the necking took place in math class. This guy is now washing windshields in the Esso station in my home town.

My mother still lives in my home town. It's called Oliver, British Columbia, on the government maps, and Lawrence in my short stories. My mother often tells people that when I was a high school kid I made her life miserable with my antisocial behaviour. I don't remember it that way at all. I always thought of myself as a secret lonely hero of virtue. Okay, I did get expelled from school a few times. In grade ten I got expelled for walking to the water fountain when they played "God Save the King," and for sticking anti-King notes in the library books. I figured this was an example of virtue: I was sticking up for a free Canada. In grade eleven I got expelled for organizing a bunch of classmates to refuse to buy another textbook halfway through the school year. I forget what I got expelled for in grade twelve. They let me into the school to write my final exams, and then out I went.

I wasn't a juvenile delinquent. In fact I once had the ambition to be a policeman, to fight crime the way my hero Batman did, to make the world safe for virtue. This ambition came to an end one day in Penticton, British Columbia, when I saw the peculiar way the policemen there got a Native man out of a restaurant and into a police car. At that moment I thought: someone ought to be writing about this. But meanwhile I was nearly always in trouble at school. I just could not keep quiet when I thought of a funny remark. I may not have been a juvenile delinquent, but I was the class clown. I could often be found standing in the hall outside a classroom I had been ejected from, or hauling rocks from the schoolyard to the rock pile. This was back when you could get punished at school. I got the strap three times, twice on the hands, once elsewhere.

The situation was a little tough on my family. My father was the chemistry teacher at that high school. He was sort of my hero.

I mean Oliver, British Columbia, was a dinky little place surrounded by orchards in the Okanagan Valley. My father was the only person I ever saw writing something. He wrote stuff on an old square black portable typewriter that he never even took out of the case, just plunked it on his little desk and opened the lid. I loved that typewriter. My father typed with his two middle fingers because he had cut his right forefinger off with a power saw. For about twenty years I typed with my middle fingers, too. I also shot a .22 rifle at Air Cadets with my right middle finger, having watched my father. My father was kind of my wounded hero. When he was umpiring baseball games it often looked as if he was indicating one-and-a-half strikes.

Here's what he typed with those two middle fingers, while he hummed some corny old dad song: sports. He was the baseball and basketball reporter for the Oliver *Chronicle* and the Penticton *Herald*. Once I learned how to make that typewriter work, I never thought of being a policeman or anything else that involved moving people from one place to another. I wanted to be a sportswriter. Forget lonely virtue, I decided, how can I ease my father out of this sportswriting job?

The teenage newspaperman. I had a green fedora with a "Press" card stuck in the band. That's my father's old brown leather jacket.

I ought to mention that I copied him in various other ways, too. He was always reading when he wasn't teaching school or picking apples or playing cards with my mother. The daily newspaper, the *Star Weekly*, including its pre-publication "novels," Erle Stanley Gardner mysteries, baseball magazines, teachers' magazines, novels about surgeons in the U.S. Civil War, and so on. I asked him about the weekly comics, and he said he read them all except "Jane Arden," so I quit reading "Jane Arden." Every week there was a cut-out dress with tabs that your sister could put on her cardboard Jane. It was also from my father that I learned that you should carry something to read in case you got stuck in a lineup at the post office.

I managed to deke him out of his sportswriting jobs, though. It started with reading. My parents got me a subscription to *Sport* magazine for Christmas. I still have every copy that ever came in the mail. Pretty soon I was spending all my change on baseball and hockey magazines. I would read every article from beginning to end, and I would read every inch of the sports pages in the Vancouver *Sun*, and pretty soon I knew how to be a sportswriter. First I wrote up some of my own versions of the ball games the Oliver teams were playing. Then I started sitting with my father while he was doing his business as "official scorekeeper." That sounded really good. At the high school basketball games in the winter we sat at a courtside table, along with the timekeeper, across from the bleachers. But baseball had its own excitement: we climbed up through a trap door onto the roof of the shaky old wooden grandstand, and crept right up to the front, to a little boarded-in room with a chicken-wire front, right over home plate. Sometimes my father let me keep score, and sometimes I filled in on the public address while the regular guy was away getting soft ice cream.

By the time I was sixteen, I was the Official Scorer and the reporter for the *Chronicle* and the *Herald*. From the *Chronicle* I got fifteen cents an inch for my stories, but from the *Herald* I was pulling in twenty-five cents an inch. My father showed me how to cut out the stories and measure them and send them in for my cheque every month.

I wasn't antisocial. I was a sportswriter. I was doing something no one else I knew was doing. I was the only sportswriter in town. Cool, I thought, because that was the word we used way back then.

So I was going to be a sportswriter. I even carried my editor's camera and made my own pictures for the paper. My buddy Will and I had a darkroom in his basement. We were the only photographer kids in town.

But I was reading a lot of different things, and sports wasn't the only thing I was writing. I read just about every western novel published in the twentieth century. I read science fiction and sports novels. The first poetry book I ever bought by myself was written by a sportswriter. I still have it. Okay, I could be a sportswriter *and* a poet. I would be the only poet in town. As it turned out I was the only poet in the Okanagan Valley, until Pat Lane showed up, a guy with a cigarette in his mouth, a pool cue in one hand, and a pen in the other. Now *there* was a juvenile delinquent. But he was from the North Okanagan. Now he is a very successful poet.

There was a weekly newspaper put out by students in my school. It was called *The Scroll*. I didn't have anything to do with it, because I was a professional reporter. But I did work on the school annual. And I did publish poems in the school annual. One of my favourites was forty stanzas long, all about headhunters in Malacca. To this day I don't know whether there were any headhunters in that part of the world. In those days there weren't any creative writing teachers in high school advising you to write about what you know. Thank goodness. If you write about what you know, you will keep on writing the same thing, and you will never know any more than you do now.

Whenever writer kids ask me what to write about I always tell them: try writing about something you don't know. And while you are at it, I say, forget that creative writing advice about using your own voice. Listen for some strange voice, I tell them. Look at the successful poet David McFadden, I tell them. He is always writing stuff he doesn't know anything about, and he is always swiping someone else's voice to write it in. He's really good, just like Susan Musgrave and Pat Lane.

When he was a kid in Hamilton, Ontario, he was usually doing something no one else in town was doing, as far as he knew.

I'll tell you something I used to do when I was twelve, as an example. In those days Nabisco Shredded Wheat used to come in that box of twelve with grey rectangles of cardboard between the layers of biscuits. Three cardboards to a box. We ate a lot of Shredded Wheat in our family.

I found out that the letter-writing paper my parents used was just the right size to cover one side of one of those grey cardboard things, with enough overlap to glue the edges on the back. It was nice paper. It was called "linen." I used it to start my famous comic strip characters collection. The comic strips in those days were quite a lot like the movies. An earlier invention of mine was the shoebox theatre: I would get a few months' worth of some comic strip such as "Steve Canyon," and glue them end to end, and make a reel to crank through a slot at one end of a shoebox. There would be a skylight right over the strip and a peephole at the other end of the shoebox. Most of the movies I saw when I was in grade three were showing in my shoebox theatre.

Anyway, I was saying that the comic strips were like the movies. For instance, some of the panels would have close-ups of the characters. I decided that I would put five close-ups on each of my famous characters cards. I used the window to trace with pencil and eventually used my father's India ink to finish off the job. So one of my cards might have pictures of Steve Canyon, Little Lulu, Donald Duck, Dagwood and Wonder Woman.

They were beautiful. I made about forty of them. I don't have a clue where they went. I also don't know where my homemade Big League Baseball game records and statistics went. I don't know why exactly, but when I make poems or stories now I feel a lot like the way I felt when I was making those comic strip cards, and I was the only person in town making them. I have found out that other writers used to make peculiar things when they were kids. David McFadden and I are big fans of Jack Kerouac, the French-Canadian writer who happened to be born and raised in the United States, and when Jack Kerouac was a kid he made all kinds of things—baseball leagues, adventure magazines, theatrical plays. He was the only kid in Lowell, Massachusetts, making these things.

Jack and David and I were nerds, I guess. Nowadays we think of nerd kids as computer freaks, making weird games and other programs. But they are not the only kids in town doing it. The real McCoy might be that strange young person down in the family basement making a relief map of Canada out of dry pasta. If I had to bet on who would turn out to be a successful writer—the pasta kid or all those people making a big noise at the 7-Eleven parking lot—I would bet on the pasta kid.

Poems for Men

The first book of poetry I ever read was volume ten of a set of books my parents had. There were volumes on geography and wildlife and astronomy and so on. Each volume was a separate colour, and volume ten was pink. I read all the books, but it was volume ten that got beaten up with use. When I think back on my childhood I am kind of surprised by that. I didn't actually buy a book of poetry till I was fifteen.

I didn't have much money to buy stuff, but I bought comic books, mainly *Detective Comics* and *Batman* and *World's Finest*. These three all had the Caped Crusader in them. My mother made me get rid of them. I never let her forget how much a *World's Finest* number one would sell for now. When I was eleven I decided that it was time to start buying movie magazines. I didn't know that boys didn't buy movie magazines. I went down to Frank's and bought *Screen Gems* and *Photoplay* for a year, reading about Lana Turner, and gazing at still photos of movies I would never see.

When I was twelve I went down to Frank's and bought sports magazines, starting with *Sport*. The first one I ever bought had Frank Brimsek on the cover, and it would be a long time till they had another hockey player there. I bought *Sport Life* and *Baseball Digest* and all the rest. It was a hobby I kept up till I was about twenty-three. I still have piles of those magazines, and I am starting to look for someone to sell them to.

When I was fifteen I went to Frank's and bought my first book of poems. Frank's was one of the two poolrooms in Oliver. The other one had a café in front. Frank's was a poolroom with a one-chair barber and a tobacco stand up front. It had an old dark wooden floor. Frank did not specialize in poetry books. He sold mainly twenty-five cent westerns, many of which I spent my pin-setting money on.

But when I was fifteen I bought *Poems for Men* by Damon Runyon. It was published by Permabooks of Garden City, New York. Permabooks were thirty-five cents each, and when they started they had those stiff covers you would find on children's picture books, though *Poems for Men* has a normal poolroom paperback cover.

Until I was twenty-two I always gave books away after I had read them. But when I was twenty-six I found a used copy of *Poems for Men*, and I have kept this one. People always hint that they would like to have it, but all they get is permission to read a poem or two.

Of course I knew Damon Runyon from the sports magazines. Next to Grantland Rice, he was my favourite sportswriter, and I wanted to be a sportswriter. I had read a lot of Runyon's short stories. My whole idea of New York City came from the settings and characters of Damon Runyon. Still does. Last year I flew to Phoenix to see a spring training baseball game. That night I stayed in my hotel and watched the movie of *Guys and Dolls* on television.

Damon Runyon joined the army when he was fourteen, and went to the Philippines to join the USAmerican war against Spain. A lot of his poems are about ordinary soldiers:

Scenery there was plenty, sir, the like I never have seen:
Some of it struck me as brownish-like, and some of it mighty green.
Some of the roads were muddy, sir, and some of them pretty fine,
As I hiked up with Dickman—old Joe Dickman—to the Rhine!

Now I am kind of hoping that in terms of form and diction I was never influenced by Damon Runyon. I never looked for a girlfriend like Lana Turner, either. But I respect Damon Runyon and the world he invented. I have never been able to decide whether his ballads are naive or cynical. I would find enough of the cynical in the book of poems I bought at Frank's when I was seventeen, *New Poems by American Poets*, edited by Rolfe Humphries and published at thirty-five cents by Ballantine Books of New York.

Poems for Men is about pool shooters and racehorse bettors and boxing pugs and dice-throwers, as everyone would expect of Damon Runyon. But I first knew Runyon as a baseball writer, and I am pretty sure that though I would be led into all of his New York and other worlds, I first checked out his baseball poems. Say, have you ever heard "Opening Day"?

> There's a bang in the whang
> If the first-round clang
> For a battle of fistic cracks.
> There's a kick in the click
> Of a barrier's flick
> As the horses tear up the tracks.
> There's a thrill in the trill
> Of the whistle shrill
> That starts the football play.
> But, say—
> Give me the thrill
> In the springtime chill
> Of baseball's opening day!

Now you are thinking of the title. I often have, ever since I first saw it. I guess that in 1951, poetry, like opera and flower shows, was mainly for women, eh? Keats and Dickinson—you can understand that. But men didn't have to shy away from the idea totally, not as long as there was a "Cremation of Sam McGee," or Damon Runyon's card sharps and racetrack touts, inhabiting ballads that bounced between witticism and pathos.

An Okanagan caballero at twenty.

Parashoot! Diary of a Novel

Whenever I pass through dry country, big stones, few trees, maybe sagebrush and cactus, the thought comes to me that this is the way landscape is supposed to be, or this is the way God meant the world to look. Growing up in that kind of country, though, I read the Bible and other such books, and there it was, God's original plan, the Garden of Eden. When Adam and Eve and all the rest of us got thrown out, it was into a kind of desert they got thrown. All through the Bible, whenever people are thrown out somewhere it is always into the desert. Of course, where the Bible was written just about all the country looks like the desert.

Where I grew up it looked a lot like the landscape in western movies. We played western movies a lot, with six-guns and all, but no horses. It helped a lot to be able to crouch with your six-gun behind a clump of real sagebrush. We wore neckerchiefs all the time. When we wanted something we pulled the neckerchiefs up under our eyes.

I didn't think of it as landscape. It was just the valley and especially the hills. There were a lot of plants I didn't know the name of, but I recognized them. I knew where there were caves. I knew what spoor was, from the books I read after I got home in the dusk. I knew what coyote shit looked like.

My mother had an interesting attitude to my solo excursions. I would often come home with dried blood on my skin and hair and clothes, but she never went into a routine about it. She would notice and then go back to her activities, dumping coffee grounds out the window over the sink, for instance. I never broke a bone running the rock slides, but I lost quite a volume of blood over the years.

I keep reading about how important bitterroot is to the Interior Salish people. It is, I read, a somewhat sacred plant, a medicinal food known to the Shuswap and all the various Okanagan bands. I read that it is the first plant gathered in the spring, that women and their daughters go up the hills and gather bitterroot on a quest that is both sacramental and famine-breaking after the snows and pit houses of winter.

For a long time I wondered what bitterroot looks like.

One of the important bitterroot places for the Okanagans is White Lake, in the hills south of Penticton. It is above the spot where the falls used to be just past the southern end of Skaha Lake. It happens that the filmmaker and poet Colin Browne made a movie about the White Lake area. His grandfather was a white pioneer in the area.

Colin Browne wrote a book of poetry called *Abraham*. It needs a glossary because Colin Browne is an erudite poet, and luckily it has one. There it is explained that bitterroot is also called rock rose. That's what we called it. Rock rose.

§

When I was a boy in the Okanagan Valley I looked around a lot. Never knew what I was looking for. Never found arrowheads or ancient Spanish coins in the dust. Found a skeleton once and put the rocks back on top. Found a little pistol once and kept it till it disappeared on me. Found a necklace made of Dutch money. But no one ever told me what to look for. I was scared of McLeans from the rumours I had heard, and I kept an eye out for them. Kenny McLean wasn't in my school anymore. I started to wonder whether he was a ghost that came and sat in my classroom for part of a winter.

There was an old woman who lived in a falling-down log house with a framed veranda. It had hollyhocks all around the veranda. A friend of mine told me that this old woman told someone that she once fed Jesse James and gave him a place to sleep overnight. Jesse was supposed to be dead with a bullet in his back, but that was all rigged. Jesse was still alive, and a lot of people knew it. Maybe the law knew it, too, but if Jesse stayed out of bank robbing they were going to let the legend continue the way it was continuing, Jesse shot in the back while he straightened a picture. When you come to think of it, was Jesse James going to turn his back on a man with a gun and straighten a picture?

So what about the McLeans? When I was a boy I was not told anything about the Okanagan Valley, but I learned a lot about the James gang and the Daltons and the Clantons. All those wild and dangerous brothers from Missouri, where my grandfather had been a boy. But what about the McLeans? Did they escape? Did Archie McLean escape? Is that a true story about the Kanaka hangman and the severed ropes and the quick horses?

When I was a boy I knew that the James gang and the Daltons were buried deep in history. That was an old, old woman who had fed Jesse and given him a bed overnight. But I kept my eyes out for McLeans. I kept my eyes open for McLeans whether they were a gang of gunslingers on the vengeance trail, or peaceful men living out their lives in the hayfields, or ghosts. I did not believe in ghosts, but I believed in God. Still, if there was a God, there was a book about him, and in that book there were a lot of stories about things that can happen even if they are hard to believe. You have to want to believe such things, I had somehow learned.

I still want to believe some things that are hard to believe. There are no gravestones for the Wild McLeans. The field where they were buried no longer exists. Who would hang a fifteen-year-old boy?

In the beer parlour in Lawrence, there is a karaoke machine in one corner, but no pool tables anymore. Now the tables do not have cigarette-burned terry cloth on them. Now there are framed pictures of famous locals all around the walls. If you look at the pictures it will not be long until you find a photograph of Windy Bone. Windy Bone is the most famous Indian in Lawrence. I don't know how old he is, but whatever his age is, he doesn't look that old. I have never heard anyone call Windy Bone an Elder. If you keep looking at the framed pictures on the walls in the beer parlour you will keep on finding pictures of Windy.

They try to call it a bar now. They once tried to call it a lounge. Someone once tried to call it a beverage room. It is one of the two beer parlours in Lawrence.

In a lot of the pictures Windy Bone is sitting on a palomino. He is wearing a wide-brimmed hat that casts his face in romantic western shadow under the bright Okanagan sun.

It is afternoon, and Windy Bone is sitting at a table in the cool shade of the beer parlour. He has a glass of beer in front of him, but he isn't drinking it. Windy says he doesn't drink beer anymore, but he likes to sit here with a glass. Before they closed the two pool halls in Lawrence, Windy Bone was the best pool shark in town. Bang, the eight ball would be gone, and Windy wasn't even looking when he shot it.

He is wearing his hat, a black stetson with silver conches making up the band around it. He is wearing strong riding boots that were polished not too long ago. He has a handsome nose and slightly puffed cheeks now. He slouches in his beer chair. If you are not too shy he will tell you stories. He does not usually tell you the legends you might expect, or the true tales you might expect. Windy has a sense of humour that tells you that you had better be content to be a white man surrounded by irony. A lot of white people in Lawrence say that Windy's a "character." They mean to be comfortable and patronizing. Boy, are they dumb!

Here is Windy Bone's account of the Indian method for catching wild deer.

An Indian rides into deer country, and leaves his horse tethered to a tree. Then he finds himself a nice spot in the shade and waits for a deer to show up. Indians are very silent and patient. When a deer shows up the Indian waits for a while. Lets the deer get over his anxiety and start cropping grass. Then the Indian begins his stalking. He is very quiet and extremely patient, making very small moves, stopping after every move to blend in with the scenery. Once in a while the deer lifts his head with the antlers on it and sniffs the air. But the Indian is blending with the scenery and he is downwind.

It takes a long time, but the Indian is slowly sneaking up on the deer. Now he is just a few steps behind him, blending in. Now comes the hardest part, and this part is what makes an Indian different from a white man. The Indian has to get right up behind the deer without the deer's noticing. Now there is nothing to hide behind.

The Indian makes a careful step and stops. The deer doesn't see him. The Indian is right behind him but the deer is looking in every other direction. Now the Indian is right behind the deer. He can reach out and touch him if he wants to. In one patient and unseen motion the Indian raises his right arm. His first finger is pointing right at the deer. The deer's tail is up. That's the way deer are. In one movement the Indian puts his finger right into the deer's hole. Quick, before the deer can move, the Indian crooks his finger.

Then the deer moves. Well, most people have seen how a deer can move. He can go from standing still and maybe quivering a little, to jumping through the forest in no time flat. You can't see him warming up. He is just gone.

This is where the Indian pays for his deer. The deer is jumping over rocks and under pine trees and between cactuses. The Indian maybe weighs just about as much as the deer, maybe a little less. He's hanging on for dear life, his finger crooked. Every time the deer comes down, the Indian comes down on rocks or cactuses or greasewood. Every time the deer jumps again, the Indian's arm is nearly torn off, and he has to concentrate all his attention on his finger. All his body's strength has to keep that finger crooked. When the deer is coming down the Indian tries to get his feet on the ground, take a few fast steps. But then he's off again.

The deer is hauling somebody that's just about his own weight. The jumps get shorter and lower. After a while the deer's taking a few steps between the jumps, and the Indian can get on his feet and run for a while. Now the deer is just walking fast. He can't jump any more. Pretty soon he can't walk either. This is when the Indian congratulates the deer for a good run, and then he has him. If he hasn't lost his knife along the way.

"That's the Indian way of deer hunting," says Windy.

"I never knew that."

"There's only one thing to look out for."

"I would have thought there were a lot of things to look out for," says the white man.

"Only one thing to look out for."

"What's that?"

"That deer, if he suddenly decides to take a quick left turn, all you've got is a brown finger," says Windy Bone, looking at the full glass of beer on his table.

Cars

Ryan Knighton, the funny blind memoirist, was my student in a few courses at Simon Fraser University. Then he was my friend in a beer parlour group called Dads and Tads, which comprised, among others, George Stanley, Willy Trump, Jamie Reid, and Maria Hindmarch among the former, and Wayde Compton, Karina Vernon, Reg Johanson, and Anne Stone among the latter. Then he was my co-editor in a little poetry magazine called *Tads*. Eventually, Ryan became my collaborator in a book of one-page memories about automobiles.

We wrote fifty pages each, commenting on one another's panels, as we called them, this Fraser Valley kid and this superannuated Okanagan Valley kid. I haven't checked to see how many of his pieces are about the Fraser Valley, but I can tell you that thirteen of my fifty are about the Okanagan Valley. Of course. That is where I learned to drive on an orchard tractor and where I first drove a lovely girl home.

from Cars

As the mercury climbs in the South Okanagan these days, such as August 11, 2001, people are awfully glad they can take their air-conditioning for granted, though of course I haven't had air conditioning in my 1990 Volvo for three summers. What does it matter? In 1959 there wasn't any air conditioning in the South Okanagan, but there were Fahrenheit degrees, lots of them. What you wished for was a convertible, and while you were at it, why not a Cadillac convertible? My

The Bowering boys, Jim, George, and Roger. I would later buy this car from my father and drive it to Veracruz. It's a two-tone green 1954 Chev Bel Air.

buddy Willy would say to a girl from Osoyoos, maybe, want to go for a spin in my snappy red convertible, and what he had was a 1954 Morris Minor with the top sawed off. This was the best joke going in the South Okanagan that summer, and to tell the truth, I was envious. A year later his stepfather had some more sawing done—well, he used to have a machine shop—and it became the smallest pickup truck in that part of the valley. Willy used it for everything. Imagine, sitting in a red Morris Minor pickup truck, ogling girls we knew.

One day a few years ago I was driving north just about at the north end of Vaseaux Lake and nearly hit a beautiful deer that was bouncing across the road in front of my car. It was the spot where my mother got hit by the flying cow. There was a dent in the front of our light green 1947 Plymouth, and my mother said a cow came flying into the front of the car. They don't fly, cows, she was informed. It must have been hit by a car coming in the opposite direction, was her conclusion. Mostly, over all these years, we have believed her, about that and other things. But one dark night we were getting ready to go home after an evening of badminton at the high school gym, my mother and I. This is how we got a dent in the back of the Plymouth. My mother backed up confidently into the rear corner of a pickup, and there was a kind of car-thunk sound. "Who put that thing there?" asked my mother. I use that line sometimes now. Once I heard my father say it when he stubbed his toe on a railroad track.

If you are going to have a head-on collision, have it at as low a speed as possible under the circumstances—that's my advice. This was how my red 1972 Datsun came to an end. It was the first new car I ever bought—twenty-five hundred dollars, with money from a novel I optioned to a filmmaker who never did. So here I was, at or really nearly at my familiar drive from Vancouver to Oliver, to see my mom in the late seventies, I guess. This would be at her new place, with her second husband Bob, up the hill a little from Oliver's little old airstrip. I was on the only straight stretch in Highway 97, getting ready to turn right, when a car coming south turned into my lane, no signal or anything, you know that nightmare. I stepped on the brake as hard as I could, thanking some being or luck that I was alone, my wife and daughter back in Van. Well, he didn't seem to share my attitude toward braking, and if I went left I'd be in a worse head-on, and to the right was a deep ditch and probably this guy still coming. Well, I can tell you, the sound of a collision is hateful. But there we were. The inside of a 1972 Datsun is not commodious, and I banged my forehead against the metal strip at the top edge of the windshield. Still, I was conscious enough to pick up the outside rear-view mirror that had been inside for a while, and drop it out the window. So the guy in the other car is also alive, and glory-be, he was to blame, a hundred percent. He was a thin guy in his eighties. I thought there was a side road there, he said. Well, I said, there isn't, and even if there was, you are required to wait until I am gone before you turn left across the highway. Now it turns out that he has no driver's licence because he did this kind of thing too often, and had it taken away from him. Even better—he turns out to be a retired dentist who years before had led a campaign including letters to the editor against me and my Oliver *Chronicle* column because I was a Communist agent and he was the local leader of Ron Gostick's Canadian Intelligence Service, a religious Cold War outfit that warned against communists, atheists, Jews, homosexuals, feminists, intellectuals, and hippies. Boy! My brother took me to the new hospital to check out my head, and took my picture in the waiting room, and I used that picture in an anthology the next year. The insurance people gave me about two thousand dollars for my car, but now it was years later and any little Japanese car would cost about ten thousand dollars. However, the only really sad part was that the radio in my Datsun was famous for its ability to pull in radio stations from halfway across the continent. My brother and my friends Dwight and Paul said I should have gone to the wrecking yard in OK Falls and snagged that radio.

By now it is just about universally agreed that 1948 was the greatest year in the history of civilization. Partly this has to do with Dior's New Look, partly with the Cleveland Indians' pitching rotation, partly even with *The Treasure of the Sierra Madre*. Plus this: have you had a relaxed look at a 1948 Mercury coupé? They can try all they want to but they will never make an automobile that looks as good as that. Especially if it is that dark blue that looks a little purple in the dry Okanagan sunlight. Were they ever any other colour? Anyway—in the summer of 1949 I loaded up my Baby Brownie and went all around Oliver and environs taking pictures of every kind of 1948 car I could find. Sometimes I had to wait for tourists or visiting baseball players to stop in town. I had to wait till 1949 because hardly anyone in Oliver ever had a brand new car. My father had quite a few cars, one after the other, but he never in his life had a brand new car. I still have those square black-and-white snapshots, a couple dozen of them. I'll bet that half of those car names don't exist any more. I was a camera boy when I was twelve. A lot of the less intelligent boys in Oliver were nuts about cars. I wasn't interested in the cars—just the pictures of the cars.

Well, Willy and I were in the back of the car, my father driving and my mother also up front. Now, Willy and I had been trying to figure out how the sunset works on a moon of Uranus, and where west is. Because Uranus tumbles along its trip around the sun—that is, its orbit is on the same plane as its rotation, and then it has a number of moons, all of them but one going around in the same direction as it tumbles. We were wondering about that moon that goes the other way. Well, you can imagine how hard this was to get ahold of while in a car on the way to Penticton. A little later my mother said, "It's not the going there that I mind; it's the getting there." Willy and I started a conversation about that. Should it be "It's not the getting there I mind; it's the going there," or the way my mother had it. We went on and on, arguing in great detail. Then my mother said, "Let's talk about the hemisphere," meaning the stuff we were onto earlier.

I can never remember whether Waterman's Hill is the road going up out of OK Falls or the road coming down into Penticton. We were going up the curvy hill out of OK Falls, my dad driving, my mother in the front seat beside him. I don't know where the rest of us were exactly, except my baby brother Jimmy. I can remember him because he opened the left rear door and there was the surface of the road going by and it looked as if he were going to step right out, probably didn't even understand that we were moving. I don't know what we were doing, probably about 40 mph, and turning a little to the right and still climbing. My dad kept on driving, but as he did so he reached behind him over the seat with his left arm and grabbed little Jimmy by the arm and yanked him back into the car and closed the door and kept the car on the right side of the road, and we drove on to Penticton or Naramata. I was in the back of the car, and while all this stuff was happening so fast I hadn't had time to do anything but see what was happening. It was just like the time my other little brother fell headfirst into the excavation, or the time the kitchen door closed on the kitten's neck and my dad had to take it out of my sight to the garage. I just saw these things happening. This was just another way in which my dad was clearly better than me.

There were two things that were naturally frightening about my father's grey four-door 1936 Ford. Well, it was either a Ford or a Chev. I was always carsick when we went to Summerland or Penticton, so my mother put the slick cold brown paper next to my chest skin. This is not repetition, this is continuity. Big inside of the dark winter car, and you like to remember it as warm, but really it was cold and if you were lucky you got a robe or a blanket or an overcoat to curl up under, but then the colder you were the less carsick, so your mother thought it was worth it to let you roll your window down, though you recognized your father's stoicism and the back of his head. How come your sister never got carsick, never had to puke out the window and along the side of the car (as I did years later in the taxi in downtown Auckland). That, and she got naturally curly hair. *And* she won a prize for her costume in the parade, a bride, for heaven's sake. The first frightening thing. It was still wartime and we lived in a soldier's house in an orchard, with a long gravel driveway to Highway 97. One time my dad had to drive somewhere, into Oliver, probably. I stood on the back bumper and held onto the trunk door, I guess. I thought to steal a ride to the end of the driveway, but now he was going faster and faster and crunching over the gravel. I didn't know that he was going for sure to stop before turning onto the highway. Had to make this choice, let go and not get foot tangled and roll hard in the gravel. Then not go for pity to my mom, because I'd be in trouble, you see? The second. He came home, and it was my sister's turn or job to bring my dad's briefcase from the car. So I pretended to go for it, and she scrambled as fast as she could, this girl, and managed to slam her little finger in the car door. It cut the end of her finger right off, except a hanging bit of skin. So we drove in this car three miles into town to Dr. Cope, and yes, he did sew it back on. I felt terrible, but it was worse than that—they thought I'd slammed the car door on her finger. I don't remember how long it was that they thought I'd done it. And anyway, it was in a way as bad as if I had. But really, I was innocent, really.

I guess that a lot of boys in the Okanagan Valley learned to drive on tractors. You've been working in the orchard for a few years, and eventually some adult gets really busy doing something else, and asks you to bring or take the tractor, maybe with a half a trailer load, somewhere. I learned on a little Ford tractor in an orchard up past the airstrip. Was it red or green or grey? But it would be on the Aikens's big orchard above Naramata that I really got going. Uncle Gerry and my father went on a hunting trip, and I was left in charge of the big grey Oliver tractor. It had only one wheel in front and huge back tires filled with water. My uncle Gerry was the ramrod of Aikens's orchard, and he could have left the Irish guy with the upside-down pipe, Paddy, or someone else to run the tractor. But I got the job. I think they were making me grow up. Forty-five years later I would buy a first edition Gertrude Stein book in a store in Penticton, and it would have John Aikens's signature in it. Well, it was probably the second day when I backed over something sharp and one of the big tires sprang a leak. Now this was the kind of thing that was always happening to me. In the air force I accidentally dyed my gym T-shirt pink and I didn't know it, for example, until the corporal started yelling at me. I was always catching trouble when it wasn't really my fault. But this turned out pretty neat, because what Paddy did was to show me how to operate the old yellow tractor with lugs instead of tires and levers instead of a steering wheel. To turn hard left between trees, you'd brake the left track and turn on a dime. It was like driving a little tank, and I just now remember the satisfactory clanking and grinding noises, and the loud exhaust that pointed straight up. It was so complicated and so enjoyable to back up with a trailer piled high with props on tilted ground around some trees on the edge of a clay cliff with Lake Okanagan below. Who would have thought that work could be so enjoyable? But a week later Uncle Gerry and my dad came back and I had to pick pears.

Cars in my home town. When there was a parade, there would be floats mounted on flatbed trucks, but there would also be a lot of cars with decorations on them going down Oliver's few blocks of main street, which was also Highway 97, and everyone pretty well knew all those cars. A few were antiques but the rest weren't exactly new, either. There were also decorated cars in shorter parades after someone's wedding. People all dressed up would fill them, and the guy in a suit in the driver's seat would be blasting the horn. If the wedding cars went past us kids we would yell all together, "You'll be sorrrrrry!" At the baseball park, before they put up the advertising boards for the outfield fence (which I thought got us a little closer to the big leagues), guys would park their cars in a big semicircle, facing home plate. Then kids like me and Willy would go from car to car, trying to sell Orange Crush and cool popcorn to the families in their automotive bleachers. All their windows were open because it was ninety-five degrees on a Sunday afternoon. Sometimes the P. A. announcer would ask the owner of the blue DeSoto to move it or put a blanket over the windshield because it was flashing in the hitters' eyes. If I didn't write these things down they would be lost from memory in no time, just like the songs Willy and I used to write. There was no drive-in movie or drive-in diner in Oliver, but they had both in Penticton. At the drive-in diner (it was called The Diner) just south of the high school and across the road there was a big sign that said in vertically rectangular capital letters, "FOR SERVICE FLICK YOUR LIGHTS." The *L* was so close to the *I* that it looked as if it said "fuck your lights." I never had the nerve to jump out and pretend to do so. But I hardly ever got to go to The Diner anyway. It was an old train car of some sort, a streetcar, maybe. Something exotic and bumpkinish. Something out of the U.S. comics that we usually didn't get here in the Canadian Okanagan Valley.

How soon after the end of the War did we start getting plastic stuff? It was fascinating, how they could make things out of this new stuff, even though you could see the line where the two halves were put together. It was also really neat when they could put a swirl of a second colour into the first colour. Well, if you do not remember, you cannot imagine. So I don't exactly remember whether Ronnie Carter's little cars and trucks were brightly coloured plastic or brightly painted metal. I think they were probably metal. We shot the shit out of them. There were two things I was not allowed to even think of in my house—motorcycles and rifles. My mother's family seemed to keep dying due to those things. But Ron Carter was like a USAmerican kid in a comic book—he had a Red Ryder Daisy BB gun. Boy, if my mother had only known. Ron Carter's dad was the town baker and also ran the Orchard Cafe, which also had a poolroom in the back, across the alley from the bakery. There was a long wooden gangplank that ran from the back alley into the upstairs of the Orchard Cafe, where I think the Carters must have lived. Now, this is a little hard to remember, but we fired from the gangplank at the little cars and trucks that were situated in a row somewhere, like the different birds you would knock off in that shooting gallery game you had when you were four. Those little metal cars and trucks, including a little tow truck were so beautiful, remember? I especially liked the yellow. That's probably why my favourite colour became yellow, though it took some courage to say so. We would fire away at those little vehicles, and if they were plastic they would get blown apart but if they were metal they would just get little dints or scraped paint. Red was pretty nice, too, especially on trucks.

There was no drive-in movie in Oliver. There was no drive-in restaurant, either, no place to flick your lights. In Penticton, along motel strip there was a drive-in and then there was another one. There was one in Osoyoos eventually. I hardly ever went to a drive-in movie. Well, I didn't have a car, and most of the time I didn't have a driver's licence. In 1958 I went to a drive-in movie somewhere near Merritt with a friend and some girls we met. I don't remember much. I think I was pretty drunk. I think that was the night I came to with the bunkhouse stove all broken apart from the fight I had apparently had with big Jeremy Crowe the Englishman. I do remember, though, going to a drive-in movie theatre in the North Okanagan, probably in Vernon,

Main Street Oliver, looking north, 1953. There is a pool hall on each side of the street.

maybe Kelowna. I was there with my buddy Red Lane and his wife. Her name was Elaine May Lane. Red said she sounded liked something at a Chinese restaurant. Red liked to be dramatic in everything, whether taking the brown paper off a bottle of wine or frying sunny side up eggs. So here is what he did at the drive-in. For some reason it was decided that Red would go to the refreshment stand and get stuff for all three of us. After a while alone with a good-looking valley girl in an automobile at a drive-in, I saw Red approaching, his hands and arms barely able to contain three really big tubs of popcorn and three really big cups of Orange Crush. I just could not help myself. As Red was carefully accomplishing the last few steps to the car, just when he was right in front of the hood ornament, I gave the horn a push. Aw, I can see it now—popcorn and Orange Crush entered the sky like fireworks over a lagoon and Red was well up in the air, his four limbs stretched in four directions. I loved Red for the way he did that, and I always looked for a horn to honk.

WRITING THE OKANAGAN

The main street of Oliver never did amount to much. It didn't even have a real name, as far as I know. It was just where Highway 97 went through the middle of town for about three blocks. We called it "Main Street," but that was more a description than a name. None of our streets had names, but some of the roads out of town did. Fairview Road, or was that just an agreed-upon description, headed up to the old ghost town of Fairview. On that model we had what people called Sawmill Road, and outside of town, every mile or so there was a road going east and/or west: Number Five Road came before Number Six Road. Someone once told me, I think, that the street in front of our house was Sixth Street, or maybe Sixth Avenue. This may have been some designation they knew about down at the village hall. There weren't any street signs in Oliver, or Lawrence, as it has been called. So getting back to "Main Street." I am going to mention one of the great moments of my life. Willy and I had been away to UBC and who knows where else, but now we were back in town. Willy had his little red Morris Minor convertible, and I think it was a Sunday, because we were driving down "Main Street," and there was hardly anyone there. At least half of the parking spaces were empty. I was sitting up on the top of the back of my seat, turning in either direction, waving to a crowd that existed in my imagination. Willy was driving without looking either right or left, under a big banner that crossed above us and existed only in our imagination. There was one person visible in the doorway of some store, some guy that was younger than we. He waved back and shouted, "Welcome home, George!"

Standing on Richards

Viking did a really nice-looking job of *Standing on Richards*, a new-and-selected, but they never produced a Penguin paperback edition. I guess it didn't wow the Canadian reading public, though Toronto's Elvis Andrus made a short movie of two of the Vancouver stories in the book. They feature Colin Mochrie, which made me happy because he is an actor I have long admired.

There are four Okanagan stories in the selected part of the volume, and two among the new works. Of these, "The Outhouse" depended on some help in the construction. As in my other fiction, Oliver is called Lawrence (because it is another first-or-last name), and Bill Trump is called Bob Small, and I am called Delsing, and so on. But here is a quick description of the way it was composed. My sweetheart Jean Baird is in Ontario, and Bill Trump and I are in our B.C. communities, and we are all on our computers emailing one another. It is during this time that Willy and I are feeding Jean the stories of our childhood together in the South Okanagan.

So the story of the outhouse and its toppling was a cross-Canada e-necdote—until Dr. Baird the "behaviour-deity" pasted it together and said there, there's a story. I can't remember whether I checked that opinion with my mother, P. B.

The Outhouse

When Bob Small and I were kids we liked going to the Lawrence Theatre to see Red Skelton movies and Bob Hope movies. We knew in our hearts that these two great men would become our role models. But Randolph Scott is the greatest movie actor of all time!

It was during this Lawrence Theatre Saturday afternoon era that I really got into Hollywood musicals. I am not interested now in *Les Miz* or *Cats* or any of that stuff, but I really liked those Howard Keel films.

No one ever threw anything in the Lawrence Theatre. The presence of Mr. Gough was enough to make us behave. Actually, we were a well-behaved generation in Lawrence in those days. Except the time I fell into the outhouse hole.

—Hey, Small, would I be doing my reputation any good by telling the behaviour-deity this story? Please advise.

—C'mon, you know you can't resist telling the story, but I'll bet you leave all my heroic efforts to save you out of it.

—Bobbo, that happened before I knew you, when I was in grade four and living at Katie's place. Do you want the behaviour-deity to think our stories are unreliable?

—Oh, I thought it happened when Mr. Laird wouldn't give us anything when we were trick-or-treating, but maybe that was just a come-to-think-of-it.

—That was just a come-to-think-of-it. You know, I think that usually outhouse holes are full of piled shit and flies and torn bits of catalogue. But this one was wet.

Well, Katie was Katie Rindisbacher, a beautiful brunette who wore pleated plaid skirts and saddle oxfords and bobby sox. We lived in a house that was in her father's orchard, and I spent a lot of time with Katie and her friend Sylvia MacNab.

Sylvia MacNab asked me to the Sadie Hawkins dance in grade nine, but I always thought it was just out of sympathy for me and my awkward trying to come to terms with a hopeless love for her. But now I think, fifty years later: what if she really liked me and wanted this relationship to blossom?

—But Dels, you never showed such sensitivity at the time. You told me she had the hots for you, and that I would never learn to handle broads nearly as adroitly as you. You said some guys just got it and some don't. But I did okay. While you were at the dance with Sylvia I was across the border in Oroville, where I almost had to beat them off with a stick when I asked, "Hoos aboot it?"

Well, years later, when there was the twentieth-year reunion of my graduating class, I was all excited because I hadn't heard from or about Sylvia MacNab for twenty years, and she didn't show. I found out from the paper they sent around that she lived in New Westminster and had several kids.

Okay, to get back to the topic—well, it was, of course, traditional, in the literature, that kids do certain things on Halloween: soap windows, steal front gates, push over outhouses. The outhouse in question on Halloween of 1944 was on a rise of dry land that rose up out of Mr. Rindisbacher's orchard, a little north and west of our house. Leonard Kovak lived down a dirt road that went east of this outhouse.

I can't remember any house nearby, so that is a little vague in my memory. That is, the terrain outside the outhouse hole's perimeter is somewhat vague to my recall.

I am pretty sure Len Kovak was one of the other outhouse pushers. There were, I think, four of us. We were in grade four, and I got the impression that these guys did this sort of stuff all the time, like the guys in stories and so on. I had been in Lawrence for only a year and a bit, so I was still learning to socialize, though I think I remember that there were times when I was a class show-off smart aleck, maybe.

Still, in addition to being a class cut-up I was also a little Jansenite boy, or at least so some Catholic kid called me, and so I had all this strict private morality, all about how I should not smoke or drink or deprive Maureen of her virginity, no matter how understanding she might be about it. So I was the kind of kid who would repair things rather than wrecking them on Halloween, and it was very odd that I should have been there, pushing on the side of that outhouse in the dark.

Leonard Kovak kept surprising me. I was surprised when he became a terrific athlete, and we were then supposed to call him Len. I was surprised when he started going steady with Joan Williams (The Student Body), and then years later I was surprised when he became a high school teacher in the Cariboo, and then I was really surprised when he became the teacher in charge of the student drama actors in his school. Amazing, every one of those moves.

So there I was with my newish Lawrence rural friends, pushing over the outhouse, just as in the books and comic books and legends and all. Soon three of those guys would be gone in the night, while I remained in situ. Now here there was no chance of explaining to Bob Small what I explained when I showed up where he didn't expect me, in the old Boy Scout Hall grounds ...

So what I am saying is: I had this personal Jansenist loathing of the idea of outhouse toppling, but I also yearned to make steady friends of my peers. It was a dilemma. Later, of course, I would see my fate as a punishment for going with the peers instead of sticking to my personal superior morality ...

Yeah, so that it becomes odd to imagine Len Kovak being a kid who would push over an outhouse. Although it must seem even stranger to think of me being such a kid, except for those blighted minds who think my genius rebellion was allied to juvenile delinquency. I wasn't thinking of that, of course, when I realized how hard it was going to be to get out of that wet hole without help.

So what could I say, but that I was a regular guy. So we rocked and pushed, and the thing came down easier than I had thought it would, among the cactus and couch grass and sagebrush and tumbleweed. Down it came, and of course it was my luck that it went over so fast that I was still pushing when there was nothing to push but air, dark fetid air with a trace of lime dust.

Now, I have looked in a lot of outhouse holes, I mean through the hole, downward, and they usually contain a mound of pretty solid shit of every hue, mixed with various kinds of paper. One would think that these things are pretty well standard.

Well, it was really hard to get out of that hole. But I came out the bottom with my rubber boots on. That was a lie I told Bob Small on any given occasion.

Okay, Mom, is that a story?

Left Hook

There have not been a lot of poets or fiction writers from the Okanagan Valley, certainly not as many as we have seen emerge from Prince George, for example. It felt all right to be a pioneer of sorts, but at times it felt kind of lonely. When I lived there I read a lot of novels by people from Chicago and London, and envied those writers who grew up in a kind of local tradition. It was not until late in the twentieth century that I found out about Mourning Dove, though she was an Okanagan storyteller who died seven months after I was born.

I don't know why we were told nothing about her when we were in high school. Or rather, I do know why. When I went looking for her grave I dropped by the tourist kiosk in Omak, Washington, and asked where her grave was. The young women there had never heard of her, a woman who should have been the most famous person ever to have lived in that town I had visited often in my youth. In high school we were told nothing about the Okanagan "Indians," not even this one who was the first ever to publish a novel.

That novel was published in 1927 by Four Seasons Co. of Boston. Ten years earlier the same publisher had published *Al Que Quiere!*, the third book of poems by William Carlos Williams. When I found this out I felt a nudge of some sort. I quite early in my life adopted Williams as my poetry father. Williams paid Four Seasons fifty dollars to publish the complete run of that little book; seventy years later I paid well over two hundred dollars for a single copy at a bookstore in London.

By the way, I have learned that Mourning Dove's gravestone was so nicely altered by Penticton writer Jeanette Armstrong and her friends. Thank you.

Mourning Dove (Christine Quintasket) (1880s–1936).

The Autobiographings of
Mourning Dove

Why do we visit graves?

Why would we travel to a place we have never been to before, and stand at the foot of a grave in which lie the remains of someone we have never seen in the flesh?

In the summer of 1992 I drove to Omak, Washington, to visit the grave of Mourning Dove, the first Native American woman ever to write a novel. At the tourist bureau they had never heard of her, but they told me that the graveyard I had mentioned was in Okanogon, the next town.

The graveyard, white and dry under the hot familiar sun, was deserted. I parked my car and got out and stood where I could see the whole place. Then I walked to the area that looked thirties-ish. The first grave I looked at was hers.

She had bought this plot out of her minimal wages from hard orchard work, a grave in a white people's cemetery. In Jay Miller's introduction to her autobiography, I had read that the words on her marker were only "Mrs. Fred Galler" (xxvi). But now I saw that someone had cut a rectangle out of the old stone and put a new marker in its place. It depicts a white dove flying over an opened book upon which appear the words:

MOURNING DOVE

COLVILLE AUTHOR

1884–1936

The revised headstone.

There I was, a still-living white male, standing, and eventually kneeling at the last narrow home of a great woman I had not heard of while I was being educated there in that Okanagan Valley.[1] She died when I was seven months old. I did not read her books until I was the age that she had attained at her death. What did I think I was doing there? I was reading.

Why do we read autobiographies?

Reading is a cultural act, and our habits of reading will accumulate into a description of our culture. As Janet Varner Gunn puts it, "The truth of autobiography is to be found, not in the 'facts' of the story itself, but in the relational space between the story and its reader" (Gunn, 143).

Traditionally we have read male autobiography as a version of history, as the story told by those statesmen and militarists who have exercised power. Traditionally we have read female autobiography as alternative history, the occluded life, domestic, personal, and perhaps solipsistic. Perhaps concerned with the permission to write such a thing at all, with an identity. Estelle Jelinek writes: "In contrast to the self-confident, one-dimensional self-image that men usually project, women often depict a multidimensional, fragmented self-image coloured by a sense of inadequacy and alienation, of being outsiders or 'other'; they feel the need for authentication, to prove their self-worth" (Jelinek, xiii). Of course many of the most successful female autobiographies have narratized the overcoming of obstacles, and the attainment of an identity that is quite satisfactory, thank you.

Of course if you were a woman, and if you were from the Interior Plateau country, and if you were aboriginal, you were triply marginalized. You might be exotic, but if you wanted to be a writer, you had to do your writing with whatever skills you had managed to develop, in a tent or a shack, after ten hours of working in an orchard and after cooking the meals for your husband and yourself at least. That is why a still-living white male will think more than twice before trying to apply normal academic, theoretical, or ethnographic methods to your autobiography.

There have been several versions of the main facts assigned to Mourning Dove's life, the disagreements caused by her fictionalizing and through the errors made by white academics coming from their various angles to use her story. She was most likely born in 1885 in Idaho, the first daughter of Lucy and Joseph Quintasket (Dark Cloud). Lucy was the daughter of a woman from the Colville Tribe, one of the tribes who share the enormous Colville[2] Reservation in northeastern Washington, and of a man who came from the Lakes people of eastern British Columbia. Mourning Dove's other grandmother was from the Nicola, a somewhat mysterious people who lived among the Okanagans near Merritt, British Columbia. Her other grandfather was probably an Okanagan, though for literary and political reasons Mourning Dove suggested that he was a white man named Haynes. There were white people named Haynes in the area. My mother used to work in Haynes's packing house in Testalinda, a mile from the Indian school at which Mourning Dove taught in 1917.

The Quintaskets usually lived on or near the Colville Reservation, among people of several Salish tribes[3] who had been reduced to poverty and the meanest of jobs in agriculture by the policies of the powerful whites in the Eastern States. Christine Quintasket managed to get some schooling. First she went to a boarding school and was introduced to the English language by French-Canadian nuns. Later she went to the Colville Mission school in Fort Spokane. When her widowed father married a young woman, Christine went to Montana, to trade menial work for a chance to go to an Indian school there.

But she spent more time at home than she did at schools. At home she learned a love for narrative from her two most important teachers, an adopted grandmother and an adopted white brother.

These two instilled in the Indian girl a desire to be a storyteller and a writer. For her last formal schooling she went to a business college in Calgary, where she endured the typical racism of that city, and learned things such as shorthand and typing, skills that would prove handy later while she was gathering traditional stories or writing her life by coal-oil light in the night cabin. The school in Calgary did not make her spelling and grammar perfect.

But Mourning Dove wrote three important books that are in print now: *Cogewea the Half-Blood*, a novel that has been aptly called a "protest romance" (Larson, 177); *Coyote Stories*, her versions of tales she collected from elders on both sides of the International Boundary; and *Mourning Dove: A Salishan Autobiography*, which was not to be published until a half century after her death. The three books are equally autobiographical, and they are all about something other than Mourning Dove's life.

Mourning Dove worked herself to death. She died at the age of about fifty-one, though by her own construction she would have been forty-eight. She left no children. In the grave she was for decades named Mrs. Fred Galler. Now the name on the stone is Mourning Dove, and the occupation is author rather than Mrs. For any reader standing over that stone she has no age.

Sometimes I used to ask students what their first and last names mean. Hardly any of them knew. So this is what a name means in non-aboriginal society: a few words on an ID card. But in a Salishan world, a name means a great deal more, whether the name of a place or the name of a person, and everyone knows this. A name is a gift, or it is family property. It is bestowed or it is earned. It is an act of honour.

When she was a little girl her parents called her Kee-ten. When an old neighbour woman named Ka-at-qhu died without passing her name to a grandchild, Kee-ten became Ka-at-qhu. A few years later a shaman woman who was pleased with the girl's help gave her her name to carry on, so now Kee-ten was also Ha-ah-pecha. Mourning Dove said that people on the reservation still used those names when speaking to her decades later.

But by this time in history Indian girls were also carrying Christian names. In the white world she was known by equivalents of her name Kee-ten. She was Christine and Christal and Cristal and Catherine Quintasket. At the convent school she was enrolled as Christine Joseph, because her father's name was Joseph. When she was first married she signed her letters Cristal MacLeod. During her second marriage she was Christine or Catherine Galler. But Christine Quintasket wanted to be a writer, and she wanted to be an Indian writer who would be read by white readers. She decided that as a storyteller she would take the name Hum-ishu-ma. Then she decided that the English version of her writer's name would be Morning Dove, because that bird is, in Colville legend, the faithful wife of Salmon, and welcomes him upstream every year. Salmon fishing is the sustenance of life for the peoples of the great Interior Plateau. In a museum in Spokane, Christine saw that the proper spelling was Mourning Dove, and though she said that it was because of that connotation not the same bird known to the Indian people, she settled on Mourning Dove as her writing name. That is the story of Mourning Dove's name.

The name Haynes does not figure at all. But these names do: Lucullus Virgil McWhorter, Heister Dean Guie, and Jay Miller. They are the names of three white men who had, in their various ways, faith in Mourning Dove's importance, and helped in the preparation of her three books, the last of course unknown to her.

When an Indian person authored a book in early twentieth-century America, she was met with two challenging responses. One: is this person really an Indian or another Grey Owl? Isn't D'Arcy McNickle really three-quarters European stock? What about Thomas King? Two: did this person really write that book, or was it done by a white anthropologist with an ear? Did Black Elk speak much?

Anyone reading *Cogewea*, especially in these latter days, notices that the language is folksy and out-westish when the spirited "half-blood" heroine is joshing with the ranch hands: "I'm a thinkin' yo' all'd make a good preacher woman. Them there kind what wants ter be made perlice wimin an' jedges an' th' main push. Wantin' to wear breeches an' boss th' hull shebang" (42). But often the reader will find a lecture about the conditions imposed on Native Americans by the U.S. governments, and find that these passages are rendered in the language one expects from a school teacher who once had to read Cato: "They lacked the perceptive sagacity of a certain great reformer of nearly two thousand years ago; who, when carrying the Message to the benighted Athenians, 'stood in the midst of Mars hill' and declared that it was of their 'Unknown God' to whom he had noticed an altar erected, that he spake" (133). This is Cogewea in conversation with the opportunist easterner she resists and then unhappily falls for.

The novel is, as it says on the title page, "Given through Sho-pow-tan," the Indian name that she and others gave to McWhorter. It is pretty clear that it was McWhorter who added the didactic diatribes against white exploitation that delay the narrative. One wonders whether the undoubtedly good-hearted McWhorter thought the stilted language was normal enough to be used by Mourning Dove the author or by her characters. Was McWhorter's grasp of fiction so poor? Of course he had a somewhat different agenda than that of his co-author. In later years, when Mourning Dove sent new manuscripts to McWhorter she asked him to stay away from the arch rhetoric, from what she called white people's big words.

It is a sad fact of life that when white anthropologists who are genuinely sympathetic with the cause of indigenous peoples become interested in their stories, they are interested in them for anthropological reasons and thus marginalize their literary qualities, hence exhibiting what could be called a subtle racism. Jay Miller says that

Mourning Dove's letters show that while she was working on the Coyote stories, "McWhorter was concerned that Indian themes and concerns be highlighted, whereas Mourning Dove wanted to express her knowledge and literary talents" (*Autobiography*, xxiii). Intelligent people on both sides of the text understand that problem and work together to make the best of an imperfect situation. There are several such problems in the area of ethnobiography. Mourning Dove's Coyote stories and autobiography would have been, perhaps, more interesting to read in scripted Interior Salish.

Mourning Dove was an Indian woman writing in the language of her white readers. Just about any of her readers were going to be more interested in her as a representative of her people than as a novelist. The same was likely to be true of her editors. Mourning Dove was also a politician. In addition to the long hours she spent on ladders in orchards, at laundry sinks in rooming houses, and at her ill-lit typewriter, she spent a lot of time working for Native people who were caught in the hard machinery of liberal democracy. She rescued families from border police. She wrote illuminating letters to newspapers and the State house. She became the first woman on the Colville Reservation Tribal Council.

In all her books one can discern her two principal social purposes— to make certain that her people's stories and the story of their life will be preserved in print while their way of life is being threatened by officially induced poverty, and to make a bridge between the Indians and the whites on their land. It is easy to assume that these two ambitions are at odds with one another. But Mourning Dove, whose view must be taken as better qualified than ours, did not think so. She was aware of the dangers one must inevitably pass through. One of the most amusing scenes in *Cogewea* concerns the heroine's anger at a white woman's fanciful book about Indian life. Some of the ranch hands joke about the misinformation they have handed to an eager female tenderfoot scribe: "Why, them there writin' folks is dead easy pickin' for the cowpunchers" (94). Finally "Cogewea found solace in consigning the maligning volumn [*sic*] to the kitchen stove" (96). Writing this novel during the second decade of the twentieth century, Mourning Dove seems to anticipate most of the arguments heard more recently about paternalism and mis-appropriation of voice.

In *Cogewea*, with its melodramatic plot and editorializing, the most interesting and accomplished passages are those in which Cogewea's grandmother, sometimes in her sweat lodge, tells the stories and trad-itions of pre-contact Salishan life. They are interesting not only because of their ethnographic information but also because of their narrative skill. They are clearly Mourning Dove's purest contribution to the novel.

And they are most clearly the nearly perfect conjoining of tradition and the individual talent. That conjunction is what Jay Miller has tried his best to produce in the autobiography. I like to notice the nice title: *Mourning Dove: A Salishan Autobiography*. Everyone has treated of that word "autobiography," and its constituent parts. James Olney has shown the way in which twentieth century reading has shifted attention from bios to autos, from life to self (Olney, 19). Miller's title tells us that in our approach here we have to look for something else, something cre-ated by the concepts of person and people among the aboriginals of the Interior Plateau, and by the dynamic of Mourning Dove's doubled ambition. It is after all a Salishan autobiography, and thus promising of a singular life. It is also a Salishan autobiography, not just that of Christine Quintasket.

It is assembled from boxes of mismatched writings that Mourn-ing Dove left to Dean Guie's attic. In the frantic and illness-filled years before her death she thought she was writing two books—one an ethnographic description of Salishan life, and the other a narrative of her own upbringing and education. The book that Miller assembled from her papers is an admirable conflation of these intentions. Curi-ously, in this "autobiography" of America's first Indian woman novelist, there is no recounting of her writing *Cogewea*, nor of the tiresome twelve-year wait to see it published.

Miller arranges the papers in three main sections: "A Woman's World," "Seasonal Activities," and "Okanogan History." The first chap-ter is called "My Life," and is the most clearly anecdotal autobiography as well as the longest chapter in the book. Yet it is filled with seemingly impersonal lore, and the later chapters on such things as salmon fishing, are narratized with memoirs of the Quintasket family and others. Miller admits his own anthropological bias, and allows that he helped to "create" the text. Perhaps the academic professionalizing of his trade has saved us from McWhorter's stentorian rhetoric. And maybe we could say that all three editors "milled" Mourning Dove's texts, somehow extending her process when she developed the Indian tales she gathered from elders. Miller says of the compromise he has fashioned: "the autobiography does represent a personal ethnography of lasting value" (*Autobiography*, xxxiv).

Mourning Dove said that she wrote to prove to her white audience that Indian people were not the savage stoics that had been created in the white romances, that Indian people felt strong emotions, just as strong as those felt by the recently arrived aliens. She said that the Coyote stories were "set down by me for the children of another race to read" (*Coyote Stories*, 12). It was not only Indian education that she was interested in. Though any text can offer only a momentary joining of understandings, she hoped that each of these joinings would contribute toward a world in which tolerance and familiarity would replace the systemic racism that characterized official life in her part of the country.

What about the danger of appropriation that seems now to accompany more interracial knowledge? It is obvious that any autobiography invites appropriation: here is my life for your dollar. Appropriation, if it is a problem, is not the big problem. For the First Nations of America, the problem has been misappropriation, and expropriation. Autobiographies and autobiographical fictions are going to be read, one hopes. If the reader somehow then becomes a writer, his writing will be about his experience. His experience here will be reading the book.

Do you remember when we were kids and we wondered whether what other people called "green" might be what we would see as "red"? As kids we learned that we had to accept the fact that we joined in our understanding only through words, through the text. Reading Indian stories, having good Indian friends, putting headbands around our heads, will not make us Indians. If we try to write or rewrite Indian narratives we will not do it. Autobiography is a narrative of mortality, and we all have our own deaths to do. Yet the pleasant thing about autobiography is that old-fashioned closure is impossible. Perhaps the author is dead, in Roland Barthes's sense, but she is also never dead. At the "end" of her book one is left hanging, alive, expecting the truth to be revealed eventually but perhaps by another. A Salishan autobiography, then, should imply that the Salishan peoples are alive, that no one has written their epitaph.

Remember what Barthes wrote at the beginning of his essay "The Death of the Author": "in ethnographic societies the responsibility for a narrative is never assumed by a person but by a mediator, shaman or relator whose 'performance'—the mastery of the narrative code—may possibly be admired but never his 'genius' " (Barthes, 142). That is what we have to understand about Mourning Dove's doubleness: when she wants us to appreciate her writing ability as well as the ethnographic information she is imparting, it is not originality she wants us to scrutinize, but performance. She is not trying to get us to know that she has deep feelings, but that Indian people, the Okanagans and the Colvilles, have deep feelings.

Mourning Dove knew how important it was to the very lives of her family and tribe that she understand the function of the reader. She knew the principle that Barthes invokes near the end of his essay: "a text is made of multiple writings, drawn from many cultures and entering into mutual relations of dialogue, parody, contestation, but there is one place where this multiplicity is focused and that place is the reader, not, as was hitherto said, the author ... a text's unity lies not in its origin but in its destination" (148).

So how do we North American white men read Mourning Dove without looking for Pocahontas?

Pocahontas has always haunted American literature. And there has always been a kind of ethno-pornography in the response of white poets and other writers. First she was wild, savage, naked, lewd. Then she was romanticized, penny-dreadfulled, tom-tommed till her feet ached.

In this century she was "redeemed" by poets such as Hart Crane and William Carlos Williams, becoming the essential Native spirit still alive in the Europeanized American continent. But always she was the image of desire, the exotic removed from her society to become the object of a male gaze. She was the literary equivalent of the naked model.

Certainly Pocahontas never wrote anything. One might as well permit women to become painters rather than the painted. In American publishing there was one kind of book about Indians that was always popular. This was the captivity narrative. It was especially successful when the captured and then rescued and then autobiographical person was a woman. The stories were usually religious in denouement, and filled with anti-Indian sentiments, filled with descriptions of cruelty, paganism, and savagery. Reading them was not just a cultural act—it was a pornographic act as well.

There were no captivity narratives written by Indian women forced to live among the Christians. Not until recently.

Remember that there was in the nineteenth century (and still is in some quarters) a sentiment at large that says that all writing by women is autobiographical. Women, normally regarded as properly the object of the male gaze, would remain so in the reading of their writing. One would think that Gertrude Stein took care of that problem.

Early in the *Autobiography* Mourning Dove offers a story of her grandmother Pah-tah-heet-sa, a Nicola medicine woman. No one could make a Pocahontas of her. Once when the people were travelling over the high Nicola trail to visit in the Okanagan, Pah-tah-heet-sa went well ahead of them, gathering huckleberries.

When this brave woman drew near the berry patch, she saw a grizzly feeding. This did not stop her. She took her digging stick of dogwood and prepared to fight if the bear meant to charge at her, which the bear did not hesitate to do. With a howl that would have frozen the blood of any coward, it charged. She threw off her pack and held her stick to challenge the brute, saying, "You are a mean animal and I am a mean woman. Let us fight this out to see who will get the berry patch."

The bear did not answer her but opened its mouth wide and came at a leap. She watched for her chance and drove the sharp stick into the animal's mouth. The bear fell back in pain, then jumped at her, even more angry. The fight went on long enough that the warriors approached, not expecting to see such a sight. When they drew their arrows to shoot, she commanded them, "Don't shoot. Wait! We are fighting this to the finish. He is a mean animal and I am a mean woman. We will see who is the strongest and conqueror in this battle."

The woman roared in imitation of the angry bear and drove her stick again into the wide, wide mouth. Every time it charged, this would drive it back. The people watched the fight until the sun lay low in the western sky. Only then did the grizzly walk away, broken and bleeding. The old woman had only a few scratches.

She picked up her basket and gathered the berries she had won, while the people stood in wonderment. She died very old when she and her buckskin horse rolled down a steep embankment near Oroville. She and the horse drowned and were both buried on the bank of the Similkameen River in an unmarked grave. Thus ended a brave, mean woman (5–6).

Anyone of a comparative-literature mind will note the resemblance to European stories of the confrontations and deaths of noble knights. But I believe the story of Mourning Dove's grandmother.

I also think I know, as much as a white male reader in this latter time can know, what the story is for. I know that Pah-tah-heet-sa lives on in Mourning Dove herself, and that she continues to live in Okanagan stories. I think of Maeg, the rooted and political woman who appears toward the end of Jeanette Armstrong's novel *Slash*. Maeg is from the U.S. part of the valley, but has parents from the Canadian side. I think that she is seen to be Pah-tah-heet-sa, and Christine Quintasket and Mourning Dove and Jeanette Armstrong. I think that she may have had something to do with the transformation of that gravestone in Okanogan, Washington.

Beth Cuthand, a First Nations writer from the prairies, put the question of autobiography this way: "Often when we are writing, it's not our words that are coming. The grandmothers, the grandfathers come and write through us" (Dybikowski, 53). No need for a muse when there is a family around. And you do not need to be a writer to take part in the making of the family story, the tribal story, a story of the Okanagan land. Among the Okanagans and other peoples of the Interior Salishan, response was expected from the listeners, encouraging voices to keep the narrative going. Among the people of the Plateau, invisible property is more valuable and more lasting than visible property. Autobiography (if we post-Hellenic people can use that term here) is a care that would be failed if it were to fall simply to an individual with a unique story to tell.

But Mourning Dove's *Autobiography* is also directed toward a non-Indian audience. What can we do to respond properly, to keep these stories alive among us, too? Why do we bother visiting the banks of the Similkameen near Oroville?

Mourning Dove learned her double narrative task right at home in her Indian father's house. Teequalt, the new grandmother she brought home, taught her Salishan stories and taught her to pay attention to her own gift as a storyteller. Jimmy Ryan, the white boy her father brought into the family, was fond of yellowback novels, and taught his little sister to read the English found in them. Once her mother papered the walls with pages from a new one. Jimmy and Christine read the walls.

Mourning Dove decided that she would try to trust the white world. She knew that she was turning tales into text, the people's property into information. Janet Gunn says: "What is made present is not merely a past that is past. What is presenced is a reality, always new, to which the past has contributed but which stands, as it were, in front of the autobiographer" (Gunn, 17).

In front of the reader, too.

NOTES

1. On the U.S. side of the border the spelling is "Okanogan," while on the Canadian side it is "Okanagan."
2. The Colville Reservation in northeastern Washington is populated by several Salishan peoples. One group is called the Colviles, the spelling changed to avoid confusion between place and tribe.
3. The term "tribe" is used in the United States. In Canada we tend to use such terms as "band" or "community" or "nation."

WORKS CITED

Armstrong, Jeanette. *Slash*. Penticton, Theytus Books, 1985.

Barthes, Roland. *Image. Music. Text*. New York: Hill and Wang, 1977.

Dybikowski, Ann et al., eds. *In the Feminine: Women and Words / Les femmes et les mots*. Edmonton: Longspoon Press, 1985.

Gunn, Janet Varner. *Autobiography: Toward a Poetics of Experience*. Philadelphia: University of Pennsylvania Press, 1982.

Jelinek, Estelle C. *The Tradition of Women's Autobiography: From Antiquity to the Present*. Boston: Twayne Publishers, 1986.

Larson, Charles R. *American Indian Fiction*. Albuquerque: University of New Mexico Press, 1978.

Mourning Dove. *Cogewea: the Half-Blood*. Lincoln: University of Nebraska Press, 1981. Reprint of the 1927 ed. published by Four Seas Co., Boston.

_____. *Coyote Stories*. Edited by Heister Dean Guie. Lincoln: University of Nebraska Press, 1990. Reprint of the 1933 ed. published by The Caxton Printers, Caldwell, Idaho.

_____. *Mourning Dove: A Salishan Autobiography*. Edited by Jay Miller. Lincoln: University of Nebraska Press, 1990.

I would also like to express my appreciation of the extensive work and publications of Dr. Alanna Kathleen Brown of Montana State University. Dr. Brown is the leading scholar of Mourning Dove's writing and life, and a trusted friend of the Quintasket family. I encourage readers to seek out her work.

Vermeer's Light

These poems were written in a time that saw a lot of changes in my life. After a long series of illnesses, my wife Angela died in the fall of 1999. Two years later I retired from my teaching job and settled into a quiet life I imagined would be filled with reading and writing and watching baseball games. But life is a lot like writing: it never turns out the way you think it will. Within a year the Canadian Parliament decided to create the position of Poet Laureate, and sure enough, the first person to occupy that position would be me. After two years of criss-crossing the country carrying out my official duties I settled into a new house in Vancouver with my sweetheart Jean Baird. In 2004, I published much of what I had written in those millennial times in a book called *Vermeer's Light*. At the end of that book I included an essay on the many ways I tried to destroy my most-anthologized poem, "Grandfather." I wrote the first version of it when I was twenty-six. It has been published in innumerable anthologies, including high school and university ones, largely because it was constructed like the "Canadian" poems of my predecessors rather than according to my aesthetic. So I subjected it to various experimental revisions as suggested by the *Oulipo* group of writers and mathematicians in Paris. It was a great pleasure to avenge myself on my most successful short poem. But here's how it insists on going according to all the textbooks I have seen.

*My grandfather Jabez Harry Bowering with my grandmother
Clara (Miller) Bowering.*

Grandfather

Grandfather
        Jabez Harry Bowering
strode across the Canadian prairie
hacking down trees
              & building churches
delivering personal baptist sermons in them
leading Holy holy holy lord god almighty songs in them
red haired man squared off in the pulpit
reading Saul on the road to Damascus at them

Left home
        big walled Bristol town
at age eight
        to make a living
buried his stubby fingers in root snarled earth
for a suit of clothes & seven hundred gruelly meals a year
taking an anabaptist cane across the back every day
for four years till he was whipt out of England

Twelve years old
         & across the ocean alone
to apocalyptic Canada
           Ontario of bone bending labour
six years on the road to Damascus till his eyes were blinded
with the blast of Christ & he wandered west
to Brandon among wheat kings & heathen Saturday nights
young red haired Bristol boy shovelling coal
in the basement of Brandon College five in the morning

Then built his first wooden church & married
a sick girl who bore two live children & died
leaving several pitiful letters & the Manitoba night

He moved west with another wife & built children & churches
Saskatchewan Alberta British Columbia Holy holy holy
lord god almighty
                       struck his laboured bones with pain
& left him a postmaster prodding grandchildren with crutches
another dead wife & a glass bowl of photographs
& holy books unopened save the bible by the bed

Till he died the day before his eighty-fifth birthday
in a Catholic hospital of sheets white as his hair

Crows in the Wind

Crows in the Wind is my first publication by BookThug, which makes simply elegant books by interesting authors. It is a chapbook that is the first of twelve that I wrote, a page a day, in 2006. It would become the first twelfth of my biggest poetry work ever, *My Darling Nellie Grey* (Talonbooks, 2010).

The little poem "I watched my father" forms the twenty-ninth of thirty-one pages of that first chapbook. The event recorded in it is one that I seem to have returned to numerous times. It happened in Peachland when I was gathering my first long memories, and it is important to me in a number of ways. For example, it hints that I learned to recognize an action that showed me the overlapping edge of a previous era. By the time that I became a father no one I knew was taking a bar of soap to the lake. When we heard the word "bathing" in a reference to swimming, we just thought of it as old-fashioned.

But while suggesting that difference, the poem also speaks of inclusivity, not only of "my people," but of our fitting naturally into the Okanagan Valley, a place nowhere near as commercialized and internationalized as the wine region and resort franchises of the time we chafe in now. Of course I am afflicted by the usual old guy's nostalgia and regret, but I also know that my father's bar of soap was not going to pollute Lake Okanagan the way "the market" is doing now. In 1939 there was a lovely town just north of our beach, a place named "Kelowna," that being what the Okanagan people called the grizzly bear.

That swimsuit was made of wool.
I know, because I wore it once in Osoyoos.

I watched my father

I watched my father
    take a bar of white soap
into the lake,
      knew I was learning
another way of my people.
          We wash

in the place where we play, we
work there, too, we don't
    call it "nature," it is only
what is afforded us,
        we take

a bath and what is granted
and give back what we can.

Let me in, coach.

Baseball Love

I was recently rereading an article that the great writer Joel Oppenheimer published in *Village Voice* for the week of October 28, 1980. Oppenheimer was an inveterate New York poet and fiction writer who couldn't stop putting baseball in his books. This article was about attending a poetry conference in a Frank Lloyd Wright house in Buffalo, and noticing that I kept skipping out on the important papers and readings and going downstairs to watch the World Series (Phillies vs. Royals).

That pretty well sums up my attitude toward the mythos and practice of poetry during the baseball season. A long line of book reviewers has scoffed at my interest in such a thing. Most of them have not figured out how to read Shelley's "Mont Blanc," either.

I have two reasons to celebrate the year 2006. The book *Baseball Love* was published, and I got married to Jean Baird. If the truth be told, we had been cohabiting since 2003, during which time she had been memorizing the infield fly rule and I had been learning something just as important. In 2003 we drove from Vancouver to Port Colborne, Ontario, by way of baseball parks in the northern United States. A year or so later we drove back to Vancouver by way of St. Louis and San Diego, by way of more southerly yards. Ms Baird filled up a baseball scorebook on these trips, and since then we have made many more baseball journeys.

Baseball Love has chapters that alternate between the trips we took and other appearances of baseball in my life. The chapter excerpts reprinted here are set mainly at the ballpark in Oliver, British Columbia.

Now this fortunate old scrivener sits back and tosses off books while Jean does all the work. First she let me live in her house in Port Colborne and arranged for my beloved Red Sox to win their first World

Series during my lifetime of yearning. Eventually she took care of that other side of my life, the side that was the reason for my being in Buffalo way back then. She sits me down and makes me write and gets my manuscript ready and brings me back a good book contract.

That is why I am going to give her the pages I have just typed. I have never enjoyed an editor's deadline so much.

There's a year of Sport *magazine. Look! Johnny Lujack, Lou Boudreau, Bob Feller, Jack Robinson, Cy Young. I still have these mags in 2015. Here they're laid out on our front sidewalk. That's more or less where I took all my pictures.*

Growing up in Baseball

I never thought that baseball was a U.S. game. It was a birthright. And certainly it was normal. In the Okanagan sun, you got your baseball stuff out as soon as the ground got softer in, say, March, and you played the summer game till apple season was over in October.

The ballpark, with its big old grey grandstand made of obvious lumber, was the most important few acres in town. There was a sandy hill behind the grandstand. All along the south side, from back of the grandstand to past the left-field foul pole ran a huge wooden siphon that carried water from the east side of the valley to the irrigation ditch at the base of the hills on the west side. Out beyond right centre field was the community hall, with the scoreboard on its side.

Between the huge siphon and the ball diamond was a long row of Lombardy poplars or cottonwoods or whatever they were, enormous pointy things, and sometime during the season, the white fluff would blow off in the wind from the hot south, and the sky would be full of cotton, white puffs, like snow in the middle of summer, drifting north, descending to cover Chevrolets, hiding the white baseball that sped at 85 mph toward the plate.

My buddy Willy's kid brother Sandy recently told me to put Squeaky into my book. Squeaky was, I guess, the town drunk in Oliver. He looked and sounded like Gabby Hayes, and he never missed a ball game. At Christmas he went to church and fell asleep in the pew. While the choir was attempting a carol, Squeaky would wake up and sing, "Take me out to the ball game."

Bill, outside the fire exit of the gymnasium. I remember that
sweater. It was brown—two-tone brown, though Bill might
not have known that since he was colour-blind as a kid.

When the outfield fence went up and local businesses bought ads on it, I thought oh boy, real home runs. Not triples with an extra ninety feet of dead-out running, but real over-the-fence home runs, like those the Cleveland Indians hit. The Washington Senators. Well. Okay. There would be about one over-the-fence home run every ten games, and it would be hit by some big U.S. import playing for Trail.

Just more proof that I lived in a dinky little town that couldn't do things the way they did them in real places, especially across the line. The putting "greens" at the local golf course were made of rolled sand mixed with oil. There was no radio station. There was something ama-teurish about the high school cafeteria. It just didn't have the *confidence* of the ones we saw in U.S. movies or in *Archie* comics.

But all things considered, I figure that our baseball was as close to real as anything in Oliver. That is why I hated it when they changed the name of the team. Part of the problem was that one of the two Kamloops teams that had joined and changed the Loop's name to the Okanagan Mainline league was also called the Elks. The name had been used by baseball teams in Kamloops since the 1880s.

So the players and managers and small-town businessmen—what did they decide to call the team? Did they name it after a fact of local life, such as the rattlers? Or coyotes? They could have anticipated the seventies and given the team an ABA-like name, such as the Oliver Sage.

No. Not a chance. They called it the Oliver Baseball Club. On the hats and shirts they stitched the letters OBC. I had to call them the OBC's in my articles in the *Chronicle*. I was embarrassed again.

I haven't said anything here about *playing* baseball when I was a kid.

I didn't, much.

I was afraid to try out. I had an inferiority complex, and I had developed a superiority complex to protect it.

It was the same way with basketball. Instead of trying out for the basketball team, I became official scorer and newspaper guy. One year there was a school volleyball team and I tried out for it and made it.

There was probably something to the fact that my father had been a baseball player and a basketball player, and got his name in the papers.

So here I was, the kid who was famous for knowing everything about baseball, keeping track of the kids with natural talent who did beautiful things but didn't know who Tris Speaker was. I never had a decent glove, but some old flat thing with no pocket. I had my father's old, old spikes and my father's old, old skates, and they both hurt my feet. I had a big heavy baseball bat, which I kept in my various offices till the summer of 2003. I had a Bremerton Braves uniform, which I kept in a secret place in the basement, along with a copy of *Sunbathing for Health* magazine.

We didn't have Little League, yet. Didn't have Pony League, Babe Ruth League, Connie Mack League. Maybe if we had had Little League I might have tried out. Maybe I would have scrounged a decent glove somewhere. We didn't have much organized baseball. There was the Okanagan Mainline league, and there was the Juniors. I think the Juniors' age limit was sixteen. Maybe fifteen. Maybe seventeen. In there somewhere.

For a short time one season I played some Junior. For some reason my classmate Ron Carter was manager of the Oliver Juniors. Maybe he was just barely over the age limit. Anyway, he talked me into suiting up. I liked that part. I knew how to roll the socks inside the pants. My feet were killing me inside my father's old, old spikes. I could feel the metal spikes through the thin leather. I figured I was going to embarrass myself.

I can't remember what position I was playing, and therefore can't remember any fielding plays. I figured I would commit errors aplenty. But here is what happened my first time at bat in the late spring of some year at the beginning of the fifties.

I don't remember whom we were playing. We had the bases loaded. I was taller than a lot of the kids, having grown like a blackberry bush in the past year or so. People said that with my long legs I should be able to run like a deer. I could not figure out what long legs had to do with running fast. Once in a track meet near the community hall, I finished third in some dash, and got the red ribbon. John Lundy got the white ribbon. Ronnie Carter got the blue ribbon. We three were the only runners in the race.

The first time up in my Junior career I hit a single up the middle with the bases loaded. This can't be me, I thought.

The age limit must have been fifteen, because I was fifteen between grade ten and grade eleven. That's when I was going with Wendy, and one of the few memories I have of this Junior career was going to a road game in Penticton, where they had a beautiful fence—and lights. I remember two things there: I taught Wendy how to keep score in my scorebook, and I got her to rub my calves with wintergreen oil. I knew about wintergreen because my grandfather had moved in with us.

Early in the season I got traded to Naramata. They had a black cap with a simple white N on it, and I wish I still had that hat. Well, it was not really a trade. School was over, and cherry season was on, to be followed by apricot season, peach season, pear season, prune season, and apple season. I spent the summers on the big orchard above Naramata, where my uncle Gerry was foreman for these rich people. (Fifty years later I would buy a Gertrude Stein first edition in my favourite bookstore in Penticton, and it would say inside the cover that it had belonged to someone in that rich family.)

So I played a bit for Naramata. But then the fruit season grew hectic, and there were road games I could not make it to because we were trying to keep up with the cherries, and then there were home games I could not make it to because we were picking on Sundays and after supper, and when we weren't picking we were thinning apples and propping apple trees.

It was a funny place, Naramata. It was ten miles north of Penticton, on the east side of Lake Okanagan opposite to the highway. Unusual religious groups set up camp there, and there were a lot of people fresh from England. Naramata was a tiny place at the bottom of the clay cliffs, and playing fields were at a premium. Sometimes we had to sit there in our black caps, or play useless catch, while the cricket players finished their incomprehensible game. We would razz them. Then they would stay after their game and razz us.

I am so glad that I had that team experience that one year. But generally I was too chicken to try out. Partly it was that I was afraid of the

Naramata Cricket Club, 1950.

ball. Even before I broke my nose on one. That's why it was so amusing to come to bat that season against Ted Bowsfield.

In the late season of 1958, Ted Bowsfield would come up to the Boston Red Sox, and defeat the World Series–bound New York Yankees three times. He and Bill Monbouquette were the two Red Sox *wunderkinder* on the mound that September. Bowsfield was injury-prone, but he lasted eight years in the American League, went 11–8 for the expansion Los Angeles Angels in 1961, and carried a no-hitter into the ninth inning for the Kansas City Athletics two years later.

The year that I played for Oliver and Naramata in the Juniors, Ted Bowsfield was pitching for the Penticton team. He was bigger than anyone, and he had a pitching cage alongside his parents' house. He was, despite what *The Official Encyclopedia of Baseball* maintains, a left-hander, and therefore dangerous. We batters were clearly outclassed. We were like me in my first-year French class at Victoria College in 1953. Bowsfield threw a fastball that was plain invisible, and a big roundhouse curveball you could not afford to wait for.

I have to tell you, I was scared witless standing in the batter's box, even if I was a right-handed batter, and I was even more scared or maybe just relieved when I was sitting down on the dirt just outside the batter's box. Ted Bowsfield was wild. He walked and hit a lot of batters. He was wild *and* invisible, a combination a lot of us admired and dreaded. It *is* nice to remember playing a guy who made it to the majors. I just wished, at the time, that we were on the same team.

I don't know what Ted Bowsfield is doing now. He finished at 37–39, with an ERA of 4.35, over seven years with the Red Sox, Indians, Angels, and Athletics. He was signed after that by the Phillies, but did not see action in the National League. In later years he was manager of the Kingdome in Seattle. That would be like having your own giant pinball machine.

Here follows my favourite image from the old grandstand in Oliver.

Look at photos of stadium baseball crowds in the olden days. All the men are wearing fedoras. All the men at hockey games are wearing fedoras, which means that when a player scored a hat trick, valuable headgear came out of the stands onto the ice. These days you see a bunch of see-through plastic mesh ball caps.

Hundreds and thousands of men wearing fedoras, in black and white.

At a game in Oliver Park some Sunday in the very early fifties, a guy was sitting alone in his fedora, intent on a close game, let us say, between the OBC's and the Vernon Canadians. Behind him were sitting two teenaged girls consuming a giant bag of peanuts. Each time one of the girls cracked open a peanut she would deposit the light shell on the brim or the dented crown of the guy's fedora.

It was a work in progress. And it still is, because I don't remember seeing any outcome.

Someone recently told me that my memoirs often contain the phrase "I don't remember." It escapes me right now, who that was.

Feb. 1935

They got married on December 26, 1934, so they've been married about six weeks.

Eggs in There

In the second half of the twentieth century the USAmerican artist Joe Brainard invented the "I Remember" book. His two first such books, or really sequences of little prose poems, are back in print, I see. What you do is simply sit, say once a day, and add a piece of writing about something you remember from your childhood or some time since.

Several writers have given themselves to such a form of writing. The French *Oulipo* writer Georges Perec did one. After Perec died, Harry Matthews did one filled with his memories of Georges Perec. Some wag did an "I Don't Remember" book. I did one about the Canadian artist Greg Curnoe after he died.

For *Eggs in There*, which also had the constraint of one entry a day for a month, I wrote memories of my parents. Of course when I was a kid my parents, like me, lived in the Okanagan, where the Bowerings were. There are thirty-one of these little paragraphs, but only two of them mention the Okanagan specifically.

Both my parents were born in Alberta, but both came to the Okanagan in their childhoods. My father was brought up in West Summerland, and ten years younger than he, my mother was brought up in the hills of Trepanier, above Peachland. I was born in Penticton and did most of my school servitude in Oliver. Maybe some day I will write an "I Remember" book about Oliver. Maybe I already have.

At my grandfather's funeral in West Summerland.

I remember going to church

I remember going to church with my parents a few
times. At my grandmother's funeral in West Summerland,
where I used to go to church with her, I saw tears in my father's
eyes, and I felt guilty for once again looking with sexual
curiosity I suppose it was at a bovine pretty young woman in
the choir. I wore my thirty-dollar suit, that came with an extra pair of
trousers, at my grandfather's funeral in West Summerland, and
I had my picture taken next to a fruit tree, a cigarette in my
mouth, gel in my hair. At my father's funeral on the Ides of
March in Oliver, at the United Church, I held my sister's hand
and my mother's hand, and heard my father say, "It's all right."
And I wished that it were.

Dad in his Dick Tracy hat.

I remember being in the back seat

I remember being in the back seat, maybe with my
sister, as my parents drove home in the darkness after a visit
with my grandparents in West Summerland or my uncle and
aunt in Naramata. Those were all Bowerings, and they were the
ones who still lived in the Okanagan Valley, thirty-seven miles
away or twenty-seven miles away if they were my other aunt
and uncle in Penticton. It was cold in the back of the car, so we
were under a blanket, and I could see the aura of light from the
dashboard or my parents' heads, my father in his Dick Tracy
hat and my mother in a mother hat. There was always a clock
on the dashboard but we never had a car that the clock worked
in.

Valley

Valley was another of the page-a-day chapbooks that made up *My Darling Nellie Grey*. It was the November poem. The challenge this time was to make a poem-book that would reply to a similar item composed by the U.S. poet Lorine Niedecker.

Are you old enough to remember those little books we would get at the drugstore, a little wider than they were high, each page a different colour, their use being to gather autographs and corny remarks from our friends? Lorine Niedecker wrote a couple of poems in those books. One is called *Paean to Place*, and Niedecker said that she wanted it to be published separately. It was written in 1969, and it was published as a facsimile edition in 2003, to honour what would have been her hundredth birthday.

Her book is filled with alliteration and other rimes, beginning (in her hand, remember) this way:

> Fish
>
>   fowl
>
>   flood
>
> Water lily mud
>
> My life

I didn't lay it on quite so insistently, but I did want my piece to be a friend's response. An obvious constraint is the use of five "lines" per page. More important—in my first page you will hear the sounds a letter *a* might indicate. And so on. I don't expect anyone to make a long trip to see the place I came from and wrote about, but I like to imagine someone reading this November's poem out loud.

The place to which Niedecker wrote her paean is mostly water. She had a kind of shack/cottage on the very wet land of Black Hawk Island in the Wisconsin River. One day I was fortunate enough to see her cottage, to escape drowning, and to buy her beautiful little book.

When it came to my handwritten book's paean to my place, it would be to a land that would be described as dry. The official term I heard while growing up was "semi-arid." Well, I like that pairing. And "Black Hawk Island" sort of rimes with "Okanagan," doesn't it?

The first two times I read this whole poem out loud, I loved the feel and sound of it, and the audiences listening in Penticton and Oliver really dug it.

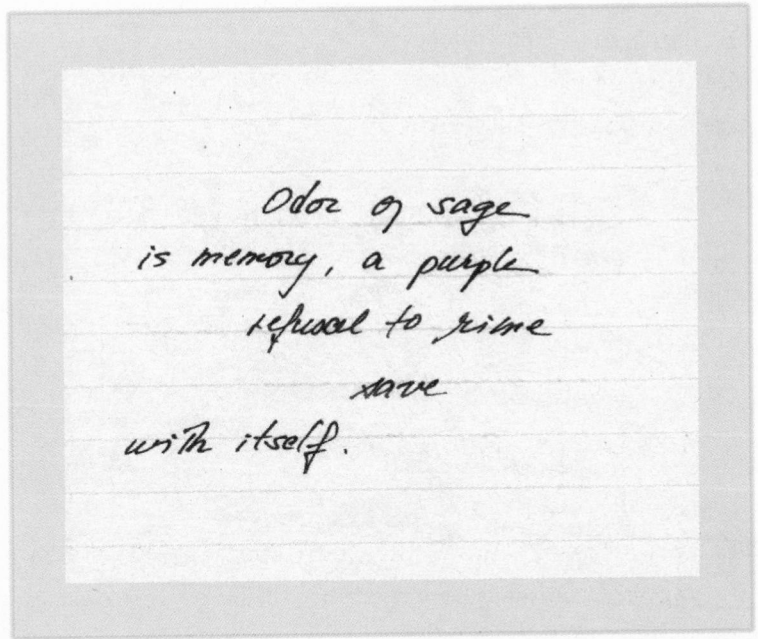

Odor of sage
is memory, a purple
refusal to rime
~~save~~
with itself.

One's automobile
   will be filled
      with the scent of sage—
how wise to drive
      my valley

south. We thought south
      our direction,
sun leaning in
         from our south
on our southern side

where the light's foot beckons
          & the brightness
begins.
          But still
we'd watch the ground

before us —
          listen for rattle
of a fast tail,
                    head down
as if humble.

carried lumber at work.
        He taught me
to sweat, a five-mile
paper route,
        cleaning green slime

from The empty town pool —
    sunstroke hospital, setting pins
with no shirt,
        okay in a small
town, lied about my age

to sweat in Mac 'n Fitz
  packing house,
toiled in orchards,
    no Eden
in this valley,   tourists

loll on beaches
    or gobble cherries,
wonder where the air
    conditioning is, if they're
Americans.

Both my parents
      were born in Alberta,
came to The Okanagan
      as kids, The earth
            now semi-vertical.

The earth
      once under a glacier,
so much made of rocks —
round as apples,
      a dry round place

where a coyote
  sits 'n grins at me.
    He wins
every race we enter.
  he's pointy faced

I'd call my little broTher
if he'd pay attention —
If he'd list me as oTher
  under The striations
    of This valley.

The Box

All my life I have heard people talking about "experimental fiction" or "experimental poetry." For some people it seems to mean another way of saying "avant-garde" or "contemporary." Sometimes I would see some of this "experimental" fiction, and I would not be able to figure out what the project was, or how the experiment was carried out. Nowadays I hear a lot of people say "unique" when they mean interesting; maybe that's what "experimental" means to these people. Sometimes it just seems to mean hard to read.

One thing I know about experiments in general is that most of them fail, as they say. That is the way science works. In fact, according to science, all theories will eventually have to be modified as more experiments are carried out. That is what makes science different from unexamined faith. That is why people with unexamined faith feel threatened by science and don't like it. I think that these same people have a similar reaction to literature, especially "experimental" literature. Or painting. Or dance.

I know that I have tried various literary experiments, and sure enough, almost all of them have failed. For example, I was going to write a book in which my "central character" visited many if not all of Ezra Pound's Cantos as if they were rooms. I tried and tried, and could barely get started. I once tried to rewrite Rilke's Elegies without the help of a dictionary or an English translation. I got something, some pages, but they just weren't interesting. They were really hard to read; I guess they were "experimental" in that sense.

Then one day I thought back to the experiments we used to do in grade-eleven chemistry classes. Our teacher, who was also my father, taught us a method that was orderly and instructive. We had to take notes and write reports on every step of the way. The order was always the same; thus we ensured reliability: hypothesis, materials, procedure, data, calculations, results, conclusions.

I grew up an innocent lad in the rural Okanagan Valley, reading novels and short stories that were often about young men or women who went to the city and were debauched or at least made less innocent. Then I went to the city and read lots more novels about that transformation. So being a fiction writer and the son of a science teacher, I inevitably or spontaneously came up with a question that might be presented as a hypothesis. I could have hypothesized that a youth moving from the city to orchard country would become purer of soul. Or I could have posited that such a youth would remain as corrupt as the city had made him, and might even taint his new Peachtree Eden with some of that corruption.

Being sometimes a realist and sometimes an anti-realist, I took the middle path. And if you say that the story is not really "experimental," I can only respond that it is a fiction in the shape of an experiment.

An Experimental Story

1. Introduction and Hypothesis

It is a commonly held belief that an innocent country boy or girl, upon moving to the city, will be exposed to temptations great in number and strong in attraction, that his or her innocence will be attacked, and in most cases, at least bruised, if not entirely battered. He or she may be debauched or hardened or criminalized or even robbed of life. Less has been said about the youth who moves from the iniquitous city to a bucolic setting. Even Émile Zola, our great founder of experimental fiction, never investigated such an eventuality.

I am a city dweller who spent his boyhood in the orchard country of south-central British Columbia. Though I have often heard people point out that I retain some of my early innocence, I also know something of the darker corners in metropolitan life, far from my mother's eye. My best friend moved from the city to my village when we were about ten, so I did not look to him for my information, although a psychologist might.

It seemed to me unlikely that a youth who has been on the relevant streets long enough to be somewhat corrupted would revert to a natural innocence upon moving to the sticks. I thought we could postulate that it was unlikely that he or she would remain at a constant level, juvenile subjectivity being as precarious as it is alleged to be. And although we should remain scientifically open to data so as not to discount the possibility out of hand that the city youth would become tainted by rural life, I was of the opinion that this outcome was least likely.

It was my hypothesis that we could expect results somewhere in the middle of the range I have described. I thought that a street-wise Vancouver youth would, after interacting with the natural setting, the social tapestry, and the native individuals of the southern Okanagan Valley, begin to develop characteristics that would make him resemble Huckleberry Finn more than Studs Lonigan, to use a couple of standards set in an earlier time in the United States.

2. Materials

I thought for some time before I decided to select a boy rather than a girl, and rather than a number of boys or girls or both. I found a fourteen-year-old white boy with an English last name who was living on West 14th Avenue near Oak Street in Vancouver, a gentle flat area not far from Vancouver General Hospital, where his mother, a single parent from the word "go," was a nurse in the maternity ward. She just plain grew tired of living in the city where you cannot find a parking spot, and the bus never comes, and accepted a position at the Royal South Okanagan Hospital in Lawrence, one of the smaller towns in the valley.

The boy's name was Drew, as were about twenty percent of the boys in his classrooms at school. He was between grades nine and ten when he and his mother moved into a two-bedroom house within walking distance of the high school. Drew had never lived in a house, and the prospect did something to alleviate his unhappiness at leaving his companions behind. He also felt a little better when he saw that the boys here in the sticks wore the same outfits as did the boys at his old school. They were just as eager as he was to wear things with the most popular brand names and logos on them. They wore long silky basketball shorts and huge sports shoes made by children their age in Asian factories.

Drew had been masturbating regularly for a year and a half, and had once placed his hand on the warmer part of a girl's thigh, but most of his sexual experience came via the Internet. He did not know that his mother, who shared the computer, could click some square and see a list of the internet sites he had visited lately.

So he was not really a debauchée, just a city kid with dirty notions. As to other measurements of innocence, well, he and his companions, or his "homeys," as he liked to call them, boosted stuff at Chinese corner stores, entering as a group of four, say, and scattering around so that the owner's teenage son at the front till could not watch them all at once. The same guys would open the door of any parked car that was not locked, and gather change or CDs or items of clothing. They would throw most of the items of clothing under a hedge, and if the CD turned out to be Mozart or Dwight Yokum, it would go sailing onto someone's roof.

I don't know whether you would call that a disappearance of innocence. I would call it stupidity, myself.

So this youth from the coast was the material that I found myself focusing on the most, but of course the village of Lawrence was pretty important in itself. Any experiment features the introduction of some material into a material that it has till then been uninvolved with.

The nature of the valley is pretty well known to anyone who has read any of those magazines that they throw onto your front porch in the western half of Vancouver. Vineyards stretch green along the formerly light brown benches of the valley's hills, and whatever orchards remain range along both sides of little Highway 97, which has been getting more and more secondary since Highway 97A was put in a few decades ago to zip travellers from the Kootenays to the coast. More than half the trees bear apples, and the rest sport, in order of their picking seasons, cherries, apricots, peaches, pears, plums and prunes, as well as a few other fruits that are more for family interest than for commercial use.

Orchardists have always been put-upon people, beset by bad weather and a sudden paucity of seasonal workers. In latter times they have had to keep up with fickle tastes on the part of the consumers, as they had come to be called. Old-time varieties of apples, Winesaps and Newtons, for example, had to be rooted out and replaced by Galas and Ambrosias or something like that. The tall trees that had once been negotiated with twenty-four-foot ladders, had to be yanked out and replaced by small trees close together, reachable by an average-sized itinerant labourer from Quebec.

When Drew and his mother moved into the valley, it was pear and prune season. When Drew's mother first heard about this she complained that someone must have got it wrong. Prunes, she said, are dried plums. Old people eat them or drink their juice in order to regularize their excretion. She is a nurse, after all, so her son nearly avoided this argument. But he was a teenager.

"Well, I have a job starting tomorrow," said Drew, "and I am supposed to be picking prunes. Drew Bartkowski told me that prunes are just about the easiest thing to pick, because the trees are low and there are tons of prunes on every branch, and you take them all off. With peaches you have to go over the tree three or four times, apparently."

His mother was astonished. It had been a long time since she had heard him say three sentences in a row.

"Plums," she replied. "You will probably be picking plums."

"Drew said prunes, and he lives here."

"So do we," said his mother. "Well, a job. Now, let's see—what will you need?"

"Sunblock and a lunch," said Drew.

3. Procedure

Mrs. Van Hoorn had a five-acre orchard up behind the little airstrip, and it was pretty evenly divided between cherries and Italian prunes, a rather unusual combination in this part of the country. She had the good old-fashioned giant Bing cherry trees, now offering only leaves and hardened sap along old wounds in their trunks. The prune trees were short, and could be handed easily with a ten-foot ladder.

Drew had told her up front that he was new to this kind of work, but she said that Paddy would show him how it's done. Work starts at eight and goes to five, she said, with half an hour for lunch and two breaks. He got the idea that Paddy was not a relative, but some kind of old friend, or uncle, or employee from an earlier time. There did not seem to be any Mr. Van Hoorn, or at least if there was, he was somewhere else.

Most of the orchard women around here would be up in a tree picking, or driving the tractor around, but Mrs. Van Hoorn did not do that sort of thing. She was a painter, she said, and worked on the shaded patio of her little square stucco house in the middle of the orchard, or inside the house itself. She left Drew to Paddy, who had thick curly white hair that he did not put a hat on despite the desert sun, and a pipe that was always in his mouth, sometimes with the bowl upside down.

He showed Drew how to move his ladder in the high grass, where to hang his picking pail. Mainly he showed him how to handle the fruit. He said that you should not yank the prunes off the branch, but lift them off backward. It's the same with everything, cherries, pears, and all. And don't drop them into the pail. You don't want to handle fruit the way you see guys throwing it into bins at the supermarket in Vancouver.

"You want to hold it gently, as if it was your girlfriend's tit."

Drew didn't have a girlfriend, but he felt his face going red anyway. He had just a minute ago been thinking of Mrs. Van Hoorn's tits. He had once heard the word "breasts," and thought it was the most embarrassing word ever.

While Drew picked his pail full and carefully emptied it into the boxes and moved his ladder, he felt the hot sun on his sunblocked neck. Pretty soon he said to hell with it and took off his shirt and hung it on a low branch that had no more prunes on it. But now his white West Coast back was bared to the sun, and by later afternoon it was forty degrees in the shade and he was not in the shade all that often.

He managed to rub sunblock on the backs of his shoulders all right, and got a little, awkwardly, around the side of his ribcage, but he could already feel the burning air in the middle of his back. He couldn't ask Paddy to rub it on, could he, Paddy, who didn't wear a hat. Drew was wearing a green baseball cap with some incomprehensible skateboard logo on the front.

By lunchtime he was already pink and red all over his back. Sweat was running down his legs, and he decided that tomorrow he would wear shorts instead of jeans, and he would sunblock his legs. He sat down on the trailer that was hooked to Mrs. van Hoorn's little tractor, and looked at the pitiful little stack of prune boxes he had filled. Paddy had filled four for each one he had managed, and Paddy's boxes did not have leaves mixed in with the purple fruit. He smelled the tobacco from Paddy's pipe, and contemplated bringing cigarettes tomorrow.

Mrs. van Hoorn came out with a jug of ginger beer and two tall plastic cups. Drew sniffed at the liquid in his cup.

"Best thing in the world for this climate," said Paddy in an accent that may have been Irish and may just have been old-timer. "That and salt tablets. I never bother with the salt tablets, but there's them that does."

Mrs. van Hoorn was wearing old-fashioned white pleated tennis shorts and a man's shirt. There was a streak of blue paint on the outer side of one thigh. She had put the jug down on the trailer beside Drew, and was turning to head back to the house, when she stopped and looked at him.

"You are going to have a bad burn on that back. It's going to peel something awful. You should have sunblock on it," she said.

"I can't reach," he said, and he had not started eating his sandwich.

"Well, you have to have some protection. The sun in this part of the country is nothing to joke about."

And she spied his tube of sunblock in the grass below his shirt. When she bent to pick it up, Drew felt that he should be looking elsewhere, but he was not fast enough. Then she was squeezing a big gob of sunblock cream onto the palm of her hand. She rubbed her palms together and approached him.

"Give me your back," she said.

He could not speak, really, but he managed a kind of throat sound with his mouth closed. Then he felt her hands on his back. They were strong and unhesitating. It must be because she is an artist, he thought. He felt like a piece of art. He didn't know what he was feeling. Her hands moved all over his back, from the back of his neck to just a little in at the top of his jeans. Her hands seemed to go on forever, for a long time, anyway. She lives in the Okanagan Valley. She understands how to do this sunblock business. He felt her hands on the sides of his waist, and the fingers went just a little around front.

He was going to have to sit here for a while. There was no chance of standing up, not just now. Paddy was nowhere in sight.

"There you go," she said, and she was walking back to the house, holding her hands in the air in front of her.

4. Quantitative Data

Number of flats or boxes of prunes picked by Drew between
 8:00 A.M. and 5:00 P.M. on his first day – 19
Number picked by Paddy – 79
Minimum temperature between 8:00 A.M. and 5:00 P.M. – 18°C
Maximum temperature between 8:00 A.M. and 5:00 P.M. – 41°C
Number of prunes eaten by Drew between 8:00 A.M.
 and noon – 21
Number of prunes eaten by Drew between 1:00 P.M. and
 5:00 P.M. – 1
Number of erections experienced by Drew before noon – 4
Number of erections experienced by Drew after noon – 22
Number of erections experienced by Paddy – 0

We should factor in a chance of error in this compilation, of perhaps plus or minus two erections for Drew, the count becoming questionable as I myself had at least one and perhaps two while thinking of Mrs. van Hoorn. This occurred by accident as my mind drifted away from the scene in the orchard and over to and inside the little stuccoed and vine-covered house, where it was cooler than it was in the sunlight, but still warm enough to induce the shedding of some clothing, as for instance by Mrs. van Hoorn, who was unbuttoning her shirt and moving her shoulders to get free of it, until she wore nothing but the tennis shorts and one of those scalloped bras that do not enclose the breasts (there's that word) so much as they hold them up a little from underneath. Mrs. van Hoorn, being of average height, stood on a chair and raised herself upon her tiptoes to bring down the curtain rod for the living-room window. It was, I suppose, time to wash that off-white curtain.

It was Heisenberg, wasn't it, who proclaimed that during a scientific observation, the observer affects the experiment in observing it. In the sharp formulation of the law of causality—"if we know the present exactly, we can calculate the future"—it is not the conclusion that is wrong but the premise. The path comes into existence only when we observe it.

Cause and effect was such a revolutionary idea when the scientists and then the medical doctors and then Émile Zola got a hold of it. Then along came those white pleated tennis shorts. They were old-fashioned—that means they had buttons rather than a zipper.

All right—we are doing Quantitative Data. There were four white buttons.

5. Qualitative Data

There are, in all experiments that involve human subjects, or even subjects from the animal kingdom, except for, perhaps, insects and fish, certain data that cannot be quantified, even data that is unexpected. Having placed a city boy in an orchard just outside a little town in the August heat, we realize that our desire to see whether he becomes more innocent, or stays about the same, or somehow continues his path away from the "visionary gleam" is not going to be satisfied quickly. We know that we are but beginning a long process of observation, and that many laboratory reports such as this one will have to be piled up before we can venture any thorough conclusion.

A lot depends, for example, on the nature of desert sunlight between the branches of fruit trees. Drew had not brought his sunglasses, or "shades" as he and his "homeys" called them. They would have made things only more difficult in the cool dark under the laden trees. But if you look up at a wall of white stucco blasted by white sun, you will not truly be seeing, but only shone upon. If you see a window in that wall, it will appear as a square of blackness. In that square of blackness, Drew saw a little bit of white rise and stay and descend. This white was Mrs. van Hoorn's tennis shorts.

Drew did not know that. He was standing on the fourth step of his ladder and picking prunes without thinking about them. What he saw was folded into his imagination, which a moment earlier had displayed his rising and rising from the polished floor and jamming a basketball, one-handedly, into the middle of a hoop that it was hard to believe had exactly twice the diameter of a basketball.

The white blur was an egret rising silently and skating away in the south wind.

Drew stopped, three prunes in his right hand, and stared at the black rectangle on the white glare. The egret did not reappear. Nor did anything else. He returned to the world of boxes and grass and pails and trees. This was a work space. For a lot of people it or something like it, would be a piece of calendar art, a dream of Eden, what I did on my summer holidays. I have a job, he had told his mother, and it was the first time he had ever done such a thing on his own. This might not be the onset of adulthood, but it was definitely the goodbye to childhood.

This was a conclusion he was led to during the afternoon appearance of the ginger beer. Mrs. van Hoorn was barefoot in the dust, and she was wearing the white shorts and a halter top, a bright parrot-patterned piece of cloth with an extravagant bow tied in back. When she put the jug and glasses down on the trailer bed, Drew was going to look away, polite boy that he was, but something made him remain attentive and he saw a bead of perspiration descend between her tanned breasts, and disappear. There was also perspiration in the hair combed back above her ears, and that, too, was something to see.

He didn't know it but he was beginning to conclude that that was it for childhood. He drank the ginger beer, and told Paddy that he had never tasted it before.

"Aye, boy," said the white-haired man. "At your age you will be tasting a lot of things for the first time."

The remark was of such an obvious nature that even Drew got an inkling of what Paddy was saying through him to the owner of this fruit ranch.

Or he may have just been a hoping boy, hoping for something he really knew nothing about. That would be my interpretation of qualitative data, anyway.

One tug, the boy thought, as he watched Mrs. van Hoorn walk barefoot and carefully back up the slight grade to her house.

Readers of my report might be somewhat skeptical regarding my observations, especially as they would seem to be made from the point of view of my subject, young Drew. One could argue, though I admit faultily, that as quantitative data would seem to be objective, so qualitative data would appear subjective. That is not going to be my tack, as I have recently done some light reading about the theoretical and experimental work of Werner Heisenberg.

All I will tell you is that I used to be fourteen years old, and when I was fourteen years old I worked in more than one orchard in the southern Okanagan Valley. If you think that that disqualifies or disquantifies me as an observer, I will say that this is a post-Heisenbergian experiment. It is careful as can be, nevertheless.

I can tell you, for example, that young Drew had a stomach ache for about an hour in the later part of the afternoon. It would be reasonable to surmise that the cause was the unusual number of prunes he had eaten during the forenoon. When he went to have a pee behind a distant tree, he paused in his walking for a few seconds while the ache tapered off a bit.

Drew liked to read a moderate number of books and magazines, but he was not a boy to analyze overmuch regarding what he had read and how he saw his position in the world. Thus he did not, not even fleetingly, compare himself to Adam in the Garden. Thoughts of innocence and its loss did not approach him. Perhaps it was a Creator that was missing from the scenario.

The city is west of there, anyway.

6. Calculations

On his first day on the job the youngster from the coast picked 19 boxes of Italian prunes. Each box weighs 24 pounds net. (The box size was created before Canada's adoption of worldwide measurements.) That means that he picked 456 pounds of prunes. As he was being paid 10.5 cents per pound, he earned $47.88 for a first day's pay. He started at 8:00 a.m. and finished at 5:00 p.m., with a half hour for lunch and two fifteen-minute breaks for ginger beer. So his hourly wage for that first day amounted to $5.98 and a sliver an hour. Back on the coast he could have made about that much for cleaning smears off tables in a hamburger joint.

He had been in a lot of those hamburger joints, pizza joints, chicken joints, and he had never seen anyone like Mrs. van Hoorn running any of them. I am not saying that that is an observation that belongs in "Calculations," but it did come to mind, his and mine.

The conclusion we want to come to, remember, has something to do with the change in innocence and behaviour that might be observed when a subject is moved from an urban environment to a rural one. The trick is to organize one's data and make one's calculations and remain clear of any undo attention to ephemeral facts or images.

All right. Paddy smoked tobacco twelve times during the working day. Drew did not use any tobacco except some second-hand smoke, which was not unpleasant, Paddy favouring a sweet mixture with a trace of cypress.

Drew was not lazy. Nor was he greedy. He was about as good a worker as you could expect given his age and experience and place of origin. That is what Paddy thought, in any case. The boy may have been momentarily guilty of some vice of which an observer might not be aware, such as avarice, or lust. Well, there *was* the beer, but surely that might be set down to usage and tradition sooner than to vice.

Mrs. van Hoorn brought out the beer, three bottles of Kokanee, with heavy dew on the outside of the brown glass, just as she had twice brought out the ginger beer. This time, though, there was no pitcher to empty into the glasses. She did the pouring in the shade of a prune tree that had been picked that day. There were leaves on the trampled grass under the tree. The beer made nice foam that almost spilled over the rim of the glass that Drew was holding, his long day's work done. Unlike ginger beer, Kokanee was something that he had tasted before, though he had never had one poured for him by an adult person.

He kind of liked the flavour, or as they call it in beer circles, the taste. He watched Paddy to see how fast you were supposed to drink it, but Paddy had his pocket knife out and was carving the plug out of the bowl of his pipe. Mrs. van Hoorn took a moderate sip and looked at him over the rim of her glass, upon which the sun, still pretty high in the sky at the end of the workday, glistened enough to make things disappear from sight.

Drew had had a beer before, as I mentioned, or rather he had shared a beer or two from time to time, on those nights when he stayed later than usual at a friend's place and there was beer in the fridge, or someone brought a bottle or two to the beach. This was his first daylight beer, and there was an understanding that it was meant to put something back into his body that had been expended in a hard day's work under the hot sun. He had his shirt back on now, but he could feel the sweat in it. It would be impossible to calculate the amount of stuff that had come out of him, and though it might be possible to measure the 375ml that were entering his stomach and so on, there was no way of figuring out how much necessary stuff he was replenishing himself with.

Before he knew it his glass and his bottle were empty and foam stains were disappearing. Now he would jump on his mountain bike and head for home, where his mother would have pasta and salad and milk ready and would be too busy to smell his breath.

So he calculated.

Mrs. van Hoorn's halter top was securely tied, it would appear. When she got up to gather the bottles and glasses, her *breasts* swung inside the cloth a little. Drew felt as if he should be apologetic for something. He remembered to pick up his lunch kit and walked two rows over to his bike. Here in the country his mother had not yet nagged him to wear his helmet.

7. Results

"What do you think?" asked Paddy. "Will this one be a sticker?"

"I expect we'll see him at 8:00 tomorrow," said Mrs. van Hoorn.

"How was the first day on the job?" asked his mother. She was still wearing her string-tied white sports trousers and discount sports shoes from work.

"I can handle it," he replied.

She thought of that as a pretty good start. He might manage another sentence at dinner. They were going to eat in the back yard, where the television was not a factor.

"Would you like to stay for supper?" asked Mrs. van Hoorn. "There's corn on the cob."

"Ah, I would," Paddy said. "But I've got a Lodge dinner at the hotel."

"You will probably be a little stiff tomorrow," said his mother, as she used the edge of the big spoon to pull some peas onto his plate.

His lips lifted a little at the edges.

"Oh, I expect so," he said. "From time to time."

Mrs. van Hoorn was alone now as the sun found its place behind a mountain that always brought an early twilight to this part of the valley, alone except for her large muscular cat to whom she had bequeathed the name "Frankie."

"I believe that I will have one more glass of beer," she told him.

Drew went off to his bedroom earlier than usual. He had to get up early for work.

When she opened his lunch kit to clean it out, she found it almost full of ripe plums.

8. Conclusions

I understand that any generalization I might make as a result of this experiment will, at best, serve as a hypothesis for another experiment, whether conducted by me or by another observer. I also understand that more than one conclusion might be made following the results seen above.

Did young Drew experience and exhibit any changes regarding his innocence as a result of moving from the west side of Vancouver to Lawrence in the Okanagan? Or were any changes only those that might be expected of any boy that age?

It is my tentative conclusion, if such a phrase be allowed (and why would it not, in a world that hears people talk about "cautious optimism"?), that the climate and weather in the orchard country during autumn served to arouse in Drew's daytime whim and nighttime fancy, thoughts and images that were in an earlier time called "lewd." (And here is another factor prompting relativism: how can we make conclusions concerning innocence and its loss when standards regarding social behaviour have gone through such thorough changes?)

The climate and weather, perhaps as much as the personalities involved, had their effect on attire, perspiration, and post-work libation.

On the one hand, the boy, Drew, might be said to have given in to lustful thoughts. But we must also remember that he became an honest worker. I recall a similar balancing-off when I was that age and did the self-examination one might expect in such a reflective youth as I was. What I assume he will assume? Which of us is even now in her dark orchard, trying to get a glimpse of the lighted interior? In any experiment one tries to shine a light there. But I am not here to construct conclusions about myself. Or am I? Does Heisenberg reach that far?

Thea gets her feet wet, circa 1972.

Horizontal Surfaces

It took me years to write this book. *Horizontal Surfaces* is one of those books with a number of short takes on one-word subjects gathered alphabetically. Actually the number of topics in the book is forty-eight. It's not the first time that I have used that number. Over the years I would occasionally return to the manuscript of this book and add a page or a page and a half. That wouldn't be a bad way of reading it, either.

Here the entries run from "Accessible" to "West." Most of them have something to do with composition, a word that means something like "placing side by side." The one entry I have chosen to reprint here is "Lawrence," purportedly about my fictionalized home town in the South Okanagan.

The title of the book was given to me by my daughter, Thea, the fiction writer. It is mysterious and obvious.

Lawrence

Quite often I write a story that takes place in the southern Okanagan Valley, and when I do, I call my home town Lawrence. I grew up, mainly, in Oliver, British Columbia, a little orchard town in the desert. I did what you always used to do in realist fiction—made up names that are something like the names of the people and places you were using as models. Is that trying for some sort of sympathetic magic? In my older stories and novels I wrote about a young guy named George

Delsing. I got the George easily, as Jack Kerouac called his stand-in Jack Duluoz, counting syllables. It turned out that in his autobiographical novels, Kerouac had his character go to or at least mention the next town over—Lawrence, Massachusetts! I used Lawrence because it, like Oliver, was a first name or a last name. I think that I remember that on a few occasions I have reported in notes on contributors or elsewhere that I spent my boyhood in Lawrence, British Columbia. I do like it when fiction intertwines with what we take to be the actual. Have I told this story? Once, when an East German magazine, desirous of making Teutonically tidy contributors' notes, pointed out to me that in various publications it was reported variously that I had been born in Princeton, Keremeos, Penticton, and Oliver. I replied that it had been a slow birth in a fast car. In one story set in an orchard, there is a reference made to a writer-lover named Oliver. It was a matter of necessity, the fictive name I put on the fellow I modelled on D. H. Lawrence. There are hundreds of such worthless little japes in my writing. I know that some will never be remarked.

The Diamond Alphabet

One of my favourite ways to organize a book is by the alphabet. I guess I learned that partly from the great French writer Roland Barthes. It was either he or another intelligent structuralist who pointed out that almost all of us know the order of the letters in the alphabet despite the fact that the order is not otherwise significant.

One of my favourite kinds of book is the one made up of a gathering of short pieces about something: poetry, friends, cars—baseball. So for my fifth baseball book I decided on the alphabet. *B*, you're so beautiful. We decided that twenty-six chapters with five subjects to each chapter would make a nice length, and thank goodness, we got a beautifully made book because Jay MillAr, the publisher of BookThug, had recently been introduced to the beauties of baseball by his son. Way to go, son!

Then Jean, who did most of the work again, rounded up twenty-six baseball caps for chapter headings, and got permission from the teams represented. Are you wondering about the letter *X*? It is worn by my favourite team in the Veracruz winter league, the Xalapa Chileros. Way to go, Jean!

You will know by now that baseball is one of my favourite subjects, and that I have been writing about baseball in the Okanagan nearly all my life. It ain't what it used to be, but last spring we went to a game in Kelowna, where the Falcons were hosting the Corvallis Knights in a West Coast League game. I think I shared memories with a little old white-haired guy up high in the bleachers on the first base side.

For a while we had a choice between the Legion and the Oliver Theatre but eventually the sloped floor and actual seats won the day.

Babe

Before they built the new Oliver Theatre on Main Street, we went to see movies in the Legion Hall. We would sit on two-by-twelves resting on upturned apple boxes, and listen to the projector laying out our western or our Disney. For a while after they opened the new Oliver Theatre, across the side road and on Main Street, too, both places showed movies.

On Saturdays most of the boys went to the new Oliver Theatre with the folding padded seats and the projector you could hear only during the really quiet and suspenseful scenes. And because they did, I preferred to go to the Legion.

Most of those boys preferred Roy Rogers, so I preferred Gene Autry. Champion rather than Trigger. No one rather than Dale. "Back in the Saddle Again" rather than "Happy Trails to You."

Most of those boys liked to see Lash LaRue, but I held out for the underdog Whip Wilson. Looking back, I might have chosen the former because he was Cajun, but I just thought he was trying to be fawncy with a French name.

Those boys chose Superman with his up up and away business, so of course I became a Batman fan. Har dee har, they said, he hasn't even got any superpowers. Exactly, I replied, trying to sound mysteriously wise.

Here we were in a little podunk in the far west of Canada, and those boys were all New York Yankees followers. Not I. I became a Red Sox fan at the age of ten.

So I extolled the fiery and aloof Ted Williams, while they were all of them gaga for Joe DiMaggio.

And when it came to the all-time history of our great game, I held out for the little-known Ty Cobb while they all confidently announced the eminence of Babe Ruth.

Donkeys

You could pile up a lot of great memories while growing up in a hot dry valley 250 miles and a couple of mountain ranges from Vancouver and the rest of the coast. A lot of them had to do with the baseball park with its rickety old grandstand down across the river. Normally there was the Okanagan Mainline Baseball League, with its games on Saturdays, and then when everyone got a little less religious, on Sundays. When I was really young there was the kind of softball called fastball, with my dad as the catcher for the Oliver Elks. Then there was the baseball league that included teams from towns up and down the Okanagan Valley on both sides of the forty-ninth parallel. Kelowna, British Columbia, and Omak, Washington, for example. Then for reasons I never learned, we had the eight-team OMBL, that stretched from Kamloops in the north to Trail in the southeast.

Eight teams, just like the two major leagues. In other words, real. If the major leagues ever changed from eight teams to something less or more, they would not be exactly real any more.

But in addition to league play there were the visitations of trick teams. I scorned them but I would never miss them. A barnstorming team of U. S. Negroes (remember, this was in the late forties) came to town, and I saw my first ever Black man up close. He had bloodshot eyes, and I took it for granted that all Negroes had bloodshot eyes. But then I wondered, because my many pictures of Jackie Robinson and Larry Doby didn't show me any such thing.

These trick teams would always take on the locals, of course. One group was made up of guys with long beards. They called themselves the House of David. I had no idea what that could possibly mean, who David was, why a House? Of course, I could have asked one of them, but I was not the sort of boy who could work up the nerve to do such a thing. Then there was Eddie Feigner, the King and his Court. He was from just south of us, in Walla Walla, and he was the greatest softball pitcher in history. His team was made of four guys, and he would strike out your best hitters from second base. They were the Globetrotters of the diamond.

But the goofiest barnstormers were the donkey baseball guys. In a donkey baseball game the outfielders all have donkeys and the offensive team has donkeys. If an outfielder has to chase a ball down he has to do it on donkey back. A hitter has to hop onto the back of his donkey to get down to first, and if he makes it, he is a base runner with an animal. Of course these barnstorming donkeys have all been trained to have certain personalities. There's Wrong Way Corrigan, who wants to head for third instead of first. There's the guy who will not move, no matter how animated you become on his back. There's the one that sits down on his bum and won't get up again. I guess you could say that they are a lot like the Washington Nationals.

*Eddie Steffen was the ace of the Oliver pitching
rotation around 1949. In the background is the
grandstand that would be around long after
baseball was no longer played in front of it.*

Okanagan

What killed semi-pro baseball all over the map was the infestation of television. When television was new to the Okanagan Valley, people who used to go out and watch the baseball game on Sunday afternoon stayed home and watched whatever the one or two television stations had to offer, old Bowery Boys movies, maybe.

That's what happened to the Okanagan Mainline Baseball League in the late fifties or early sixties. For the life of me, I can't understand why people would give up the excitement of a sunny afternoon at the park, the Summerland Macs in town with the amazing Kato brothers around the infield, to go home and pull the curtains and watch a little black-and-white game show. It just goes to show what happens when a new drug hits town. It would happen again later with video games and cellphones.

The Okanagan Mainline Baseball League had two teams in Kamloops, and one each in Vernon, Kelowna, Summerland, Penticton, Oliver, and Trail. In those days it was just normal to have eight teams in a league, because that was what happened in the Majors. Before the formation of the OMBL there was an outfit called the Okanagan League, with four teams in British Columbia (Vernon, Kelowna, Penticton, and Oliver) and four in Washington (Omak, Brewster, Tonasket, and either Chelan or Republic). I had mixed feelings when we went all Canadian.

There were a lot of Protestants in town who said that we shouldn't have ball games on Sundays, ball games you had to pay fifty cents to see. I sort of agreed with them, but I loved baseball so much that I was willing to step a little closer to Hell. I wasn't even averse to making a bit of money on the Sabbath. Sometimes I joined the boys chasing foul balls for the dimes you got for returning them. Later I roamed the stands and autos with bottles of pop for sale. Still later I got to the roof of the grandstand to keep score and make notes for stories in the *Chronicle*.

What the heck is Mainline, I wondered. I have it figured out now: it must be the CPR geography that passes through Kamloops. I generally didn't go on road trips to Kamloops or Trail, so that I had to make up stories on those games from the anecdotes I gathered from the players on Monday.

And now I remember that Princeton was in the league for a while. The ball players there had jobs working in the Princeton Brewery. That was the first beer I ever had, and once in a blue moon I have a sip of beer that reminds me of how good it tasted. Each bottle in the case of twelve was wrapped in a kind of grey asbestosy paper. Now when I drive to Oliver to see my family I pass the remains of the old Princeton baseball stadium. I think Princeton was in the league when Trail wasn't.

In the Okanagan Mainline Baseball League there was a lot of talk about "imports." These were USAmerican ballplayers who would be brought to town and given a job so they could be paid for playing ball. Some years back when I was doing research for a novel set in Kamloops, I found out that the baseball teams around there were bringing in USAmerican "imports" in 1889. I remember feeling a little ashamed that we went to the States to get good ballplayers.

But I wish I could go back and see a game in Tonasket on a hot dusty July Sunday afternoon—and have one of those USAmerican soda pops you couldn't get back home.

Words, Words, Words

The subtitle of this book gets it right: *Essays and Memoirs*. "To essay" something is to give it a try, I guess, which means "starting out." Then when you get older there is more time behind you, more to remember. Or as it says in the beginning of the first part of *Words, Words, Words*, "A Writer in the Family": "Now in my mellow years I just write when I write and dote on my sweetheart, Jean, when I am doting."

I would like to tell you how this autobiographical essay was generated, but being in my mellow years I can't quite recall. It had its source in one of those interviews you find yourself taking part in if you have been around long enough. I once did some rapid typing while sitting there with many wires attached to my skull, part of a research event for someone else's discipline, and then managed to reshape that typing into some real writing. The sequence I am concerned with now was not that dramatic in its birth, but what emerged seemed good enough to be the leadoff to a collection. It has five constituent parts, and here we include the second part of the first, "The Family Son." It tells the story of a boy growing up in a town unfamiliar with the arts and hoping to find out which of them he will pursue.

The Family Son

When I moved away from home at age seventeen, the first thing I saved for and bought myself was a portable typewriter.

Because back home with my dad's typewriter, there on a card table

I guess that's my dad's typewriter. In Oliver, in our front yard,
just outside the dining room.

or out on the lawn, where I would get my picture taken, long-haired fellow sweating out the paragraphs, I could imagine making books, figuring out how to assemble gatherings or signatures, not knowing those words. Also the other way round—when I was buying paperbacks at the drugstore or pool hall I was interested in the whole package, reading all the stuff in the front pages and back pages, noticing whether there was stitching as on White Circle paperbacks, seeing the way the cheapo lines had typefaces that looked like typewriter letters. When the New American Library Signet Books became taller in proportion to their breadth, I favoured Pocket Books and Bantam Books, which stayed short, but eventually they went for the taller shape.

I was a lone boy in all this. I had two friends, John Jalovec and Art Fraser, who gobbled up westerns and other paperbacks, and they were both a long way from our English teachers' approval lists, but I never knew whether they were turning into writer boys. They certainly didn't write for the paper, or even the school paper. Despite all his typing, my father never did any "creative" writing. No one in Oliver did, except my buddy Willy's mother, who wrote some kids' stories for the weekend Vancouver *Province*.

So there was no "writing community," that's for sure. In fact it never entered my mind that such a thing was possible. There were no painters in town, as far as I knew, and certainly no place to see paintings. I once had a commission to do giant cartoons of the firemen for a firemen's ball, but I didn't even see those when they were installed. Outside of high school the only musicians I knew were a couple of dance bands, one with accordions for polkas, the other with saxophones for dancing, led by Gar McKinley, my high school music teacher. I was in the school band and the school choir, working off the bass clef for both of them.

Well, I also wrote songs with my buddy Willy. Usually I would write the words and he would make up the melody. These were on the model of the hit parade at the time, romantic love songs, two verses, a chorus, and a third verse. Later at university we wrote the songs for a musical comedy about the opening of Japan by the Americans in the nineteenth century. It featured great tunes such as "I'm yo Daimyo," and

"I'm the Shogun with the Slogan."

In high school Willy and I would hardly ever perform our songs, mainly because though Willy had a great voice, I was shy, partly because I had more style than voice. But Willy and my girlfriend Wendy and another couple formed a quartet that I baptized The Troubadours, and they sometimes sang our songs.

But I knew all the words of all the songs on the hit parade. I still know most of those fifties songs, and so does my daughter, because I sang them with her when she was a kid. I don't know the words to any of today's songs, or maybe they don't have words, I don't know. People were amazed that I'd memorized all these songs, but they never told me I should be a professional singer. In fact, years later, at reunions, they told me they thought I would have become a stand-up comedian.

I was an actor. In high school I was always in a play, on one occasion in two at once, dashing from rehearsal to rehearsal. I played the lead in Oscar Wilde's *The Importance of Being Earnest*, of all things. There was an adult acting organization in town, and though I went to their plays, I don't think I was ever in one of them, or was I?

Well, I wanted to do all those things—write, sing, paint, photograph (Willy and I had a darkroom in his basement), be in a band, whatever there was. But when you are in a small town, and you are the kind of kid who goes on mountain hikes alone, the one that is easiest to do is to write. You can keep it a secret. Unlike acting and singing and cracking wise and all those things, writing was something you could do alone. Besides, I had an inferiority complex and a superiority complex at the same time. I felt socially inferior and intellectually superior, and did everything I could to pretend the opposite.

But though I wrote some poems and stories when I was a high school kid, I imagined myself as a sportswriter. I collected sports magazines (I still have them packed away in boxes), so I knew the names of all the sportswriters in the United States. I even wrote to one I liked a lot, Bob Broeg of the St. Louis *Post-Dispatch*, asking him what I should do. He said to come to Columbus and the University of Missouri, the best journalism school in the United States. Of course I could not have afforded such a thing, even though my mother's family was from Missouri. Besides which, the girl I loved was going to go to normal school in Victoria. The normal school shared a building with Victoria College, and my uncle Jack lived within walking distance, so that's where I went. I have made all the important decisions in my life for love.

ST. LOUIS POST-DISPATCH
THE PULITZER PUBLISHING COMPANY

Feb. 24

Dear George:

Pardon the delay in answering your letter.

If you don't mind my saying so, George, you've got
the ~~dog~~ *tail* wagging the ~~dog~~ when you talk about getting a position
with a large eastern paper before you have attended college and
studied journalism.

To show your interest, however, I would drop into
the New York and Boston newspapers---preferably New York---whenever
the opportunity presents itself and try to see the sports editors.
It might not be easy, but try. If you succeed, tell them you're
aware you're not ready now, but that you're planning to go to
college and that, if they don't mind, you'll write to them from
time to time---not expecting an answer---and will ~~send~~ send them
school-paper clippings. *The contacts are important.*

If you haven't set yourself on a choice elsewhere, I
can recommend highly the University of Missouri School of Journalism,
the first in the U.S., located at Columbia, Mo., which is halfway
between St. Louis and Kansas City. Because of its reputation, the
Mizzou Jay School has a cosmppolitan enrollment you would appreciate.
For further information, I suggest you write Dean ~~Earl~~ Earl English
at the school.

As for your interests in baseball and football, try to
learn all sports, George, and remember that a sports section is
a newspaper within a newspaper, that it's absolutely essential to
be adept in reading copy, writing heads and laying out and making up
pages. I can't stress too much the necessity for skill as an "inside"

man as the opening wedge into a sports department, large or
small, and the foot-in-the-door necessary to get the juicy
outside assignments you dream about.

Take my word for the above. You've got to generalize,
to be a triple threat, before you can specialize. Become a
good all-around newspaperman and you enhance your chances of
getting what you want.

Study newspaper headline and layout techiques as well
as writing methods. The best of luck, George, and if you
get through St. Louis, look me up.

Sincerely

Bob Broeg

Bob Broeg

My famous Georgie hat, in the hills east of Oliver.

Pinboy

Some people say that *Pinboy* is a memoir. Others say it is a novel. Still others try to find a word that will properly categorize it in bookstores and libraries—a fictobiography, maybe, a non-fiction novel. In a recent essay Marc Coté, who was the book's publisher, argues that it is a memoir and does some fancy stepping that reminds me of my own.

Whatever *Pinboy* is, it takes place entirely in the Okanagan Valley, primarily in Oliver, because it tells the story, in the first person, of a boy who went to high school there, as did I. The letter featured in this excerpt, and the classmate's poem alluded to, are two examples of unreliable writings. In a way, this passage is filled with clues about the novel and its authorship.

from Pinboy

If you have managed to read or skim this far, you will know that things happen or don't happen to me in threes. Mickey's rabbit punch was scary because I had blacked out. Delsing's poem was embarrassing because I could never persuade anyone that I didn't write it, and more than that, there were parts of it that seemed familiar. I almost felt as if I could have written it. It sounded like a guy who is inwardly noble and romantic and uses tough humour to disguise that fact. But I would happily have accepted the cowardly blow and the snide plagiarism if I had never found Wendy's letter.

You remember how the beloved's handwriting could put goose-bumps on your heart? You remember that I often roamed the brown rocky hills up behind the elementary school, with or without my dog Dinky? Usually I had a drugstore paperback novel in my back pocket, sometimes a magazine. I have a photo that Will took of me up in the hills. I am wearing my Georgie Hat and reading a copy of *Hit Parader*. My Georgie Hat was not to be confused with my reporter hat. My Georgie Hat was also a fedora, probably found in the cloakroom of the community hall, but it had the front brim turned up and pinned to the crown. Sometimes the back brim, too. In the cooler months I would have a scarf tied over the top and around my chin. Now I remember that the other lyrics magazine was *Song Hits*. You can't believe how thrilling it was when these mags arrived in Frank's pool hall in Oliver. I pretty well knew all the lyrics of all the hit tunes, which used to amaze my friend Roy Collett, who wound up playing bass in his own cocktail jazz trio ten years later, but these wonderful mags, made and sold cheap by the Charlton company, along with its lesser-known comic books, connected me with the shiny two-bit world of the eastern United States, where I almost felt that I belonged. Like most U. S. magazines, the November 1951 issue of *Hit Parader* reached small-town Okanagan news racks in September 1951.

This one likely had the lyrics for Tony Bennett's "Because of You" and the Four Aces's "Tell Me Why," with Al Albert bending the note on "me" and making sure there was a lot of light on his teeth for the group photo, while the rhythm section kept the doo-dum doo-dum going behind him.

"I keep fooling my heart."

I have probably figured this narrative all out by now, or if I haven't, I shouldn't be allowed to write this memoir, or at least to pretend that I am capable of analysis in its composition, as they say.

I mean, how did the letter get there?

And how come I was the one that found it?

I guess that at the time I thought my hiking alone in these hills was a fully private and lonesome activity, known to me and my Creator.

I will not, as some might do, peg Him as the one who arranged for my finding of the letter. But there is a sliver of my brain that leaves room for that exigency.

To fold back again, just for a bit, I'll say that I don't right now remember whether I told you about the frozen guy and the fingers. This is something I haven't talked to anyone about for over a half century. He was a year or more likely two ahead of me in school, some kind of athletic hero I didn't know, and why would that be? Anyway, he was a patterned-sweater-wearing skier, and a climber and all that. You will remember that around that time or a bit earlier, the best young swimmer in Oliver drowned in the river, fell off a chair he was sitting on in the water, and the best young skater in Oliver fell through the ice on Tuc-el-Nuit Lake and was pulled under the thicker ice by a current and disappeared. I felt safe because I wasn't the best at anything physical in that town. But now there was this story.

There was a big windy snowstorm in the mountains I had never climbed, on the west side of the valley between Oliver and Osoyoos. It was not until this moment that I noticed I never climbed up and back in those mountains. I wonder whether this was why. The guy in question, tall, fit, went, as they say, missing, and crews went out looking for him, a grade-twelve boy or man, who could take care of himself, people thought. Were there others who did get out, did get found? Why don't I remember more of this? Did it really happen?

Well, the story we heard from each other was that he had eventually been found, released by the snow, and it had been a long time. He had chewed off the ends of his fingers.

Did this really happen? Was it a story whose edge had been caught by some boy from some uncle reading a newspaper story out loud? Was that it, something like that?

But such stories did fall away, didn't they? My classmate Tibor Palley died in the hospital, and the story we heard was that he said over and over "I love you, Jesus." A few years later no one ever mentioned Tibor Palley. The kids a couple of grades younger than us probably didn't hear his name much.

Okay, but this manly boy. There was another step in the foggy story. Supposedly, before I met her and got to love being with her, Wendy had been this guy's girlfriend for a while. Now you have to remember that Wendy was a grade ahead of me in school, but a year and a month younger.

I could not ask her.

Especially when the story hinted a little further (and where did I get this, did I imagine it or did I hear it whispered from a friend or enemy?), that Wendy had gone all the way with this romantic, doomed young man.

It seems silly now, because it is easy to think back and do the arithmetic. If Wendy had gone all the way with him it would have happened a year or so back, and back then she would have been barely into her teenage years. Nowadays it would seem at least possible, but not then, at least not with an intelligent and wholesome daughter of the Anglican Church and the English community that ran orchards south of Oliver in the fifties.

Anyway, I don't think there was any question that Wendy's letter was addressed to that guy. Which only makes it worse, I guess, though I thought: what if this is a fake? But then I knew Wendy's handwriting as well as I knew anyone's, or almost as well as I knew my father's, say, or mine. No, it had to be her handwriting. In pale blue ink on an even paler blue letter paper. Under a rock on top of a larger rock in my favourite little cave in Cryhat Valley, where Will and I used to eat our oranges and practise cowboy dialogue.

So someone had put it there, in all likelihood someone who was watching me even as I went into the little cave and lifted the smaller rock. Someone who apparently didn't much like me, or who maybe just liked the opportunity to bother the ears off someone who thinks he is alone in his hike or his daydream.

When I first unfolded the light blue paper and saw the handwriting and saw that it was a letter, I assumed that it was addressed to me, that this was an elaborate gesture of affection. But I soon saw that though someone meant me to read it, the letter was addressed to someone else. Unless Wendy herself was at the helm of the ruse—which was an eventuality I did not want to entertain then, and which I don't much like to consider now.

I would or would not like to reproduce the letter here. But it has disappeared. Maybe I balled it up and threw it over a cliff. Maybe I burned it. Maybe I put it on the ground and pissed on it. I know that it is not among my papers at the National Library, which do contain letters I wish I had never got. Well, it wasn't addressed to me, so it wouldn't have gone there anyway. You will notice that I am putting this off. Okay, I cannot, for whatever reason, present it here in its original shape. Suffice it to say that I was hurt as only a teenage boy on a mountain can be hurt.

Funny verb, that, now that I come to remember the first time I heard it. It was from Wendy herself, sometime over the preceding year. I don't want you to be hurt, she said, I think. And I wondered about that: does it mean hurt feelings? But it sounded more serious than that, more intimate. But then I got to thinking about the word "intimate," which always made me think of inside the brassiere.

Okay, the letter. It was not addressed to anyone, or rather, there was no salutation at the beginning. But it said this and that, in Wendy's handwriting, in Parker's blue ink. I will not say much more, except that it referred to "you," whoever that was, being inside her. My girl.

Now that I think about it, the person who put this little blue folded paper under that rock was probably watching me open and read it, watching from behind a rock, with field glasses. Smiling. I can't see a face. I never thought till this moment—maybe a female person?

No, female persons did not hike around these hills. I never ran across any. But who knew about my favourite cave? Will did, but he was out of the question. Maybe he told someone. Not likely.

Anyway, this letter, I did not know this then, but I grew to know it, or maybe to admit it, this letter was worse than getting judo chopped or misrepresented in doggerel.

I imagined my beloved naked that night and in nights to follow, but now in my imagination she was not alone.

Teeth

The only overt mention of the Okanagan in the collection *Teeth* is in the poem "Tie."

One thing about "Tie" is that it is an early example of the post-Ashbery one-page poems I began writing late in the first decade of the twenty-first century. These poems, the first of which was "I Like Summer," are usually made of one longish stanza in which the mind runs away with itself, the new line springing off detail from its predecessor. Gone is my earlier interest in short regular stanzas, and gone is my interest in the sharp, clear Levertovian image. The first line, taken from a popular song of my high-school days, may turn out to be ironical later in the poem, but I had no idea that that would happen.

Another thing is an Okanagan experience I have mentioned in various novels and stories. The village of Oliver was created to service orchard-owners who had come from Britain to work their tree-fruit homesteads. Eastern Europeans arrived, too, and tried to get in on the act. As an anti-imperial boy, I harboured a bit of animus for the Limeys. I was pretty sure that they were ordinary louts who came over here and put on blazers and regimental ties and became the local aristocracy. This picture is full of holes, of course. My grandfather came as a homeboy from England, and I fell in love with a British-raised girl, and the poem in question makes something of rumours we schoolboys heard.

Tie

It's paradise to be near you like this,
away from the ice, close to Charley and Keith
the fire angels, believing in afternoon shopping,
the humour of traffic in no hurry.
I write poetry when there's nothing important to do,
but Tom Walmsley can touch a bubble with
a needle and not pop it. That's how near you
it's paradise to be.
                    But then poems and bubbles,
what kind of shopping is this? My grade-eleven
English teacher never cracked a smile, her teeth
in trouble because the oaf in a regimental tie
banged her with his fat hand, hair on his
fat knuckles. It was, easy to say, a hell
we selfish grammar kids knew nothing of.
High school was for sissies, similes, seldom cowboys,
seldom people who really knew what a noun was.
And down by the bend of the Okanagan River
no English dick in a fake blue blazer would go,
his ventures in the bedroom dark, no ice in that drink.

What was I? Eight?

The World, I Guess

Early in the second decade of the twenty-first century, Toronto's Ryerson University asked me to come and say something to some of their literature people, students, and teachers. So I sat down and started writing something about whatever it was that made me become a writer. The way things are going now that I am an old hand, I found myself writing little narratives about moments in my early life that took me past the boundary line of comfort into a psyche-region that required not so much words as a realization that something like organized alarm is called for.

I kept going till I had six of these stories. Four of them take place in the Okanagan Valley. One of them involves hanging out the door of an airplane while holding a camera. Another tells about a seven-year-old boy reading in a mountain-top tent while some animal sniffs around outside. I guess I might be talking about fear, and then about the beauty that so often attends fear and vice versa.

I was thinking of writing ten of these little things, but I ran out of steam after six, and when I got to Ryerson I had time for only two. There's a truth about the writing life there somewhere.

The Giant Snowball

The other day while Jean was driving us to lunch with my childhood pal Willy, I saw three boys on a front lawn fingertipping a volleyball to each other in the afternoon sunshine. It made me momentarily happy, and I remarked to Jean that it was a welcome change—more commonly these days one would see three young heads bent over small screens. I don't care that this happened while the Olympic Games were being contested. Those boys, as far as I could tell while our car drove past them, were not contesting—they were just playing, and relying on one another for fun.

We sure did that when I was an elementary schoolboy. In Oliver our school had a girls' playground to its south and a boys' playground to its north. Either playground was made up of about ten acres of semi-arid land, mostly composed of sand and rocks, with sagebrush and antelope brush and greasewood growing slowly and sparsely. There were rattlesnakes and cactus to watch out for, but that was true in just about every vacant lot in Oliver. Occasionally we had rattlesnakes in our back yard, down the hill from the school.

In those days the boys in Oliver usually played "swords." We had wooden swords that would be held to us by our belts, hardly ever any shields, once in a while cardboard-box armour. Sometimes we made bows and arrows, but we seldom used them against each other, because really, you could put an eye out, just as our parents said. We snaffled laths from the lumberyard and employed them as javelins, but only if the other guys had cardboard shields.

Swordfights went on all over town, and sure enough, boys did come home with skinned knuckles and a bit of blood in the crewcut. But the parents usually knew as well as we did that we boys made up the rules around here and agreed to them.

We saw in the comic books that kids back east made snow forts in the winter. We usually didn't get enough snow for any such thing, but we made another kind of fort in that big boys' playground north of the school. It took a lot of teamwork and time to make these forts. To begin with, they were pits, not surface structures. We dug our holes in the sifting dirt, then acquired planks or shiplap from somewhere for a roof, then did the best we could to lay the crumbling sod on top of the boards, complete with cactuses. The idea was to make it seem as if there were no pit there. Usually we had two crawly holes for entrance and exit. I think that nowadays no such enterprise would be allowed because of safety "issues."

I don't remember whether we raided each other's pits, or tried to destroy them. Probably not, because the teamwork involved was more enjoyable than any hostilities. That we would come home with our hair, skin, and clothing covered in dirt didn't mean all that much. We were boys. I never knew a boy without knee-scabs and dirty fingernails. When someone told me that that brush lying on the edge of your bathtub was a fingernail brush, I didn't know whether to believe it.

But one winter we had a hell of a snowfall. It was just like the snowfalls we saw in magazine pictures from back east. It got cold, too. Someone with a back porch Fahrenheit thermometer said it went to ten below. In later years I took a picture every Christmas, of my two little brothers standing on the front lawn with their Christmas presents— skates dangling from their necks, toboggans held vertical beside them, their shoes on the bare grass of December 25th. But this winter when I was ten we finally got our chance to build snow forts. Instead, we got together and built a giant snowball.

Remember, we had acres and acres of snow in the boys' playground. Someone started a regular throwable snowball rolling, and it picked up snow until it was big enough to make the bottom ball of a snowman, but he kept going, and friends joined him, and by lunch hour the ball was a little higher than a regular ten-year-old boy. We left it outside the grade-five windows for the afternoon, and when the end of school came, we raced out into the fading Okanagan sun and pushed our snowball.

Soon it took five or six boys to push the snowball, and it was so high that you needed to climb on top of another kid to get up there. We took turns getting to the top while that was still possible, each boy seeing whether he could remain riding while the others pushed the snowball. There were old dead cactuses and elm leaves in the snow, a frozen sock and an arithmetic assignment. We pushed back and forth across the boys' playground until we could hear referees' whistles being blown—time to go home. We did not think of leaving someone to guard the nine-foot snowball. That was a Friday.

Saturday morning, just before the sun struggled up over the brown hills of the Indian reserve, there were four boys pushing the snowball. There were some slight slopes in the boys' playground, but four boys could, with a lot of loud straining and some ten-year-olds' profanity, move that ball up them. When it came to a downward slope the ball would get away a little, but the snow was so deep that eventually we could run around the other side and slow it down and get it to stop. It was early morning and it was below zero in the South Okanagan, but we were sweating inside our heavy jackets. When one of us became lieutenant for a moment and declared a rest period, we willingly complied.

Let me give a sketch of the landform involved. To the immediate west of the then village of Oliver lie some brown hills that ascend to some blue mountains. At the foot of the former is a sizeable flat bench, upon which the school rests. Then there is a sudden drop to the village (now town) itself. Along the edge of this precipice runs "the ditch," a concrete irrigation canal. Near the school is a street that runs from bench down to the town. It was near that street that we stopped pushing the giant snowball late that Saturday morning.

I should mention that boys loved pushing fair-sized boulders down hillsides in those days, and I don't remember anyone getting killed down below, though I do remember parents becoming stern-faced when the discussion turned to boulder rolling. This giant snowball perched on the edge of the drop into a snowy little town could have picked up real speed and done some real damage, especially if it followed the road right to downtown, where Highway 97 was main street. Cars could have been smashed. A house could have been demolished. A pedestrian would have been killed for sure.

But there the giant snowball perched. No one boy, no one man, could have started it rolling. It would take teamwork by a group of snowball boys, the kind that put stones in hand-sized snowballs. And it never happened. That snowball stood there on the lip of mayhem while the rest of the snow in the valley melted, while all the front yard snowmen disappeared. Finally some of us made snowballs from the handy armoury and enjoyed a once-in-a-life springtime snowball fight.

It was while the giant snowball stood sentinel on the edge of the hill just west of the house I lived in that I got a glimmer that I wanted to be someone who noticed such things and got them into something. I don't know, a poem, maybe.

Somebody's Horse

The southern Okanagan Valley of British Columbia is very dry now, a desert, in fact, where water has to be cared for, where they had to build a canal called "the ditch" to irrigate orchards, and where you were instructed to flush your toilet, if you had a flush toilet, only when it seemed absolutely necessary. You never brushed your teeth, and your father never shaved, with a running faucet.

But the valley used to be the path of a glacier that moved slowly in the southward direction taken by the Okanagan River now. You can see the presence of extremely old news in the tall clay banks on both sides of Okanagan Lake at its south end, or in the striations in the rock faces as you go farther south, toward Oliver, where I lived from grade three to grade twelve. A kid living in the southern Okanagan lived among signs of an ancient land, even while keeping track of the ground in front of him because he might be stepping where rattlesnakes wanted to be.

The valley is shaped the way a valley should be, so that you can stand at the intersection of Oliver's Main Street and Fairview Road, for example, and look up to the west and up to the east and see parallel lines of hills and then mountains. The river runs through the middle of the valley. Then on either side you now get orchards or vineyards; or in some cases you still get slopes of dusty soil with dry grass and sagebrush, right up until the hills rise seriously. The farther you go up those hills and then into the mountains, the more likely you are to find pine trees, and in the winter you will, if you keep climbing, find your share of romantic snow.

As often as I could, when I was not working, when I was still a Wordsworthian boy, I would be up in those hills, east or west, watching for rattlesnake or cactus, sometimes carrying an orange and a book that would fit into a pocket, walking around and looking for animal footprints. During the winter, when the water was turned off, I would explore the ditch, sometimes on foot, sometimes with my bike. With your bike you could ride up and down the sloping concrete sides, but there was a problem when the ditch had to cross a road—it would change from concrete to some sort of metal, and there would be planks across the top, so you had to take your bike out and down across the road and up again and so on.

There was also a problem with the slime. There was a lot of green slime in the water of the southern Okanagan—in the lakes and in the river, in the town swimming pool and in the ditch. Usually I walked when I was exploring the newly emptied ditch. Once I found a necklace made of coins. Once I found a small-calibre pistol. Despite the fact that we were only fifteen miles from the U.S. border, this was the first pistol I had ever seen. The handgrip was missing, but the rest was there. Maybe it was a .22, I don't know. Once I found a big old primitive-looking jackknife with a toad sticker. I still have it, but I don't know what happened to the pistol or the necklace.

Up in the hills I found stuff, too. Some of it was stuff I had secretly buried a year or two earlier, my secret caches that included hunting knives I had found, baseballs, I can't remember what else. I found a lot of footprints, as I said, horseshoe prints, paw prints. In my fancy under the hot sun I liked to intermingle this business with the stuff I was reading in drugstore paperbacks by Max Brand. Sometimes I would find a tuft of fur on a barbwire fence, fur or hair. There was no one else around, unless I had brought my little old dog Dinky with me, but I tried to look knowledgeable and laconic, eyes squinted and lifted to scan the near horizon.

I found an old stove door once, and a woman's boot that must have come from the late nineteenth century. I found lots of rusty old cans that must have been emptied near a campfire decades before. I found mysterious square bottles from the olden days. I found skulls, big ones and small ones, from cows and birds and coyotes, maybe.

Once when I didn't have Dinky with me, I climbed a hillside cliff made of rotting stone just for fun, and on the other side there was a little open space of no trees and no rock outcroppings, kind of like a natural corral, natural except for the remains of a wooden fence. In the middle was a dead horse.

The body had been around so long that it didn't give off that smell you hate. In fact it was pretty well flat, some brown hide with the insides all gone, eyes gone, not like a sheepskin or bearskin, because it was just horsehide lying full length on the ground where the brown grass had all been removed.

There were horse buns all around, been there a long time in the sun, and if you picked one up it would fall apart between your fingers. I stood and stared at my first dead horse. The flat neck still had a rope tied around it, and the rope was secured to a fence post. It looked so flimsy that I wondered why the horse had not pulled it loose.

Quite often in those days you might see large birds with long black wings circling around something in the hills, as in western movies or comic strips. I thought that they had probably been over this spot quite a long time ago. Since then the sun had become a tannery.

I tried not to think about the person who had tied the rope and why he had not come back. Was he saving a bullet? Did something happen to him? Had he ever given this horse a name?

After I descended into the valley and went home to fill the sawdust hopper and so on, I didn't tell anyone about the place where I'd seen something wrong. I knew that I was going to be something, a poet or something.

Twice I learned to ride on my sister's bike.

Writing That Made
It into the Book

Much of George Bowering's writing on the Okanagan Valley has been previously published in collections of poetry, prose, fiction, and non-fiction. The original publications are listed here, along with the page numbers on which to find them in those books.

The unpublished novel, *Delsing*, was written between 1959 and 1961.

Sticks & Stones (Vancouver: Tishbooks, 1962), 28, 38; reprinted (Vancouver: Talonbooks, 1989), 35, 45.

The Valley was published in *Parallel* (Montreal) 2, no. 7 (June/July 1967): 42, 44–45.

The Roy Miki bibliography is *A Record of Writing: An Annotated and Illustrated Bibliography of George Bowering* (Vancouver: Talonbooks, 1990).

"Okanagan Storm" was never published in a Bowering collection. Instead, it was used in an ad by the Hudson's Bay Company, circa 1966. Black print on a white background with a sketch of a storm; sketch by Les Simoens; designed as a page-size ad for magazines.

"Locus Solus" was published in *Points on the Grid* (Toronto: Contact Press, 1964), 39.

"Patrol" is yet another poem from the sixties that was never published in a collection. As well as appearing in the essay, *The Valley*, "Patrol" was published in *LitQuiz Weekly* (Bombay, India), no. 1 [23 June 1966]: 1.

Points on the Grid (Toronto: Contact Press, 1964), 33, 64–65.

The Man in Yellow Boots (Mexico City: El Corno Emplumado, 1965), 60.

The Silver Wire (Kington: Quarry Press, 1966).

Baseball (Toronto: Coach House Press, 1967, 2002), n.p. Used courtesy of the publisher.

The Gangs of Kosmos (Toronto: House of Anansi, 1969), 20, 26.

Autobiology (Vancouver: Georgia Straight Writing Supplement Vancouver Series #7, 1972), 7–8, 11–12, 23–24, 27–28, 35–36, 41–44, 53–54, 61–64, 67–68, 77–78, 85–86.

Flycatcher and Other Stories (Ottawa: Oberon Press, 1974), 29–37, 54–63, 96–103, 112–14.

The Catch (Toronto: McClelland & Stewart, 1976), 104, 107, 109, 111–12, 114.

Protective Footwear (Toronto: McClelland & Stewart, 1978), 9–22.

West Window (Toronto: General Publishing, 1982), 139–40, 142.

Smoking Mirror (Edmonton: Longspoon Press, 1982), 40, 42, 48.

A Way with Words (Ottawa: Oberon, 1982), 88–100.

A Place to Die (Ottawa: Oberon Press, 1983), 23–35, 52–64.

Caprice (Markham: Viking, 1987), 50–54, 60–65; reprinted (Vancouver: New Star Books, 2010), 53-57, 63–68. Used courtesy of the publisher.

Urban Snow (Vancouver: Talonbooks, 1991), 26, 92.

The Rain Barrel (Vancouver: Talonbooks, 1994), 9–49, 81–90.

Shoot! (Toronto: Key Porter Books, 1994), 88–92, 105–107; reprinted (Vancouver: New Star Books, 2008), 75–78, 89–90. Used courtesy of the publisher.

Bowering's B.C.: A Swashbuckling History (Toronto: Viking, 1996), 126–28, 393–94.

Blonds on Bikes (Vancouver: Talonbooks, 1997), 57, 59–61.

His Life, a Poem (Toronto: ECW Press, 2000), 3–4, 7, 11, 13, 16–17, 23, 28–29, 52, 83, 102. Used courtesy of the publisher.

A Magpie Life (Toronto: Key Porter Books, 2001), 12–13, 14–16, 47–52, 53–55, 168, 174–75, 185–89.

Cars (Toronto: Coach House Press, 2002), 9, 11, 17, 25, 33, 41, 43, 57, 59, 63, 87, 95, 105. Used courtesy of the publisher.

Standing on Richards (Toronto: Viking, 2004), 111–17, 205–209.

Left Hook (Vancouver: Raincoast Books, 2005), 201–216.

Vermeer's Light (Vancouver, Talonbooks, 2006), 189–90.

Crows in the Wind (Toronto: BookThug, 2006), 35.

Baseball Love (Vancouver: Talonbooks, 2006), 37–47.

Eggs in There (Edmonton: Rubicon Press, 2007), 7–8.

Valley (Calgary: No Press, 2008), n.p.

The Box (Vancouver: New Star Books, 2009), 13–28. Used courtesy of the publisher.

Horizontal Surfaces (Toronto: BookThug, 2010), 45–46.

The Diamond Alphabet (Toronto: BookThug, 2011), 15–16, 19–21, 34–36, 123–24.

Words, Words, Words (Vancouver: New Star Books, 2012), 5–9. Used courtesy of the publisher.

Pinboy (Toronto: Cormorant Books, 2012), 124–30. Used courtesy of the publisher.

Teeth (Toronto: Mansfield Press, 2013), 48.

The World, I Guess (Vancouver: New Star, 2015), 61–63, 71–74. Used courtesy of the publisher.

Writing That Didn't Make

It into the Book

"Trail" from *Sticks & Stones* (Vancouver: Tishbooks, 1962; Vancouver: Talon-books, 1989), 35.

"The Girl at the Beach," "The Bottles," "Gas Station Town," "Okanagan Winter Scenario," "Old Umbrella Tree," and "Driving to Kelowna" from "The Valley," *Parallel* (Montreal) 2, no. 7 (June/July 1967).

Some parts of "Meta Physic and Things" from *Points on the Grid* (Toronto: Contact Press, 1964).

"2nd Inning" from *Baseball* (Toronto: Coach House Press, 1967, 2002), n.p.

"Dobbin" from *The Gangs of Kosmos* (Toronto: House of Anansi, 1969), 26.

"The Pollywogs," "The Front Yard," "The Trees," and "The Fruit Ranch" from *Autobiology* (Vancouver: Georgia Straight Writing Supplement, Vancouver Series, no. 7).

"How Delsing Met Frances" in *Flycatcher and Other Stories* (Ottawa: Oberon Press, 1974), 96*ff*.

"Thinning Apples" and "Scrubbing the Pool" in *West Window: The Selected Poetry of George Bowering* (Toronto: General Publishing, 1982), 140 and 142.

"Old Bottles" in *A Place to Die* (Ottawa: Oberon Press, 1983), 52*ff*.

"Thea in Oliver" in *Delayed Mercy* (Toronto: Coach House Press, 1986), 87.

"Fairview" in *Bowering's B.C.: A Swashbuckling History* (Toronto: Viking, 1996), 252.

"Summer 1959," "Winter 1959," "Winter 1960," "Summer 1961," "Spring 1962," "Summer 1962," "Spring 1965," and "Summer 1965," in *His Life, a Poem* (Toronto: ECW Press, 2000), 5, 7, 11, 13, 16, 17, 28, and 29.

"Childhood" in *A Magpie Life: Growing a Writer* (Toronto: Key Porter Books, 2001), 12*ff*.

"Pretty as a Picture" in *Standing on Richards* (Toronto: Viking, 2004), 113*ff.*

"Bowsfield" in *The Diamond Alphabet: Baseball in Shorts* (Toronto: Book-Thug, 2011).

"Inside the Tent," "Auntie Pam," "The Swimming Hole," and "Air Camera" in *The World, I Guess* (Vancouver: New Star, 2015) 19, 35, 43, and 103.

In addition, George has written ongoing letters to the editor about establishing a national park in the South Okanagan.

About the Photos

All photos courtesy George Bowering, except as follows:

Postscript

JB: What do you think of the idea of including a map in
Writing the Okanagan?

KS: Well, I think it kind of defeats the "purpose" of the book,
which is, if I may be so succinctly bold, to make the
point that, "George Bowering's Okanagan" is a place of
the imagination. I am moved to recall a poem by Robert
Duncan, "Often I Am Permitted to Return to a Meadow,"
where the poet refers to a place "made up by the mind,"
a "made place, created by light."

     George's debt to Robert Duncan as one of his
"unacknowledged guides to poetics" is one of G. B.'s best-
kept secrets. Printing a map is as if Dante had pretended
that Virgil wasn't actually his guide throughout the *Inferno*
and the *Purgatorio* (though not, of course his *Paradiso*).

     It's because I know this (among many other things)
that I am able to edit George's work.

     So why don't we all just keep it a secret. As
George does.

GB: You know what?
I'd like it if the question
and Karl's answer appeared in the book.

George Bowering is a major Canadian literary figure and one of the most prolific writers in the country: more than eighty books to date, not including editions he has edited or contributed to, or his thirty-three chapbooks. He is a two-time winner of the Governor General's Award and has been shortlisted for the Griffin Prize for Poetry, Dorothy Livesay Poetry Prize, Stephen Leacock Medal for Humour, and B.C.'s National Award for Canadian Non-Fiction. In November 2002 he was appointed Canada's first Parliamentary Poet Laureate – in that same year he was awarded the Order of Canada. In 2004 he was awarded the Order of British Columbia. In 2011 he received the British Columbia Lieutenant Governor's Award for Literary Excellence and the UBC Alumni Achievement Award. He is a respected poet, novelist, essayist, critic, teacher, historian, editor, and tireless supporter of fellow writers.